AGELESS WISDOM

A TREASURY OF QUOTES TO MOTIVATE & INSPIRE

J. S. FELTS

ISBN: 978-0-578-87572-9 (Paperback)
Library of Congress Control Number: 2021904963

Exterior and Interior Design by Donna Cunningham of BeauxArts.Design

Printed by Plum Hill Publishing in the United States of America.

First edition printing 2021

www.PlumHillPublishing.com

Dedication

To my wife, Ashley, the most amazing woman I have ever known.

To my children and grandchildren:
In all your getting, get wisdom.

and

In memory of my brother, Marc:
A wise man, deposited into this world for a short time, but having left an impact for eternity.

CONTENTS

INTRODUCTION

"I have gathered a posie of other men's flowers, and nothing but the thread that binds them is mine own."

Montaigne, "Of Phisiognomy"

In almost every book we read, we find those few passages of wisdom, which stand up, stand out, and demand to be noticed; "One simile, that solitary shines in the dry desert of a thousand lines" as Alexander Pope put it. Those are the ones we write down because we keep coming back to them time and time again. Over the last thirty years, I've done just that, and carefully arranged my collection, into this book, Ageless Wisdom. This compilation is not meant to be the largest collection, but the wisest, which shares the greatest of thoughts. As George Eliot once poetically wrote, "A book which hath been culled from the flowers of all books."

There's something mesmerizing about being able to pick up one book, and having the wisdom of many of the world's greatest minds, at your immediate disposal. Ageless Wisdom is just that, a rich storehouse for those who love quotations. It contains a refreshing newness of quotes most have never been introduced to; not just another rearranging of old tired quotes.

I hope you find this collection thought-provoking and that it brings you many hours of reading enjoyment.

PART I

The Emotional Effects

ONE

ANGER

Anger blows out the lamp of the mind. In the examination of a great and important question, everyone should be serene, slow-pulsed, and calm.

-Robert G. Ingersoll, *The Christian Religion*

If you are patient in one moment of anger, you will escape a hundred days of sorrow.

-Chinese Proverb

What was anger when it was new became hatred when it was turned into long continuance. Anger is a weed, hatred, a tree.

-Saint Augustine, *Sermons on Selected Lessons of the New Testament*

A man that does not know how to be angry does not know how to be good.

-Henry Ward Beecher, "Moth-Eaten Garments", *Sermons*

There is a holy anger, excited by zeal that moves us to reprove with warmth those whom our mildness failed to correct.

-John Baptiste de la Salle

Anger is not argument.

-James Mills, A Letter to Sir Charles Abbott

Better a little fire to warm us than a great one to burn us.

-English Proverb

Hesitation is the best cure for anger.

-Lucius Annaeus Seneca (the younger), "On Anger", *Moral Essays*

The best fighter is never angry.

- Lao Tzu, Tao Te Ching

Anger ventilated often hurries toward forgiveness; and concealed often hardens into revenge.

-Edward Bulwer-Lytton, quoted in *Pearls of Thought* (1882) by Maturin Murray Ballou

Be ye angry, and sin not: let not the sun go down upon your wrath.

- The Bible (*KJV*), Ephesians 4:26

The bare recollection of anger kindles anger.

- Publilius Syrus, *Sententiae*

The world needs anger. The world often continues to allow evil because it isn't angry enough.

-Bede Jarrett, "Love's Restraint", *The Vocation to Marriage*

Anger is an acid that can do more harm to the vessel in which it is stored than to anything on which it is poured.

-Mark Twain

How great a matter a little fire kindleth!

-The Bible (*KJV*), James 3:5

Anger itself is much more hurtful for us than the injury that provokes it.

– Lucius Annaeus Seneca (the younger), "On Anger", *Moral Essays*

When angry, count ten, before you speak; if very angry, an hundred.

-Thomas Jefferson, letter to Thomas Jefferson Smith, 21 Feb 1825

It is easy to fly into a passion - anybody can do that - but to be angry with the right person and to the right extent and at the right time and with the right object and in the right way - that is not easy, and it is not everyone who can do it.

-Aristotle, *Nicomachean Ethics*

Do not teach your children never to be angry; teach them how to be angry.

- Lyman Abbott, *The Christian Union*, 11 Sept 1884

He that is soon angry dealeth foolishly.

-The Bible (*KJV*), Proverbs 14:17

Wise anger is like fire in a flint: there is great ado to get it out; and when it is out, it is gone again immediately.

-Matthew Henry, The Life of Mr. Philip Henry

I was angry with my friend;
I told my wrath, my wrath did end.
I was angry with my foe:
I told it not, my wrath did grow.

-William Blake, *A Poison Tree*

For he who gives no fuel to fire puts it out, and likewise he who does not in the beginning nurse his wrath and does not puff himself up with anger takes precautions against it and destroys it.

- Plutarch, *Moralia*

He that is slow to wrath is of great understanding: but he that is hasty of spirit exalteth folly.

-The Bible (*KJV*), Proverbs 14:29

He submits to be seen through a microscope, who suffers himself to be caught in a fit of passion.

- Johann Kaspar Lavater, *Aphorisms on Man*

How much more grievous are the consequences of anger than the causes of it.

-Marcus Aurelius, *Meditations*

Surround yourself with those who are slow to anger, not those who are free from anger.

-J.S. Felts

TWO

APATHY

A little neglect may breed great mischief: For want of a nail, the shoe was lost; for want of a shoe, the horse was lost; and for want of a horse, the rider was lost.

- Benjamin Franklin, Poor Richard's Almanack

None so deaf as those who will not hear.

-Thomas de Quincey, "Casuistry", Theological Essays and Other Papers

There are few signs in a soul's state more alarming than that of religious indifference, that is, the spirit of thinking all religions equally true — the real meaning of which is, that all religions are equally false.

- Frederick William Robertson, sermon, Brighton, England. 24 June 1849

They have mouths, but they speak not: eyes have they, but they see not. They have ears, but they hear not.

-The Bible (*KJV*), Psalms 115:5-6

Our lives begin to end the day we become silent about the things that matter.

-Unknown

Thou shalt not be a victim. Thou shalt not be a perpetrator. Above all, thou shalt not be a bystander.

-Inscription, U.S. Holocaust Memorial Museum in Washington, D.C.

The worst sin towards out fellow creatures is not to hate them, but to be indifferent to them: that's the essence of inhumanity.

-George Bernard Shaw, *The Devil's Disciple*

By far the most dangerous foe we have to fight is apathy - indifference from whatever cause, not from a lack of knowledge, but from carelessness, from absorption in other pursuits, from a contempt bred of self-satisfaction.

-William Osler, "Unity, Peace and Concord", *Aequanimitas*

Bad men need nothing more to compass their ends, than that good men should look on and do nothing.

-John Stuart Mill, inaugural address at the University of St. Andrews, 1 Feb, 1867

Science may have found a cure for most evils; but it has found no remedy for the worst of them all - the apathy of human beings.

-Helen Keller, *My Religion*

THREE

Emotions

When dealing with people, let us remember we are not dealing with creatures of logic. We are dealing with creatures of emotion.

-Dale Carnegie, How to Win Friends and Influence People

Until you learn to control your emotions, you will never control your life.

-J.S. Felts

The taste for emotion may, however, become a dangerous taste; and we should be very cautious how we attempt to squeeze out of human life, more ecstasy and paroxysm than it can well afford. It throws an air of insipidity over the greater part of our being, and lavishes on a few favored moments the joy which was given to season our whole existence.

-Sydney Smith, Elementary Sketches of Moral Philosophy

Men are oftener treacherous through weakness than design.

-Francois de La Rochefoucauld, *Moral Maxims*

When you live next to the cemetery, you cannot weep for everyone.

-Russian Proverb

Mobs in their emotions are much like children, subject to the same tantrums and fits of fury.

-Euripides, *Orestes*

Human nature is the same everywhere; the modes only are different.

- Lord Chesterfield, *Letters to His Godson*

Emotion, without knowledge, is dangerous.

- J.S. Felts

No emotion, any more than a wave, can long retain its own individual form.

-Henry Ward Beecher, "Conduct the Index of Feeling", *The Sermons of Henry Ward Beecher*

Men, as well as women, are much oftener led by their hearts than by their understandings.

-Lord Chesterfield, letter to his son, 21 June 1748

I don't want to be at the mercy of my emotions. I want to use them, to enjoy them, and to dominate them.

-Oscar Wilde, *The Picture of Dorian Gray*

The passions are like fire, useful in a thousand ways and dangerous only in one, through their excess.

-Christian Nestell Bovee, *Intuitions and Summaries of Thought*

The best and most beautiful things in the world cannot be seen nor even touched, but just felt in the heart.

-Helen Keller, *The Story of My Life*

Unfruitful emotion is to be suspected. Feeling acts as an impulse, as a spur, as a spring, and when feelings are excited, and they put nothing forward, they are sometimes even dangerous to a man.

-Henry Ward Beecher, *Proverbs from Plymouth Pulpit*

We have lost confidence in reason because we have learned that man is chiefly a creature of habit and emotion.

-John Dewey, "What I Believe"

FOUR

Fear

We often suffer more from our response to a difficulty, than from the difficulty itself. Panic and anxiety don't lessen what we are facing, they magnify it.

- J.S. Felts

'Tis safest, when in fear, to force the attack.

-Lucius Annaeus Seneca (the younger), "Hippolytus", *Tragedies*

This fear of any future difficulties or misfortune is so natural to the mind, that were a man's sorrows and disquietudes summed up at the end of his life, it would generally be found that he had suffered more from the apprehension of such evils as never happened to him, than from those evils which had really befallen him. To this we may add, that among those evils which befall us, there are many which have been more painful to us in the prospect than by their actual pressure.

-Joseph Addison, *The Spectator*, 9 October 1712

The mass of men lead lives of quiet desperation.

-Henry David Thoreau, *Walden*

When a resolute young fellow steps up to the great bully, the world, and takes him boldly by the beard, he is often surprised to find it comes off in his hand, and that it was only tied on to scare away the timid adventurers.

- Oliver Wendell Holmes Sr., *Elsie Venner*

There is a great beauty in going through life fearlessly. Half our fears are baseless - the other half discreditable.

-Christian Nestell Bovee, *Intuitions and Summaries of Thought*

The absent danger greater still appears less fears he who is near the thing he fears.

–Samuel Daniel, “The Tragedy of Cleopatra”, *The Poetical Works of Mr. Samuel Daniel*

Fear always springs from ignorance.

-Ralph Waldo Emerson, speech, “The American Scholar”, 31 August, 1837

He who fears being conquered is sure of defeat.

-Napoleon Bonaparte, *Aphorisms and Thoughts*

The wounded limb shrinks from the gentlest touch; and to the nervous the smallest shadow excites alarm.

–Ovid, *Epistulae ex Ponto*

Neither a man nor a crowd nor a nation can be trusted to act humanely or to think sanely under the influence of a great fear.

-Bertrand Russell, "An Outline of Intellectual Rubbish"

No passion so effectually robs the mind of all its powers of acting and reasoning as fear.

-Edmund Burke, *A Philosophical Enquiry into the Origin of Our Ideas*

The only thing we have to fear is fear itself - nameless, unreasoning, unjustified terror which paralyzes needed efforts to convert retreat into advance.

-Franklin Delano Roosevelt, first inaugural address, 4 March 1933

It is better by noble boldness to run the risk of being subject to half the evils we anticipate than to remain in cowardly listlessness for fear of what might happen.

-Herodotus, *The Histories*

Fear makes the wolf bigger than he is.

-German Proverb

Fear, like courage, is contagious. It must be resisted as soon as shown.

–Charles Wagner, *Courage*

He who fears something gives it power over him.

-Moorish Proverb

We are more often frightened than hurt: our troubles spring more often from fancy than reality.

-Lucius Annaeus Seneca (the younger), *Moral Letters to Lucilius*

He who fears he shall suffer, already suffers what he fears.

-Michel de Montaigne, "Of Experience", *Essays*

Fear to let fall a drop and you spill a lot.

-Malay Proverb

There are those who are so scrupulously afraid of doing wrong that they seldom venture to do anything.

-Joseph Farrell, “About Impartiality”, *The Lectures of a Certain Professor*

The most drastic and usually the most effective remedy for fear is direct action.

-William Henry Burnham, *The Normal Mind*

Just as courage imperils life, fear protects it.

-Leonardo da Vinci, *The Notebooks*

A good scare is worth more to a man than good advice.

-Edgar Watson Howe, *Plain People*

It is only the fear of God, which can deliver us from the fear of men.

-John Witherspoon, "Ministerial Character and Duty", *Sermons*

Fear not that thy life shall come to an end, but rather fear that it shall never have a beginning.

-John Henry Newman, quoted in *Character Lessons in American Biography* (1909) by James White

Were the diver to think on the jaws of the shark, he would never lay hands on the precious pearl.

-Sa'di, *Gulistan*

He that will not sail till all dangers are over must never put to sea.

-English Proverb

As a rule, what is out of sight disturbs men's minds more seriously than what they see.

-Gaius Julius Caesar, *The Gallic War*

The concessions of the weak are the concessions of fear.

-Edmund Burke, speech, "On Conciliation with the American Colonies", 22 March 1775

Knowledge is the antidote to fear.

-Ralph Waldo Emerson, "Courage", *Society and Solitude*

To fear the examination of any proposition appears to me an intellectual and moral palsy that will ever hinder the firm grasping of any substance whatever.

-George Eliot, letter to Mrs. Pears, February 1842

Once men are caught up in an event they cease to be afraid. Only the unknown frightens men.

-Antoine de Saint-Exupery, *Wind, Sand and Stars*

Better hazard once, than be always in fear.

-Thomas Fuller, *Gnomologia*

I don't like these cold, precise, perfect people, who, in order not to speak wrong, never speak at all, and in order not to do wrong, do nothing.

-Henry Ward Beecher, "The Faults of Character", published in *The Herald of Health* (1870)

"I will have no man in my boat," said Starbuck, "who is not afraid of a whale." By this, he seemed to mean not only that the most reliable and useful courage was that which arises from the fair estimation of the encountered peril, but that an utterly fearless man is a far more dangerous comrade than a coward.

-Herman Melville, *Moby Dick*

He feared man so little because he feared God so much.

-Inscription on the monument to Lord Lawrence at Westminster Abbey

The timid fear before danger, the cowardly in the midst of it, and the courageous after it is over.

-Jean Paul Richter, quoted in *Library of the World's Best Literature* (1896) by Charles Warner

He who fears to suffer, suffers from fear.

-French Proverb

For God hath not given us the spirit of fear; but of power, and of love, and of a sound mind.

-The Bible (*KJV*), 2 Timothy 1:7

Our doubts are traitors, and make us lose the good we oft might win by fearing to attempt.

-William Shakespeare, *Measure for Measure*

If your cause is just, if your principles are pure, and if your conduct is prudent, you need not fear the multitude of opposing hosts.

-John Witherspoon, sermon, "The Dominion of Providence over the Passions of Men", 17 May 1775

Those who fear nothing, love nothing.

-Saying

If evils come not, then our fears are vain; and if they do, fear but augments the pain.

-Benjamin Franklin, *Poor Richard's Almanack*

Courage is resistance to fear, mastery of fear - not absence of fear.

-Mark Twain, *Pudd'nhead Wilson*

Every man is scared in his first battle. If he says he's not, he's a liar! Some men are cowards but they fight the same as the brave men or they get the hell slammed out of them watching men fight who are just as scared as they are. The real hero is the man who fights even though he is scared.

-George S. Patton, speech to the Third Army before the invasion of France, June 1944

Audacity augments courage; hesitation, fear.

-Publilius Syrus, *Sententiae*

The great masses of people are timid by nature, and thereby danger is invariably exaggerated.

-Carl Von Clausewitz, *On War*

FIVE

Grief

While grief is fresh, every attempt to divert only irritates.

-Samuel Johnson, quoted in *Life of Samuel Johnson* (1791) by James Boswell

Grief is like a physical pain which must be allowed to subside somewhat on its own

-Plutarch, "*In Consolation to His Wife*"

There is a sacredness in tears. They are not the mark of weakness, but of power. They speak more eloquently than ten thousand tongues. They are messengers of overwhelming grief, of deep contrition, of unspeakable love.

-Samuel Johnson, quoted in *The Mother's Assistant* (1845)

He that conceals his grief finds no remedy for it.

-Turkish Proverb

It is better to drink of deep griefs than to taste shallow pleasures.

-William Hazlitt, *Characteristics*

Immoderate grief is selfish, harmful, brings no advantage to either the mourner or the mourned, and dishonors the dead.

-Plutarch, *"In Consolation to His Wife"*

Grief drives men into habits of serious reflection, sharpens the understanding, and softens the heart.

-John Adams, letter to Thomas Jefferson, 6 May 1816

When you are sorrowful, look again in your heart, and you shall see that in truth you are weeping for that which has been your delight.

-Khalil Gibran, "Joy and Sorrow", *The Prophet*

Grief is itself a medicine.

-William Cowper, "Charity", *Poems*

It is foolish to tear one's hair in grief, as if grief could be lessened by baldness.

-Marcus Tullius Cicero, *Tusculan Disputations*

No greater grief than to remember days of joy, when mis'ry is at hand.

–Dante Alighieri, *The Divine Comedy*

He that lacks time to mourn lacks time to mend.

-Henry Taylor, *Philip Van Artevelde*

If our inward griefs were seen written on our brow, how many would be pitied who are now envied!

–Pietro Metastasio, *Giuseppe Riconosciuto*

Happiness is beneficial for the body but it is grief that develops the powers of the mind.

-Marcel Proust, *In Search of Lost Time*

It's the great mystery of human life that old grief passes gradually into quiet tender joy.

-Fyodor Dostoevsky, *The Brothers Karamazov*

Grief knits two hearts in closer bonds than happiness ever can; and common sufferings are far stronger links than common joys.

-Alphonse de Lamartine, *Raphael*

What an argument in favor of social connections is the observation that often by communicating our grief we have less, and by communicating our pleasure we have more.

-Fulke Greville, *Maxims, Characters, and Reflections*

To weep excessively for the dead is to affront the living.

-Thomas Fuller, *Gnomologia*

SIX

Happiness

It is necessary to the happiness of man that he be mentally faithful to himself.

-Thomas Paine, *The Age of Reason*

I don't know what your destiny will be, but one thing I do know: the only ones among you who will be really happy are those who will have sought and found how to serve.

-Albert Schweitzer

There is only one way to happiness, and that is to cease worrying about things which are beyond the power of our will.

-Epictetus, *Discourses*

Give a man health and a course to steer, and he'll never stop to trouble about whether he's happy or not.

-George Bernard Shaw, *Captain Brassbound's Conversion*

If you work at that which is before you . . . expecting nothing, fearing nothing, but satisfied with your present activity according to nature, and with heroic truth in every word and sound which you speak, you will live happy. And there is no man who is able to prevent this.

-Marcus Aurelius, *Meditations*

In vain do they talk of happiness who never subdued an impulse in obedience to a principle. He who never sacrificed a present to a future good, or a personal to a general one, can speak of happiness only as the blind do of colors.

-Horace Mann, *The Common School Journal*, 2 January 1843

True happiness consists not in the multitude of friends, but in the worth and choice.

-Ben Jonson, *Cynthia's Revels*

Those who seek for something more than happiness in this world must not complain if happiness is not their portion.

-James Anthony Froude, *Thomas Carlyle: A History of the First Forty Years*

It is not how much we have, but how much we enjoy, that makes happiness.

-Charles Haddon Spurgeon, *John Ploughman's Talk*

There is only one happiness in life, to love and be loved.

-George Sand, letter to Lina Calamatta, 31 March 1862

Happiness in this world, when it comes, comes incidentally. Make it the object of pursuit, and it leads us a wild-goose chase, and it is never attained.

–Nathaniel Hawthorne, “The American Notebooks” *The Works of Nathaniel Hawthorne*

We act as though comfort and luxury were the chief requirements of life, when all that we need to make us really happy is something to be enthusiastic about.

-Anonymous, quoted in *The Smart Set*, August 1914

The grand essentials to happiness in this life are something to do, something to love, and something to hope for.

-George Washington Burnap, *The Sphere and Duties of Woman*

Five great enemies to peace inhabit us: avarice, ambition, envy, anger and pride. If those enemies were to be banished, we should infallibly enjoy perpetual peace.

-Petrarch, quoted in *The Amusing Instructor* (1727) by Antonio Montucci

If an Arab in the desert were suddenly to discover a spring in his tent, and so would always be able to have water in abundance, how fortunate he would consider himself; so too, when a man who is always turned toward the outside, thinking that his happiness lies outside him, finally turns inward and discovers that the source is within him; not to mention his discovering that the source is his relation to God.

-Soren Kierkegaard, *Journals*

Pleasure is very seldom found where it is sought. Our brightest blazes are of gladness are commonly kindled by unexpected sparks.

-Samuel Johnson, *The Idler*, 26 May 1759

The man of pleasure, by a vain attempt to be more happy than any man can be, is often more miserable than most men are.

-Charles Caleb Colton, *Lacon*

Make happy those who are near and those who are far will come.

-Chinese Proverb

This is the true joy in life, the being used for a purpose recognized by yourself as a mighty one; the being thoroughly worn out before you are thrown on the scrap heap; the being a force of Nature instead of a feverish selfish little clod of ailments and grievances complaining that the world will not devote itself to making you happy.

-George Bernard Shaw, *Man and Superman*

A man's as miserable as he thinks he is.

-Lucius Annaeus Seneca (the younger), *Moral Letters to Lucilius*

He is happiest, be he king or peasant, who finds peace in his home.

-Johann Wolfgang von Goethe, *Iphigenia in Tauris*

The supreme happiness of life is the conviction that we are loved.

-Victor Hugo, *Les Miserables*

To be without some of the things you want is an indispensable part of happiness.

-Bertrand Russell, *The Conquest of Happiness*

I look at what I have not and think myself unhappy; others look at what I have and think me happy.

-Joseph Roux, *Meditations of a Parish Priest*

Happiness always looks small while you hold it in your hands, but let it go, and you learn at once how big and precious it is.

-Maxim Gorky, *The Zykovs*

If people only wanted to be happy it would be very easy; but they want to be happier than other people, and this is almost always difficult, because we imagine other people happier than they really are.

-Charles de Montesquieu, quoted in *Montesquieu* (1888) by Albert Sorel

I am still determined to be cheerful and happy in whatever situation I may be, for I have also learnt that the greater part of our happiness or misery depends upon our disposition, and not upon our circumstances.

-Martha Washington, letter to Mrs. Mercy Otis Warren, 26 December 1789

The extent, to which you are happy, is in direct proportion to your recognition of what you have to be thankful.

- J.S. Felts

Happiness does not depend on external conditions, but on the way we see them.

-Leo Tolstoy, *Boyhood*

To render ourselves insensible to pain we must forfeit also the possibility of happiness.

-John Lubbock, *The Pleasures of Life*

People can have many different kinds of pleasure. The real one is that for which they will forsake the others.

-Marcel Proust, *In Search of Lost Time*

We are never so happy or so unhappy as we think.

-Francois de La Rochefoucauld, *Reflections or Sentences and Moral Maxims*

The most unhappy of all men is he who believes himself to be so.

-Henry Home, *The Art of Thinking*

He that is of a merry heart hath a continual feast.

-The Bible (*KJV*), Proverbs 15:15

Very little is needed to make a happy life.

-Marcus Aurelius, *Meditations*

There is something better for us in this world than happiness, whatever there may be beyond. We will take happiness as the incident of this, gladly and gratefully. We will add a thousand-fold to the happiness of the present in the fearlessness of the future which it brings, but we will not place happiness first, and thus cloud our heads with doubt and fill our hearts with discontent. In the blackest soils grow the richest flowers, and the loftiest and strongest trees spring heavenward among the rocks.

-Josiah Gilbert Holland, *Gold-foil: Hammered from Popular Proverbs*

If the chief part of human happiness arises from the consciousness of being beloved, as I believe it does, those sudden changes of fortune seldom contribute much to happiness.

-Adam Smith, *The Theory of Moral Sentiments*

SEVEN

HATE

We are more inclined to hate one another for points on which we differ, than to love one another for points on which we agree.

-Charles Caleb Colton, *Lacon*

What was anger when it was new became hatred when it was turned into long continuance.

-Saint Augustine, *Sermons on Selected Lessons of the New Testament*

I would permit no man . . . to narrow and degrade my soul by making me hate him.

-Booker T. Washington, *Up from Slavery*

We hate some persons because we do not know them; and will not know them because we hate them.

-Charles Caleb Colton, *Lacon*

In time we hate that which we often fear.

-William Shakespeare, *Antony & Cleopatra*

Take care that no one hates you justly.

-Publilius Syrus, *Sententia*

Hatred is the coward's revenge for being intimidated.

-George Bernard Shaw, *Major Barbara*

Love blinds us to faults, hatred to virtues.

-Moses ibn Ezra

Whoever claims to love God yet hates a brother or sister is a liar. For whoever does not love their brother and sister, whom they have seen, cannot love God, whom they have not seen.

-The Bible (*NIV*), 1 John 4:20

The greatest hatred, like the greatest virtue ... is quiet.

-Jean Paul Richter, *Hesperus*

Folks never understand the folks they hate.

-James Russell Lowell, *The Biglow Papers*

If you must hate a man for the many things about which you disagree, remember that you should also love him for the many things about which you agree.

-Ivan Panin, *Thoughts*

EIGHT

HOPE

Hope for the best, get ready for the worst, and then take what God chooses to send.

-Matthew Henry, *The Christian Sentinel*, June 1867

Of all delusions perhaps none is so great as the thought that our past has ruined our present, that the evils we have done, the mistakes we have committed, have made all further Hope impossible.

-Alban Goodier, *The School of Love and Other Essays*

Without vision, there's no hope, and without hope, life is nothing more than a mere existence.

- J.S. Felts

What we call our despair is often only the painful eagerness of unfed hope.

-George Eliot, *Middlemarch*

Hope deferred makes the heart sick, but a longing fulfilled is a tree of life.

-The Bible (*NIV*), Proverbs 13:12

The grand essentials to happiness in this life are something to do, something to love, and something to hope for.

-George Washington Burnap, *The Sphere and Duties of Woman*

At first we hope too much, later on, not enough.

-Joseph Roux, *Meditations of a Parish Priest*

Hope is the best possession. None are completely wretched but those who are without hope. Few are reduced so low as that.

-William Hazlitt, *Characteristics: In the Manner of Rochefoucault's Maxims*

Never give out while there is hope; but hope not beyond reason, for that shows more desire than judgment.

-William Penn, *Some Fruits of Solitude*

If we hope for what we are not likely to possess, we act and think in vain, and make life a greater dream and shadow than it really is.

-Joseph Addison, *The Spectator*, 13 November 1712

There are situations in which hope and fear run together, in which they mutually destroy one another, and lose themselves in a dull indifference.

-Johann Wolfgang von Goethe, *Elective Affinities*

Hope is necessary in every condition. The miseries of poverty, sickness, of captivity, would, without this comfort, be insupportable.

-Samuel Johnson, *The Rambler*, 6 November 1750

I am prepared for the worst, but hope for the best.

-Benjamin Disraeli, *The Wondrous Tale of Alroy*

NINE

Jealousy

In jealousy there is more of self-love than love.

-Francois de La Rochefoucauld, *Reflections or Sentences and Moral Maxims*

It is in the character of very few men to honor without envy a friend who has prospered.

-Aeschylus, *Agamemnon*

Jealousy is sustained as often by pride as by affection.

-Charles Caleb Colton, quoted in *Notable Thoughts about Women* (1882) by Maturin Ballou

A slowness to applaud betrays a cold temper, or an envious spirit.

-Hannah More, quoted in *Memoirs of the Life of Mrs. Hannah More* (1839) by William Roberts

As a moth gnaws a garment, so does envy consume the heart of man.

-John Chrysostom, quoted in *The Anatomy of Melancholy* (1621) by Robert Burton

Love may exist without jealousy, although this is rare: but jealousy may exist without love, and this is common; for jealousy can feed on that which is bitter no less than on that which is sweet, and is sustained by pride as often as by affection.

–Charles Caleb Colton, *Lacon*

Prospect is often better than possession.

-English Proverb

Jealousy, that dragon which slays love under the pretense of keeping it alive.

-Havelock Ellis, "Husbands and Wives", *Little Essays of Love and Virtue*

Jealousy is a terrible thing. It resembles love, only it is precisely love's contrary. Instead of wishing for the welfare of the object loved, it desires the dependence of that object upon itself, and its own triumph.

-Henri Frederic Amiel, *Journal Intime*, 28 December 1880

Just as iron is eaten away by rust, so are the envious consumed by their envy.

- Antisthenes, quoted in *The Lives and Opinions of Eminent Philosophers* by Diogenes Laertius

For where you have envy and selfish ambition, there you find disorder and every evil practice.

-The Bible (*NIV*), James 3:16

Jealousy is that pain which a man feels from the apprehension that he is not equally loved by the person whom he entirely loves.

-Joseph Addison, *The Spectator*, 14 September 1711

Envy is based on an incomplete understanding of the other person's situation.

-George Chapman

The jealous are troublesome to others, but a torment to themselves.

-William Penn, *Fruits of Solitude*

TEN

Laughter

Good-humor makes all things tolerable.

-Henry Ward Beecher, quoted in *Cavanagh's Phrenology* (1895)

A good laugh and a long sleep are the best cures in the doctor's book.

-Irish Proverb

There is nothing in which people more betray their character than in what they find to laugh at.

-Johann Wolfgang von Goethe, *Elective Affinities*

He is not always at ease who laughs.

-Dante Alighieri, *The Divine Comedy*

ELEVEN

Love

The way to love anything is to realize that it might be lost.

-G.K. Chesterton, *Tremendous Trifles*

'Tis better to have loved and lost, than never to have loved at all.

-Alfred Tennyson, *In Memoriam*

Be kind, for everyone is fighting a hard battle.

-John Watson, "Ian Maclaren": *The Life of the Rev. John Watson* (1909) by William Nicoll

Such ever was love's way: to rise, it stoops.

-Robert Browning, "A Death in the Desert", *Dramatis Personae*

You can accomplish by kindness what you cannot do by force.

-Publilius Syrus, *Moral Sayings*

I expect to pass through this world but once. Any good thing, therefore, that I can do or any kindness I can show to any fellow human being, let me do it now. Let me not defer nor neglect it, for I shall not pass this way again.

-Quaker Proverb

We are most of us very lonely in this world; you who have any who love you, cling to them and thank God!

-William Makepeace Thackeray, quoted in *Catholic World*, July 1898

How far that little candle throws his beams! So shines a good deed in a naughty world.

-William Shakespeare, *The Merchant of Venice*

It is astonishing how little one feels poverty when one loves.

-Edward Bulwer-Lytton, *My Novel*

The springs of conflict cannot be eliminated through institutions, but through the reform of the individual human being.

-Douglas MacArthur, speech in Washington, D.C., 14 July 1935

If we could read the secret history of our enemies, we would find in each man's life sorrow and suffering enough to disarm all hostility.

-Henry Wadsworth Longfellow, "Driftwood", *Table-Talk*

Absence lessens ordinary passions and augments great ones, just as the wind blows out a candle and makes a fire blaze.

-Francois de La Rochefoucauld, *Reflections or Sentences and Moral Maxims*

The lonely one offers his hand too quickly to whomever he encounters.

-Friedrich Nietzsche, *Thus Spoke Zarathustra*

If one were given five minutes' warning before sudden death, five minutes to say what it had all meant to us, every telephone booth would be occupied by people trying to call up other people to stammer that they loved them.

-Christopher Morley, *Religio Journalistici*

Love is not love
Which alters when it alteration finds.

-William Shakespeare, *As You Like It*

We should measure affection, not like youngsters, by the ardor of its passion, but by its strength and constancy.

-Marcus Tullius Cicero, *De Officiis*

Where there is love, there is pain.

-Spanish Proverb

Absence sharpens love, presence strengthens it.

-Thomas Fuller, *Gnomologia*

All things whatsoever ye would that men should do to you, do ye even so to them.

-The Bible (*KJV*), Matthew 7:12

Life has taught us that love does not consist in gazing at each other but in looking together in the same direction.

-Antoine de Saint-Exupery, *Wind, Sand and Stars*

Thou shalt love thy neighbor as thyself.

-The Bible *(KJV),* Leviticus 19:18

Nothing is so strong as gentleness, nothing so gentle and loving as real strength.

-Saint Francis de Sales, quoted in *My Sermon-notes* (1884) by Charles Haddon Spurgeon

We put our love where we have put our labor.

-Ralph Waldo Emerson, *Journals*

Love is patient, love is kind. It does not envy, it does not boast, it is not proud.

-The Bible (*NIV*), 1 Corinthians 13:4

To love a person means to see him as God intended him.

-Fyodor Dostoevsky

Be not overcome of evil, but overcome evil with good.

-The Bible (*NIV*), Romans 12:21

There is no disguise which can hide love for long where it exists, or simulate it where it does not.

-Francois de La Rochefoucauld, *Reflections or Sentences and Moral Maxims*

Only in the agony of parting do we look into the depths of love.

-George Eliot, *Felix Holt, the Radical*

We cannot help conforming ourselves to what we love.

-Saint Francis de Sales, *Treatise on the Love of God*

How far you go in life depends on your being tender with the young, compassionate with the aged, sympathetic with the striving and tolerant of the weak and strong, because someday in your life you will have been all of these.

-Unknown

Our virtues are dearer to us the more we have had to suffer for them. It is the same with our children. All profound affection admits a sacrifice.

-Luc de Clapiers, Marquis de Vauvenargues, quoted in *Gleason's Pictorial* (1853)

Recompense hatred with justice, and recompense kindness with kindness.

-Confucius, *The Analects*

With love one can live even without happiness.

-Fyodor Dostoevsky, *Notes from Underground*

Treasure each other in the recognition that we do not know how long we shall have each other.

-Joshua Loth Liebman, *Peace of Mind*

Hurt people, hurt people!

-Saying

You will find as you look back on your life, that the moments that stand out, the moments when you have really lived, are the moments when you have done things in a spirit of love.

-Henry Drummond, *The Greatest Thing In the World*

Let all bitterness, and wrath, and anger, and clamour, and evil speaking, be put away from you, with all malice: And be ye kind one to another, tenderhearted, forgiving one another, even as God for Christ's sake hath forgiven you.

-The Bible (*KJV*), Ephesians 4:31-32

No act of kindness, no matter how small, is ever wasted.

-Aesop, "The Lion and the Mouse", *Fables*

A good character is the best tombstone. Those who loved you, and were helped by you, will remember you when forget-me-nots are withered. Carve your name on hearts, and not on marble.

-Charles Haddon Spurgeon, *John Ploughman's Talk*

Write your name, by kindness, love, and mercy, on the hearts of thousands you come into contact with year by year, and you will never be forgotten.

-John Harvey, *The Golden Chain*

I say unto you, Love your enemies, bless them that curse you, do good to them that hate you, and pray for them who despitefully use you, and persecute you.

-The Bible (*KJV*), Matthew 5:44

The greatest evidence of love is in action, not words.

- J.S. Felts

Could a greater miracle take place than for us to look through each other's eyes for an instant?

-Henry David Thoreau, *Walden*

TWELVE

Passion

Nothing great in the world has been accomplished without passion.

-Georg Hegel, *Lectures on the Philosophy of History*

Without passion man is a mere latent force and possibility, like the flint which awaits the shock of the iron before it can give forth its spark.

-Henri Frederic Amiel, *Journal Intime*, 17 December 1856

Be still when you have nothing to say; when genuine passion moves you, say what you've got to say, and say it hot.

-D.H. Lawrence, *Studies in Classic American Literature*

Reason, ruling alone, is a force confining; and passion, unattended, is a flame that burns to its own destruction.

-Khalil Gibran, "On Reason and Passion", *The Prophet*

When the passions become masters, they are vices.

-Blaise Pascal, *Pensées*

Absence lessens ordinary passions and augments great ones, just as the wind blows out a candle and makes a fire blaze.

-Francois de La Rochefoucauld, *Reflections or Sentences and Moral Maxims*

Knowledge is indispensable, but it's passion that persuades.

- J.S. Felts

It is not good to have zeal without knowledge, nor to be hasty and miss the way.

-The Bible (*NIV*), Proverbs 19:2

Passion makes us feel, but never see clearly.

-Baron de Montesquieu, quoted in *Within an Ace* (1875) by Camilla Jenkin

The passions are like fire, useful in a thousand ways and dangerous only in one, through their excess.

-Christian Nestell Bovee, *Intuitions and Summaries of Thought*

Man is only truly great when he acts from the passions.

-Benjamin Disraeli, *Coningsby*

A wise man rules his passions, a fool obeys them.

-Publilius Syrus, *Sententiae*

THIRTEEN

Pride

The weakest spot in every man is where he thinks himself to be the wisest.

-Nathanael Emmons, *The Works*

He, who thinks his place below him, will certainly be below his place.

-Henry Savile, "Maxims of State", *Miscellanies*

A man wrapped up in himself makes a very small bundle.

-Saying

To know a man, observe how he wins his object, rather than how he loses it; for, when we fail, our pride supports us, when we succeed, it betrays us.

-Charles Caleb Colton, *Lacon*

People seldom improve when they have no other model but themselves to copy.

-Oliver Goldsmith, "On Our Theatres", *The Bee*, 13 October 1759

Those who never retract their opinions love themselves more than they love truth.

-Joseph Joubert, *Pensées of Joubert*

Shall a man go and hang himself because he belongs to the race of pygmies, and not be the biggest pygmy that he can?

-Henry David Thoreau, *Walden*

For where the fear of God is wanting, destruction is sure to follow.

-Niccolo Machiavelli, *Discourses on Livy*

The greatest of faults, I should say, is to be conscious of none.

-Thomas Carlyle, *On Heroes, Hero-worship, and the Heroic in History*

Pride goeth before destruction, and an haughty spirit before a fall.

-The Bible (*KJV*), Proverbs 16:18

Glory is like a circle in the water,
Which never ceaseth to enlarge itself,
Till, by broad spreading, it disperse to nought.

-William Shakespeare, *King Henry VI*

The third clause of the Lord's Prayer is repeated daily by millions, who have not the slightest intention of letting any will be done except their own.

-Aldous Huxley, *The Perennial Philosophy*

Let another man praise thee, and not thine own mouth.

-The Bible (*KJV*), Proverbs 27:2

It may easily come to pass that a vain man may become proud and may imagine that he is pleasing to all, when in reality he may be an annoyance to all.

-Baruch Spinoza, "The Origin and Nature of the Emotions", *The Ethics*

Sometimes it's necessary to step back in order to go forward.

-Saying

Whosoever shall exalt himself shall be abased; and he that shall humble himself shall be exalted.

-The Bible (*KJV*), Matthew 23:12

If you act like an ass, don't get insulted if people ride you.

-Yiddish Proverb

Let him that thinketh he standeth take heed lest he fall.

-The Bible (*KJV*), 1 Corinthians 10:12

He that will not be counseled cannot be helped.

-Thomas Fuller, *Gnomologia*

When pride comes, then comes disgrace, but with humility comes wisdom.

-The Bible (*NIV*), Proverbs 11:2

Pride perceiving humility honorable, often borrows her cloak.

-Thomas Fuller, *Gnomologia*

The labor of self-love is a heavy one indeed . . . The heart's fierce effort to protect itself from every slight, to shield its touchy honor from the bad opinion of friend and enemy, will never let the mind have rest.

-A.W. Tozer, *The Pursuit of God*

We do not dare to classify or compare ourselves with some who commend themselves. When they measure themselves by themselves and compare themselves with themselves, they are not wise.

-The Bible (*NIV*), 2 Corinthians 10:12

When flowers are full of heaven-descended dews, they always hang their heads; but men hold theirs the higher the more they receive, getting proud as they get full.

-Henry Ward Beecher, *Life Thoughts*

A beggar's rags may cover as much pride as an alderman's gown.

-Charles Haddon Spurgeon, sermon "The Healing of One Born Blind", 11 August 1872

God resisteth the proud and giveth grace to the humble. Humble yourselves therefore under the mighty hand of God, that he may exalt you in due time.

-The Bible (*KJV*), 1 Peter 5:5-6

Seest thou a man wise in his own conceit? There is more hope of a fool than of him.

-The Bible (*KJV*), Proverbs 26:12

It is a revenge the devil sometimes takes upon the virtuous, that he entraps them by the force of the very passion they have suppressed and think themselves superior to.

-George Santayana, letter to Guy Murchie, 12 March 1896

Vanity and pride are different things, though the words are often used synonymously. A person may be proud without being vain. Pride relates more to our opinion of ourselves; vanity, to what we would have others think of us.

-Jane Austen, *Pride and Prejudice*

Pride only breeds quarrels, but wisdom is found in those who take advice.

-The Bible (*NIV*), Proverbs 13:10

Those who err in one direction, always take care to let you know that they are quite free from error in the opposite direction.

-Arthur Helps, "Short Essays", *Good Words*

Idleness and pride tax with a heavier hand than kings and parliaments.

-Benjamin Franklin, letter to Charles Thomson, 11 July 1765

Arrogance is a weed which grows upon a dunghill. It is he that has nothing else to commend him, who would invade men's good opinions, by an unbecoming haughtiness.

-Owen Felltham, *Resolves, Divine, Moral and Political*

A man's pride shall bring him low: but honour shall uphold the humble in spirit.

-The Bible (*KJV*), Proverbs 29:23

One thing pride has, more than any vice, that I know; it is an enemy to itself. The proud man cannot endure to see pride in another.

-Owen Felltham, *Resolves, Divine, Moral and Political*

There are no friends more inseparable than pride and hardness of heart, humility and love, falsehood and impudence.

-Johann Kaspar Lavater, quoted in *The Golden Treasury of Thought* (1873) by Theodore Taylor

If he could only see how small a vacancy his death would leave, the proud man would think less of the place he occupies in his lifetime.

-Ernest Legouve, quoted in *Many Thoughts of Many Minds* (1896) by Louis Klopsch

Men are sometimes accused of pride, merely because their accusers would be proud themselves were they in their places.

-William Shenstone, *Essays On Men And Manners*

Of all the causes which conspire to blind man's erring judgement, and misguide the mind ... is PRIDE, the never-failing vice of fools.

–Alexander Pope, *An Essay on Criticism*

FOURTEEN

REVENGE

Whoso diggeth a pit shall fall therein.

-The Bible (*KJV*), Proverbs 26:27

A man that studieth revenge keeps his own wounds green, which otherwise would heal and do well.

-Francis Bacon, "Of Revenge", *Essays*

Revenge is a confession of pain.

-Latin Proverb

Revenge is a kind of wild justice; which the more man's nature runs to, the more ought law to weed it out.

-Francis Bacon, "Of Revenge", *Essays*

Revenge is always the weak pleasure of a little and narrow mind.

-Juvenal, *Satires*

Men often make up in wrath what they want in reason.

-William R. Alger, quoted in *Treasury of Thought* (1872) by Maturin Murray Ballou

In taking revenge, a man is but even with his enemy; but in passing it over, he is superior.

-Francis Bacon, “Of Revenge”, *Essays*

FIFTEEN

SUFFERING

What does not destroy me makes me stronger.

-Friedrich Nietzsche, "Maxims and Arrows", *Twilight of the Idols*

The reward of suffering is experience.

-Aeschylus, *Oresteia*

There is no man in the world free from trouble or anguish, though he were King or Pope.

-Thomas a' Kempis, *The Imitation of Christ*

Weeping may endure for a night, but joy cometh in the morning.

-The Bible *(KJV),* Psalms 30:5

He jests at scars that never felt a wound.

-William Shakespeare, *Romeo and Juliet*

Cast thy burden on the Lord, and he shall sustain thee.

-The Bible (*KJV*), Psalms 55:22

Those things that hurt, instruct.

-Saying

Who has never tasted what is bitter does not know what is sweet.

-German Proverb

We often learn more of God under the rod that strikes us, than under the staff that comforts us.

-Stephen Charnock, *A Discourse of the Knowledge of God*

Men are as much blinded by the extremes of misery as by the extremes of prosperity.

-Edmund Burke, letter to a member of the National Assembly, 19 January 1791

I walked a mile with Pleasure,
She chattered all the way,
But left me none the wiser,
For all she had to say.
I walked a mile with Sorrow,
And ne'er a word said she,
But, oh, the things I learned from her
When Sorrow walked with me!

-Robert Browning Hamilton, "Along the Road"

The difficulties of life are intended to make us better, not bitter.

-Saying

Difficulties are things that show what men are.

-Epictetus, *Discourses*

Not only so, but we also rejoice in our sufferings, because we know that suffering produces perseverance; perseverance, character; and character, hope.

-The Bible (*NIV*), Romans 5: 3-4

Affliction, like the iron-smith, shapes as it smites.

-Christian Nestell Bovee, *Summaries of Thought*

Once you discover something worth suffering for, suffering ceases to be relevant.

- J.S. Felts

God hath not promised skies always blue,
Flower-strewn pathways all our lives through;
God hath not promised sun without rain,
Joy without sorrow, peace without pain.
But God hath promised strength for the day,
Rest for the labor, light for the way,
Grace for the trials, help from above,
Unfailing sympathy, undying love.

-Annie Johnson Flint, "What God Hath Promised"

The agony of man's affliction is often necessary to put him into the right mood to face the fundamental things of life. The Psalmist says: "Before I was afflicted I went astray, but now have I kept Thy Word."

-Oswald Chambers, *The Shadow of an Agony*

The Lord gets his best soldiers out of the highlands of affliction.

-Charles Haddon Spurgeon, *Gleanings Among the Sheaves*

After crosses and losses, men grow humbler and wiser.

-Benjamin Franklin, *Poor Richard's Almanack*

Those who do not feel pain, seldom think that it is felt.

-Samuel Johnson, *The Rambler*, 1 September 1750

We could never learn to be brave and patient, if there were only joy in the world.

-Helen Keller, *The Story of My Life*

It matters not how strait the gate,
How charged with punishments the scroll,
I am the master of my fate:
I am the captain of my soul.

-William Ernest Henley, “Invictus”

They that sow in tears shall reap in joy.

-The Bible (*KJV*), Psalms 126:5

God whispers to us in our pleasures, speaks in our conscience, but shouts in our pain: it is His megaphone to rouse a deaf world.

-C.S. Lewis, *The Problem of Pain*

It is a great thing, when our Gethsemane hours come, when the cup of bitterness is pressed to our lips . . . to feel that it is not fate or necessity, but divine love working upon us for good ends.

-Edwin Hubbel Chapin, *Living Words*

It is good for me that I have been afflicted, that I might learn thy statutes.

-The Bible (*KJV*), Psalms 119:71

For our light affliction, which is but for a moment, worketh for us a far more exceeding and eternal weight of glory.

-The Bible (*KJV*), 2 Corinthians 4:17

Men think God is destroying them because he is tuning them. The violinist screws up the key till the tense cord sounds the concert pitch; but it is not to break it, but to use it tunefully, that he stretches the string upon the musical rack.

-Henry Ward Beecher, *Life Thoughts*

We are troubled on every side, yet not distressed; we are perplexed, but not in despair; Persecuted, but not forsaken; cast down, but not destroyed.

-The Bible (*KJV*), 2 Corinthians 4:8-9

SIXTEEN

VANITY

Vanity and pride are different things, though the words are often used synonymously. A person may be proud without being vain. Pride relates more to our opinion of ourselves; vanity, to what we would have others think of us.

-Jane Austen, *Pride and Prejudice*

Praise has different effects, according to the mind it meets with: it makes a wise man modest, but a fool more arrogant.

-Owen Felltham, *Resolves, Divine, Moral and Political*

Vanity; it is the quicksand of reason; it is on that all merit makes shipwreck and disappears.

-George Sand, *Mademoiselle Merquem*

Nothing ought more to humiliate men who have deserved great praise than the care which they still take to boast of trifles.

- La Rochefoucauld, *Moral Maxims*

The desire of glory is the last infirmity cast off even by the wise.

-Tacitus, *Histories*

No really great man ever thought himself so.

-William Hazlitt, *The Plain Speaker*

Those who are greedy of praise prove that they are poor in merit.

-Plutarch, quoted in *A Book of Thoughts* (1865) by Henry Attwell

How quickly the glory of this world passes away!

-Thomas a' Kempis, *The Imitation of Christ*

There is no limit to the vanity of this world. Each spoke in the wheel thinks the whole strength of the wheel depends upon it.

-Josh Billings, "Saws", *The Complete Works of Josh Billings*

Applause is the spur of noble minds, the end and aim of weak ones.

-Charles Caleb Colton, *Lacon*

Fame has also this great drawback, that if we pursue it, we must direct our lives in such a way as to please the fancy of men.

-Baruch Spinoza, *On the Improvement of the Understanding*

The truest characters of ignorance
Are vanity, and pride, and arrogance.

-Samuel Butler (17th Century), "Miscellaneous Thoughts", *Genuine Poetical Remains*

Those who err in one direction, always take care to let you know that they are quite free from error in the opposite direction.

-Arthur Helps, "Short Essays", *Good Words*

Fools take to themselves the respect that is given to their office.

-Aesop, "The Jackass in Office", *Fables*

A vain man may become proud and imagine himself pleasing to all when he is in reality a universal nuisance.

-Baruch Spinoza, *Ethics*

SEVENTEEN

WORRY

There is only one way to happiness, and that is to cease worrying about things which are beyond the power of our will.

-Epictetus, *Discourses*

Suspense is worse than disappointment.

-Robert Burns, letter to Thomas Sloan, 1 September 1791

The beginning of anxiety is the end of faith, and the beginning of true faith is the end of anxiety.

-George Muller, quoted in *The Baptist Missionary Magazine*, September 1896

Suspicion always haunts the guilty mind;
The thief doth fear each bush an officer.

-William Shakespeare, *King Henry VI*

Only man clogs his happiness with care, destroying what is, with thoughts of what may be.

-John Dryden, quoted in *A Dictionary of Thoughts* (1891) by Tryon Edwards

This we might easily manage, if we would only take the burden appointed for us each day; but we choose to increase our troubles by carrying yesterday's stick over again today, and adding tomorrow's burden to our load, before we are required to bear it.

-John Newton, *The Life of Rev. John Newton*

Which of you by taking thought can add one cubit unto his stature?

-The Bible (*KJV*), Matthew 6:27

Some of your hurts you have cured,
And the sharpest you still have survived,
But what torments of grief you endured,
From evils that never arrived!

-Ralph Waldo Emerson, "Borrowing", *May-day, and Other Pieces*

Therefore do not worry about tomorrow, for tomorrow will worry about itself. Each day has enough trouble of its own.

-The Bible (*NIV*), Matthew 6:34

Learn to do thy part, and leave the rest to Heaven.

-John Henry Newman, "St. Paul at Melita", *Verses on Various Occasions*

Our Heavenly Father never takes anything from His children unless He means to give them something better.

-George Muller, *The Life of Trust*

Do not be miserable about what may happen tomorrow. The same everlasting Father, who cares for you today, will care for you tomorrow and every day. Either He will shield you from suffering or He will give you unfailing strength to bear it.

-Saint Francis de Sales, letter to lady, 16 January 1619

Don't be afraid of the day you have never seen.

-English Proverb

Never let the future disturb you. You will meet it, if you have to, with the same weapons of reason which today arm you against the present.

-Marcus Aurelius, *Meditations*

Worry gives a small thing a big shadow.

-Swedish Proverb

Courage for the great sorrows of life, and patience for the small ones. And then when you have laboriously accomplished your daily tasks, go to sleep in peace. God is awake.

-Victor Hugo, letter to Savinien Lapointe, March 1841

Cast all your cares on God; that anchor holds.

-Alfred Tennyson, *Enoch Arden*

One of the illusions of life is that the present hour is not the critical decisive hour. Write it on your heart that every day is the best day of the year.

-Ralph Waldo Emerson, "Works and Days", *Prose Works of Ralph Waldo Emerson*

The great masses of people are timid by nature, and thereby danger is invariably exaggerated.

-Carl Von Clausewitz, *On War*

When a thing is done, it's done.

-Saying

Anxiety is the rust of life, destroying its brightness and weakening its power. A childlike and abiding trust in Providence is its best preventive and remedy.

-Tryon Edwards, *A Dictionary of Thoughts*

It is impossible for that man to despair who remembers that his Helper is omnipotent.

-Jeremy Taylor, *The Rule and Exercises of Holy Living*

The bow cannot remain always bent, and relaxation, both of body and mind, is indispensable to all.

-Miguel de Cervantes, *Don Quixote*

Light burdens borne far become heavy.

-French Proverb

If that is how God clothes the grass of the field, which is here today and tomorrow is thrown into the fire, will he not much more clothe you.

-The Bible (*NIV*), Matthew 6:30

Apprehensions are greater in proportion as things are unknown.

–Livy, *History of Rome*

PART II

The Spiritual Journey

ONE

Charity

You will find as you look back on your life, that the moments that stand out, the moments when you have really lived, are the moments when you have done things in a spirit of love.

-Henry Drummond, *The Greatest Thing In the World*

I cannot do everything,
But still I can do something;
And because I cannot do everything,
I will not refuse to do the something that I can do.

-Edward Everett Hale, *Ten Times One is Ten*

Do all the good you can,
In all the ways you can,
To all the people you can,
As long as you can.

-*The Sunday School Repository* (1813)

It is the greatest of all mistakes to do nothing because you can only do little.

-Sydney Smith, lecture "On the Conduct of the Understanding" at. Royal Institution

He who awaits the call, but sees the need, already sets his spirit to refuse it.

-Dante Alighieri, "Purgatorio", *The Divine Comedy*

It is more blessed to give than to receive.

-The Bible (*KJV*), Acts 20:35

No one has ever become poor by giving.

-Anne Frank, *Diary of Anne Frank*

He who waits to do a great deal of good at once, will never do anything.

-Samuel Johnson, quoted in *The Visitor* (1844)

I hate the giving of the hand unless the whole man accompanies it.

-Ralph Waldo Emerson, *Journals*

This is what is hardest: to close the open hand because one loves.

-Friedrich Nietzsche, *Thus Spoke Zarathustra*

Who will sacrifice nothing, and enjoy all, is a fool.

-Johann Kaspar Lavater, *Aphorisms on Man*

When you give to the needy, do not let your left hand know what your right hand is doing.

-The Bible (*NIV*), Matthew 6:3

An old man, going a lone highway,
Came at the evening, cold and gray,
To chasm, vast and deep and wide,
Through which was flowing a sullen tide.
The old man crossed in the twilight dim;
The sullen stream had no fears for him;
But he turned when safe on the other side
And built a bridge to span the tide.
"Old man," said a fellow pilgrim near,
"You are wasting strength with building here;
your journey will end with the ending day;
You never again must pass this way;
You have crossed the chasm, deep and wide –
Why build you the bridge at the eventide?"
The builder lifted his old gray head:
"Good friend, in the path I have come," he said,
"There followeth after me today
A youth whose feet must pass this way.
This chasm that has been naught to me
To that fair-haired youth may a pit-fall be,
He, too, must cross in the twilight dim;
Good friend, I am building the bridge for him."

-Will Allen Dromgoole, "The Bridge Builder"

Be not forgetful to entertain strangers: for thereby some have entertained angels unawares.

-The Bible (*KJV*), Hebrews 13:2

The Sea of Galilee and the Dead Sea are made of the same water. It flows down, clear and cool, from the heights of Hermon and the roots of the cedars of Lebanon. The Sea of Galilee makes beauty of it, for the Sea of Galilee has an outlet. It gets to give. It gathers in its riches that it may pour them out again to fertilize the Jordan plain. But the Dead Sea with the same water makes horror. For the Dead Sea has no outlet. It gets to keep.

-Harry Emerson Fosdick, *The Meaning of Service*

If you asked twenty good men today what they thought the highest of the virtues, nineteen of them would reply, unselfishness. But if you asked almost any of the great Christians of old he would have replied, love. Do you see what has happened? A negative term has been substituted for a positive and this is of more than philological importance. The negative ideal of unselfishness carries with it the suggestion not primarily of securing good things for others, but going without them ourselves, as if our abstinence and not their happiness was the important point. I do not think this is the Christian virtue of love.

-C.S. Lewis, "The Weight of Glory", address at Oxford University Church, 8 June 1941

Benefits, like grain, should be followed from the seed to the harvest... delay not doing a benefit for fear of ingratitude; by which you neglect a duty to yourself. It is another's fault if he be ungrateful, but it is mine if I do not give.

-Lucius Annaeus Seneca (the younger), "On benefits", *Moral Essays*

There are two kinds of charity, remedial and preventive. The former is often injurious in its tendency; the latter is always praiseworthy and beneficial.

-Tryon Edwards, *A Dictionary of Thoughts*

All the beautiful sentiments in the world weigh less than a single lovely action.

-James Russell Lowell, *Rousseau and the Sentimentalists*

Petting scorpions with a compassionate hand will only get you stung.

-Saying

The greatest pleasure I know is to do a good action by stealth, and to have it found out by accident.

-Charles Lamb, "Table Talk by the late Elia" in *The Athenaeum*, 4 January 1834

A bone to the dog is not charity. Charity is the bone shared with the dog, when you are just as hungry as the dog.

-Jack London, "Confession", *The Road*

Every man according as he purposeth in his heart, so let him give, not grudgingly, or of necessity; for God loveth a cheerful giver.

-The Bible (*KJV*), 2 Corinthians 9:7

A blind man will not thank you for a looking glass.

-Thomas Fuller, *Gnomologia*

TWO

CHASTITY

Chastity, once lost, cannot be recalled; it goes only once.

-Ovid, *The Heroines*

A man who governs his passions is master of the world. We must either command them or be enslaved to them. It is better to be the hammer than the anvil.

-Saint Dominic, quoted in *The Lives* (1833) by Alban Butler

So long as chastity is preserved, it is respected; it is despised only after having been lost.

-Jean Jacques Rousseau, *Emile*

Who doth desire that chaste his wife should be,
First, be he true, for truth doth truth deserve.

-Philip Sidney, *The Countess of Pembroke's Arcadia*

To the pure, all things are pure, but to those who are corrupted and do not believe, nothing is pure.

-The Bible (*NIV*), Titus 1:15

Sensuality often makes love grow too quickly, so that the root remains weak and is easy to pull out.

-Friedrich Nietzsche, *Beyond Good and Evil*

The way to avoid evil is not by maiming our passions, but by compelling them to yield their vigor to our moral nature.

-Henry Ward Beecher, *Life Thoughts*

THREE

CHRISTIANITY

The The Christian ideal has not been tried and found wanting; it has been found difficult, and left untried.

-G.K. Chesterton, *What's Wrong with the World*

He, who begins by loving Christianity better than the truth, will proceed by loving his own sect or Church better than Christianity, and end by loving himself better than all.

-Samuel Taylor Coleridge, "Moral and Religious Aphorisms", *Aids to Reflection*

There's not much practical Christianity in the man . . . who lives on better terms with angels and seraphs than with his children, servants and neighbors.

-Isaac Taylor, *Natural History of Enthusiasm*

If my people which are called by my name shall humble themselves and pray, and seek my face and turn from their wicked ways then I will hear from heaven and forgive their sins and will heal their land.

-The Bible (*KJV*), 2 Chronicles 7:14

If a man cannot be a Christian in the place where he is, he cannot be a Christian anywhere.

-Henry Ward Beecher, *Life Thoughts*

You are to follow no man further than he follows Christ.

-Bartholomew Ashwood, *The Heavenly Trade*

His religion was not a thing like a theory but a thing like a love affair.

-G.K. Chesterton, *St. Francis of Assisi*

Every man is a priest, even involuntary; his conduct is an unspoken sermon, which is forever preaching to others.

-Henri Frederic Amiel, *Journal Intime*, 2 May 1852

He that can apprehend and consider vice with all her baits and seeming pleasures, and yet abstain, and yet distinguish and prefer that which is truly better, he is the true warfaring Christian.

-John Milton, *Areopagitica*

Are the things you are living for worth Christ dying for?

-Leonard Ravenhill, inscription on his tombstone

Though I am not what I ought to be, nor what I wish to be, nor I am not what I hope to be, I can truly say, I am not what I once was.

-John Newton, quoted in *The Christian Spectator*, April 1821

The Gateway to Christianity is not through an intricate labyrinth of dogma, but by a simple belief in the person of Christ.

-William Lyon Phelps, *Human Nature and the Gospel*

I consider that the chief dangers which confront the coming century will be religion without the Holy Ghost, Christianity without Christ, forgiveness without repentance, salvation without regeneration, politics without God, and heaven without hell.

-William Booth, *The War Cry*, 5 Jan 1901

I believe in Christianity as I believe that the sun has risen, not only because I see it, but because by it I see everything else.

-C.S. Lewis, "The Weight of Glory", address at Oxford University, 8 June 1941

When I read the life of such a man (Apostle Paul), how I blush to think how sickly and dwarfed Christianity is at the present time.

-Dwight L. Moody, *Heaven*

The test of every religious, political, or educational system is the man which it forms.

-Henri Frederic Amiel, *Journal Intime*, 17 June 1852

Expect great things from God; attempt great things for God.

-William Carey, "Deathless", sermon, 31 May 1792

Let my heart be broken with the things that break the heart of God.

-Robert "Bob" Pierce, written inside the cover of his bible

FOUR

CHURCH

Ye are the salt of the earth: but if the salt have lost his savor, wherewith shall it be salted? It is thenceforth good for nothing, but to be cast out, and to be trodden under foot of men. Ye are the light of the world. A city that is set on an hill cannot be hid. Neither do men light a candle, and put it under a bushel, but on a candlestick; and it giveth light unto all that are in the house. Let your light so shine before men, that they may see your good works, and glorify your Father which is in heaven.

-The Bible (*KJV*), Matthew 5:13-16

"I beseech ye in the bowels of Christ, think that ye may be mistaken." I should like to have that written over the portals of every church, every school, and every courthouse, and, may I say, of every legislative body in the United States.

-Learned Hand, *The Spirit of Liberty*

The Lord showed me, so that I did see clearly, that he did not dwell in these temples which men had commanded and set up, but in people's hearts . . . his people were his temple, and he dwelt in them.

-George Fox, *Journal*

Religious externals may have meaning for the God-inhabited soul; for any others they are not only useless but may actually become snares, deceiving them into a false and perilous sense of security.

-A.W. Tozer, *Man: The Dwelling Place of God*

One hundred religious persons knit into a unity by careful organization do not constitute a church any more than eleven dead men make a football team. The first requisite is life, always.

-A.W. Tozer, *Man: The Dwelling Place of God*

We Christians too often substitute prayer for playing the game. Prayer is good; but when used as a substitute for obedience, it is nothing but a blatant hypocrisy, a despicable Pharisaism...To your knees, man! And to your Bible! Decide at once! Don't hedge! Time flies! Cease your insults to God. Quit consulting flesh and blood. Stop your lame, lying, and cowardly excuses.

-Charles Thomas Studd, *The Chocolate Soldier*

The devil is a better theologian than any of us and is a devil still.

-A.W. Tozer, *Man: The Dwelling Place of God*

Give me a hundred men who fear nothing but sin, and desire nothing but God, and I will shake the world. I care not for straw whether they be clergymen or laymen; and such alone will overthrow the kingdom of Satan and build up the Kingdom of God on earth.

-John Wesley, quoted in *The Baptist Reporter*, January 1843

We find not in the Gospel, that Christ hath anywhere provided for the uniformity of churches, but only for their unity.

-Roger Williams, *The Bloudy Tenent of Persecution*

The soul's safety is in its heat. Truth without enthusiasm, morality without emotion, ritual without soul, make for a Church without power. Destitute of the Fire of God, nothing else counts; possessing Fire, nothing else matters.

-Samuel Chadwick, *The Way to Pentecost*

And this is the mission of the church – not civilization, but salvation – not better laws, purer legislation, social elevation, human equality and liberty, but first, the "kingdom of God and His righteousness;" regenerated hearts, and all other things will follow.

-Abbott Eliot Kittredge, quoted in *Dictionary of Burning Words of Brilliant Writers* (1895) by Josiah Gilbert

That sermon that makes everyone go away silent and grave, and hastening to be alone, to meditate or pray over the matter of it in secret, has had its true effect.

-Gilbert Burnet, *A Discourse of the Pastoral Care*

The trouble with organizing a thing is that pretty soon folks get to paying more attention to the organization than to what they're organized for.

-Laura Ingalls Wilder, *Little Town on the Prairie*

'Tis mad idolatry
To make the service greater than the god.

-William Shakespeare, *Troilus and Cressida*

For religion all men are equal, as all pennies are equal, because the only value of any of them is that they bear the image of the King.

-G.K. Chesterton, *Charles Dickens*

The way to preserve the peace of the church is to preserve the purity of it.

-Matthew Henry, *An Exposition of the Old and New Testaments*

Depend upon it, as long as the church is living so much like the world, we cannot expect our children to be brought into the fold.

-Dwight L. Moody, "Where Art Thou?" *Twelve Select Sermons*

Do you recall the laughter of the Philistines at the helpless Sampson? You can hear the echo of that laughter to-day, as the church, shorn of her strength by her own sin, is an object of ridicule to the world.

-Abbott Eliot Kittredge, quoted in *Dictionary of Burning Words* (1895) by Josiah Gilbert

There is nothing more pitiable ... a soulless, sapless, shriveled church, seeking to thrive in a worldly atmosphere, rooted in barren professions, bearing no fruit, and maintaining only the semblance of existence, such a church cannot long survive.

-George C. Lorimer, *Isms Old and New*

What is ministerial success? Crowded churches, full aisles, attentive congregations, the approval of the religious world, much impression produced? Elijah thought so; and when he found out his mistake, and discovered that the Carmel applause subsided into hideous stillness, his heart wellnigh broke with disappointment. Ministerial success lies in altered lives, and obedient, humble hearts; unseen work recognized in the judgment-day.

-Frederick William Robertson, sermon, "Elijah", 13 October 1850

The conduct of our lives is the true mirror of our doctrine.

-Michel de Montaigne, "The Education of Children", *Essays*

Since the days before Pentecost, has the whole church ever put aside every other work and waited upon Him for ten days, that the Spirit's power might be manifested?. . .
We give too much attention to method and machinery and resources, and too little to the source of power.

-Hudson Taylor, speech, "The Source of Power for Christian Missions", 23 April 1900

We are too busy to pray, and so we are too busy to have power. We have a great deal of activity, but we accomplish little; many services but few conversions; much machinery but few results.

-R.A. Torrey, *How to Obtain Fullness of Power in Christian Life and Service*

One scabby sheep is enough to spoil the whole flock.

-French Proverb

An unholy church! It is useless to the world, and of no esteem among men. It is an abomination, hell's laughter, heaven's abhorrence. The worst evils which have ever come upon the world have been brought upon her by an unholy church.

-Charles Haddon Spurgeon, *Evening by Evening*

Our great problem is the problem of trafficking in unlived truth. We try to communicate what we've never experienced in our own lives.

-Dwight L. Moody

FIVE

Faith & Belief

I would rather walk in the dark with God than go alone in the light.

-Mary Gardiner Brainard, "Not Knowing"

All I have seen teaches me to trust the Creator for all I have not seen.

-Ralph Waldo Emerson, "Immortality", *Letters and Social Aims*

Therefore do not seek to understand in order to believe, but believe that thou mayest understand.

-Saint Augustine, *Tractates on the Gospel of John*

A faith that sets bounds to itself, that will believe so much and no more, that will trust so far and no further, is none.

-Julius Charles Hare, *Guesses at Truth*

What is divine escapes men's notice because of their incredulity.

-Heraclitus, *Fragments*

Though he slay me, yet will I trust in him.

–The Bible (*KJV*), Job13:15

He who believes is strong; he who doubts is weak. Strong convictions precede great actions.

-James Freeman Clarke, *Common-sense in Religion*

Can a faith that does nothing be called sincere?

-Jean Racine, *Athalie*

Faith without works is dead.

-The Bible (*KJV*), James 2:26

He does not believe, that does not live according to his belief.

-Thomas Fuller, *Gnomologia*

To be an atheist requires an infinitely greater measure of faith than to receive all the great truths which atheism would deny.

-Joseph Addison, *The Spectator*, 8 March 1711

They that worship God merely for Fear,
Would worship the Devil too, if he appear.

-Thomas Fuller, *Gnomologia*

Strong meat belongeth to them that are of full age.

-The Bible (*KJV*), Hebrews 5:14

Faith is a living and unshakeable confidence, a belief in the grace of God so assured that a man would die a thousand deaths for its sake.

-Martin Luther, preface to his translation of *St. Paul's Epistle to the Romans*

Faith is precious, feeling is fickle. Believing, we stand firm; but by feeling we are tossed about.

-Charles Haddon Spurgeon, sermon, "Stand Fast", 27 August 1882

He that will believe only what he can fully comprehend, must have a very long head, or a very short creed.

-Charles Caleb Colton, *Lacon*

I believe in the sun even when it isn't shining.
I believe in love even when I feel it not.
I believe in God even when he is silent.

-inscription on the wall of a cellar in Cologne, Germany where Jews had been hiding during WWII

A man may be a heretic in the truth; and if he believe things only because his pastor says so, or the assembly so determines, without knowing other reason, though his belief be true, yet the very truth he holds becomes his heresy.

-John Milton, *Areopagitica*

There comes a time when you've used your brains, your training, your technical skill, and the die is cast and the events are in the hands of God, and there you have to leave them.

-Dwight D. Eisenhower, statement before battle for Sicily, 10 July 1943

Question with boldness even the existence of a God; because, if there be one, he must more approve of the homage of reason, than that of blind-folded fear.

-Thomas Jefferson, letter to Peter Carr, 10 August 1787

Doubt, indulged and cherished, is in danger of becoming denial; but if honest, and bent on thorough investigation, it may soon lead to full establishment in the truth.

-Tryon Edwards, *A Dictionary of Thoughts*

It is so fatally easy to confuse an aesthetic appreciation of the spiritual life with the life itself - to dream that you have waked, washed, and dressed & then to find yourself still in bed.

-C.S. Lewis, letter to Arthur Greeves, 15 June 1930

Sometimes the Lord calms the storm. Sometimes he lets the storm rage and calms his child.

-Saying

Our belief or disbelief of a thing does not alter the nature of the thing.

-John Tillotson, *The Wisdom of Being Religious*

We are half-hearted creatures, fooling about with drink and sex and ambition, when infinite joy is offered to us, like an ignorant child who wants to go on making mud pies in the slum because he cannot imagine what is meant by the offer of a holiday at the sea. We are far too easily pleased.

-C.S. Lewis, "The Weight of Glory", address at Oxford University Church, 8 June 1941

Thou wilt keep him in perfect peace, whose mind is stayed on thee: because he trusteth in thee.

-The Bible (*KJV*), Isaiah 26:3

There lives more faith in honest doubt,
Believe me, than in half the creeds.

-Alfred Tennyson, *In Memoriam*

I was young and now I am old, yet I have never seen the righteous forsaken or their children begging bread.

-The Bible (*NIV*), Psalms 37:25

That the universe was formed by a fortuitous concourse of atoms, I will no more believe, than that the accidental jumbling of the alphabet, could fall by chance into a most ingenious and learned treatise of philosophy.

-Jonathan Swift, *A Critical Essay upon the Faculties of the Mind*

How many (Christians) estimate difficulty in the light of their own resources, and thus attempt little, and often fail in the little they attempt. All God's giants have been weak men who did great things for God because they reckoned on His power and presence to be with them.

-Hudson Taylor, *China's Millions*

SIX

FORGIVENESS

The weak can never forgive. Forgiveness is the attribute of the strong.

-Mahatma Gandhi, *Young India*, 2 April 1931

Many promising reconciliations have broken down because while both parties came prepared to forgive, neither party came prepared to be forgiven.

-Charles Walter Stansby Williams

A good garden may have some weeds.

-English Proverb

It is a severe rebuke upon us that God makes us so many allowances, and we make so few to our neighbor.

-William Penn, *Some Fruits of Solitude*

He that cannot forgive others, breaks the bridge over which he must pass himself; for every man has need to be forgiven.

-Edward Herbert, *The Life of Edward Lord Herbert of Cherbury*

A God all mercy is a God unjust.

-Edward Young, *Night-Thoughts*

Take heed to yourselves: If thy brother trespass against thee, rebuke him; and if he repent, forgive him.

-The Bible (*KJV*), Luke 17:3

The best may err.

-Joseph Addison, *Cato*

Bear with each other and forgive whatever grievances you may have against one another. Forgive as the Lord forgave you.

-The Bible (*NIV*), Colossians 3:13

Teach me to feel another's woe,
To hide the fault I see;
That mercy I to others show,
That mercy show to me.

-Alexander Pope, "The Universal Prayer"

SEVEN

God

God is preparing his heroes still, and when the opportunity comes He can fit them into their place in a moment, and the world will wonder where they came from.

-Albert Benjamin Simpson, *The Holy Spirit*

Though God's attributes are equal, yet his mercy is more attractive and pleasing in our eyes than his justice.

-Miguel de Cervantes, *Don Quixote*

The most beautiful of all emblems is that of God, whom Timaeus of Locris describes under the image of "A circle whose centre is everywhere and whose circumference is nowhere."

-Voltaire, *A Philosophical Dictionary*

It is the heart which experiences God, and not the reason.

-Blaise Pascal, *Pensées*

Nothing hath separated us from God but our own will, or rather our own will is our separation from God.

-William Law, *The Grounds and Reasons of Christian Regeneration*

Without the assistance of the Divine Being. . . I cannot succeed. With that assistance, I cannot fail.

-Abraham Lincoln, address in Springfield, Illinois, 11 February 1861

The things which are impossible with men are possible with God.

-The Bible (*KJV*), Luke 18:27

Thus speaketh Christ, our Lord, to us:
Ye call me Master, and obey me not;
Ye call me light, and seek me not;
Ye call me life, and desire me not;
Ye call me wise, and follow me not;
Ye call me fair, and love me not;
Ye call me rich, and ask me not;
Ye call me eternal, and seek me not;
Ye call me gracious, and trust me not;
Ye call me noble, and serve me not;
Ye call me mighty, and honor me not;
Ye call me just, and fear me not;
If I condemn you, blame me not.

-ancient inscription in the cathedral at Lubeck, Germany

Be still, and know that I am God.

-The Bible (*KJV*), Psalms 46:10

A man with God is always in the majority.

-John Knox, inscription on the Reformation Monument in Geneva, Switzerland

Trust in the Lord with all thine heart, and lean not unto thine own understanding. In all thy ways acknowledge Him, and He shall direct thy paths.

-The Bible (*KJV*), Proverbs 3:5-6

A true love to God must begin with a delight in his holiness.

-Jonathan Edwards, *A Treatise Concerning Religious Affections*

What a long way it is between knowing God and loving Him!

-Blaise Pascal, *Pensées*

If God be for us, who can be against us?

-The Bible (*KJV*), Romans 8:31

Christ is not valued at all, unless he is valued above all.

-Saint Augustine, quoted in *Dictionary of Burning Words of Brilliant Writers* (1895) by Josiah Gilbert

God is as great in minuteness as in magnitude.

-Charles Caleb Colton, *Lacon*

Little is much if God is in it.

-Amy Carmichael, *From Sunrise Land: Letters from Japan*

God sees hearts, as we see faces.

-George Herbert, *A Priest to the Temple*

Those who seek me early shall find me.

-The Bible (*KJV*), Proverbs 8:17

Whatever your heart clings to and confides in, that is really your God.

-Martin Luther, "Ten Commandments", *Large Catechism*

Don't measure God's mind by your own.

-George MacDonald, *David Elginbrod*

Draw nigh to God, and he will draw nigh to you.

-The Bible (*KJV*), James 4:8

An unknown God is an untrusted God.

-Charles Haddon Spurgeon, sermon, "Two Good Things", 17 June 1880

There are things in Christ which you can never learn or see until you have knelt at his feet.

-Harrington C. Lees, quoted in *Bible Truths Illustrated* (1917) by J. C. Ferdinand Pittman

EIGHT

HOLINESS

No man can serve two masters: for either he will hate the one, and love the other; or else he will hold to the one, and despise the other.

-The Bible (*KJV*), Matthew 6:24

He who does not weep does not see.

-Victor Hugo, *Les Miserables*

Give not that which is holy unto the dogs, neither cast ye your pearls before swine, lest they trample them under their feet, and turn again and rend you.

-The Bible (*KJV*), Matthew 7:6

Whitewashing the pump won't make the water pure.

-Saying

Blessed is the man that walketh not in the counsel of the ungodly, nor standeth in the way of sinners, nor sitteth in the seat of the scornful. But his delight is in the law of the Lord; and in his law doth he meditate day and night. And he shall be like a tree planted by the rivers of water, that bringeth forth his fruit in his season; his leaf also shall not whither; and whatsoever he doeth shall prosper. The ungodly are not so: but are like the chaff which the wind driveth away.

-The Bible (*KJV*), Psalms 1:1-4

Preaching is of much avail, but practice is far more potent. A godly life is the strongest argument that you can offer to the skeptic.

-Hosea Ballou, quoted in *Life Story of Hosea Ballou* (1854) by Maturin Murray Ballou

It is a great deal better to live holy than to talk about it. We are told to let our light shine, and if it does we won't need to tell anybody it does. The light will be its own witness. Lighthouses don't ring bells and fire cannon to call attention to their shining - they just shine.

-Dwight L. Moody, quoted in *Golden Gleams of Thought* (1881) by Rev. S. Pollock Linn

God often works more by the life of the illiterate seeking the things that are God's, than by the ability of the learned seeking the things that are their own.

-Saint Anselm, quoted in *Ages of Faith* (1840) by Kenelm-Henry Digby

How many people would like to be good, if only they might be good without taking trouble about it! They do not like goodness well enough to hunger and thirst after it, or to sell all that they have that they may buy it; they will not batter at the gate of the kingdom of heaven; but they look with pleasure on this or that aerial castle of righteousness, and think it would be rather nice to live in it.

-George MacDonald, *Paul Faber, Surgeon*

A holy life is not an ascetic, or gloomy, or solitary life, but a life regulated by divine truth and faithful in Christian duty - It is living above the world while we are still in it.

-Tryon Edwards, *A Dictionary of Thoughts*

NINE

Humility

It's only by forgetting yourself that you draw near to God.

-Henry David Thoreau, *Journal*

Whosoever shall exalt himself shall be abased; and he that shall humble himself shall be exalted.

-The Bible (*KJV*), Matthew 23:12

Plenty of people wish to become devout, but no one wishes to be humble.

-Francois de La Rochefoucauld, *Moral Maxims*

The graveyards are full of people the world could not do without.

-Elbert Hubbard, *The Philistine*

When pride comes, then comes disgrace, but with humility comes wisdom.

-The Bible (*NIV*), Proverbs 11:2

Pride perceiving humility honorable, often borrows her cloak.

-Thomas Fuller, *Gnomologia*

God resisteth the proud and giveth grace to the humble. Humble yourselves therefore under the mighty hand of God, that he may exalt you in due time.

-The Bible (*KJV*), 1 Peter 5:5-6

A man's pride shall bring him low: but honour shall uphold the humble in spirit.

-The Bible (*KJV*), Proverbs 29:23

I murmured because I had no shoes, until I met a man who had no feet.

-Persian Proverb

A humble knowledge of oneself is a surer road to God than a deep searching of the sciences.

-Thomas a' Kempis, *The Imitation of Christ*

A man should never be ashamed to own that he has been in the wrong, which is but saying, that he is wiser today than he was yesterday.

-Jonathan Swift, *Thoughts on Various Subjects*

Let us right our faults with speed, for easily righted are the hearts of the brave.

-Homer, *The Iliad*

It is well to remember your heart is not God's compass. Stop following your heart and start following God.

- J.S. Felts

Every man has had kings and slaves, barbarians and Greeks, among his ancestors.

-Plato, *Theaetetus*

We are never more in danger than when we think ourselves most secure, nor in reality more secure than when we seem to be most in danger.

-William Cowper, letter to Rev. William Unwin, 3 August 1782

If the best man's faults were written on his forehead, it would make him pull his hat over his eyes.

-Gaelic Proverb

You can always tell when a man is a great ways from God - he is always talking about himself, how good he is. But the moment he sees God by the eye of faith, he is down on his knees, and, like Job, he cries, "Behold I am vile."

-Dwight L. Moody, "Sinners Seeking Christ", *Twelve Select Sermons*

Before honour is humility.

-The Bible (*KJV*), Proverbs 15:33

Remember always that all of us, and you and I especially, are descended from immigrants and revolutionists.

-Franklin Delano Roosevelt, address to Daughters of American Revolution, 21 April 1938

If you want people to think well of you, do not speak well of yourself.

-Blaise Pascal, *Pensées*

Do you wish to be great? Then begin by being little. Do you desire to construct a vast and lofty fabric? Think first about the foundation of humility. The higher your structure is to be, the deeper must be its foundation.

-Saint Augustine, *Sermons on Selected Lessons of the New Testament*

Lord Jesus, when we are wrong, make us willing to change, and when we are right, make us easy to live with.

-Peter Marshall, *A Man Called Peter*

The first test of a truly great man is his humility.

-John Ruskin, "Of Many Things", *Modern Painters*

Conceal a flaw, and the world will imagine the worst.

-Martial, *Epigrams*

To ask is no sin and to be refused is no calamity.

-Russian Proverb

Like a man traveling in foggy weather, those at some distance before him on the road he sees wrapped up in the fog, as well as those behind him, and also the people in the fields on each side, but near him all appears clear, though in truth he is as much in the fog as any of them.

-Benjamin Franklin, *Autobiography of Benjamin Franklin*

If we could solve all the mysteries of the universe, we would be co-equal with God. Every drop of ocean shares its glory, but is not the ocean.

-Mahatma Gandhi, *Harijan,* 13 June 1936

I preached as never sure to preach again,
And as a dying man to dying men!

-Richard Baxter, "Love Breathing Thanks and Praise", *Poetical Fragments*

Always acknowledge a fault frankly. This will throw those in authority off guard and give you an opportunity to commit more.

-Mark Twain, *Notebook*

Nothing sets a person so much out of the devil's reach as humility.

-Jonathan Edwards, *Some Thoughts Concerning the Present Revival of Religion*

A generous confession disarms slander.

-English Proverb

[Even] the strongest have their moments of fatigue.

-Friedrich Nietzsche, *The Will To Power*

The true way to be humble is not to stoop until you are smaller than yourself, but to stand at your real height against some higher nature that will show you what the real smallness of your greatest greatness is.

-Phillips Brooks, "Humility", *Sermons*

All men are tempted. There is no man that lives that can't be broken down, provided it is the right temptation, put in the right spot.

-Henry Ward Beecher, Proverbs from Plymouth Pulpit

It is always the secure who are humble.

-G.K. Chesterton, "A Defense of Humility", *The Defendant*

The meek man is not a human mouse afflicted with a sense of his own inferiority. . . He has accepted God's estimate of his own life . . . In himself, nothing; In God, everything . . . He knows well that the world will never see him as God sees him and he has stopped caring.

-A.W. Tozer, *The Pursuit of God*

The weakest spot in every man is where he thinks himself to be the wisest.

-Nathanael Emmons, “Reflections of a Visitor”, *The Works of Nathanael Emmons*

True humility is not an abject, groveling, self-despising spirit; it is but a right estimate of ourselves as God sees us.

-Tryon Edwards, *A Dictionary of Thoughts*

It is no great thing to be humble when you are brought low; but to be humble when you are praised is a great and rare attainment.

-Saint Bernard, quoted in *Seed-thought* (1863) by George C. Robinson

By humility, and the fear of the Lord, are riches, honor, and life.

-The Bible (*KJV*), Proverbs 22:4

Be very slow to believe that you are wiser than all others; it is a fatal but common error. Where one has been saved by a true estimation of another's weakness, thousands have been destroyed by a false appreciation of their own strength.

-Charles Caleb Colton, *Lacon*

We need not be much concerned about those faults which we have the courage to own.

-Francois de La Rochefoucauld, *Reflections or Sentences and Moral Maxims*

Confession is good for the soul.

-Scottish Proverb

To be secure, be humble; to be happy, be content.

-James Hurdis, *The Village Curate*

What you dislike in another person, take care to correct in yourself.

-Thomas Sprat, quoted in *The Rule of Life* (1758)

Many of the Bible characters fell just in the things in which they were thought to be strongest. Moses failed in his humility, Abraham in his faith, Elijah in his courage, for one woman scared him away to that juniper-tree; and Peter, whose strong point was boldness, was so frightened by a maid, as to deny his Lord.

-Dwight L. Moody, *Best Thoughts and Discourses of D.L. Moody*

A great man is always willing to be little.

-Ralph Waldo Emerson, "Compensation", *Essays*

He, who thinks his place below him, will certainly be below his place.

-George Savile, *Miscellanies*

I believe firmly, that the moment our hearts are emptied of pride and selfishness and ambition and self-seeking and everything that is contrary to God's law, the Holy Ghost will come and fill every corner of our hearts; but if we are full of pride and conceit and ambition and self-seeking and pleasure and the world, there is no room for the Spirit of God; and I believe many a man is praying to God to fill him when he is full already with something else. Before we pray that God would fill us, I believe we ought to pray Him to empty us.

-Dwight L. Moody, *Secret Power*

TEN

Prayer

It is because of the hasty and superficial conversation with God that the sense of sin is so weak and that no motives have power to help you to hate and flee from sin as you should.

-Andrew Murray, *The Prayer Life*

Prayer does not change God, but it changes the one who offers it.

-Soren Kierkegaard, "Purity of Heart", *Edifying Discourses in Diverse Spirits*

Men of God are always men of prayer.

-E.M. Bounds, *The Weapon of Prayer*

The one concern of the devil is to keep Christians from praying. He fears nothing from prayerless studies, prayer-less work, and prayerless religion. He laughs at our toil, mocks at our wisdom, but trembles when we pray.

-Samuel Chadwick, quoted in *The Possibilities of Prayer* (1923) by E.M. Bounds

We look upon prayer as a means of getting things for ourselves; the Bible's idea of prayer is that we may get to know God Himself.

-Oswald Chambers, *My Utmost for His Highest*

The effectual, fervent prayer of a righteous man availeth much.

-The Bible (*KJV*), James 5:16

We have to pray with our eyes on God, not on the difficulties.

-Oswald Chambers, *God's Workmanship*

Do not have as your motive the desire to be known as a praying man. Get an inner chamber in which to pray where no one knows you are praying, shut the door, and talk to God in secret.

-Oswald Chambers, *My Utmost for His Highest*

When thou prayest, rather let your heart be without words than your words without heart.

-John Bunyan

Nowhere can we get to know the holiness of God, and come under its influence and power, except in the inner chamber. It has been well said: "No man can expect to make progress in holiness who is not often and long alone with God."

-Andrew Murray, *The Prayer Life*

When our will wholeheartedly enters into the prayer of Christ, then we pray correctly.

-Dietrich Bonhoeffer, *Psalms: The Prayer Book of the Bible*

We pray pious blether, our will is not in it, and then we say God does not answer; we never asked for anything . . . asking means that our wills are in it.

-Oswald Chambers, *My Utmost for His Highest*

Prayer is not eloquence, but earnestness; not the definition of helplessness, but the feeling of it; not figures of speech, but compunction of soul.

-Hannah More, quoted in *The Southern Spectator*, June 1859

If we rely on the Holy Spirit, we shall find that our prayers become more and more inarticulate; and when they are inarticulate, reverence grows deeper and deeper.

-Oswald Chambers, *If Ye Shall Ask*

The best prayers have often more groans than words.

-John Bunyan, *A Discourse Touching Prayer*

Ye lust, and have not: ye kill, and desire to have, and cannot obtain: ye fight and war, yet ye have not, because ye ask not.

-The Bible (*KJV*), James 4:2

We can never know God as it is our privilege to know Him, by brief and fragmentary and unconsidered repetitions of intercessions that are requests for personal favors and nothing more.

-E.M. Bounds, *Purpose in Prayer*

Ye ask, and receive not, because ye ask amiss.

-The Bible *(KJV),* James 4:3

Storm the throne of grace and persevere therein, and mercy will come down.

-John Wesley, letter to Mrs. Bennis, 1 March 1774

Ask, and it shall be given you; seek, and ye shall find; knock, and it shall be opened unto you.

-The Bible (*NIV*), Matthew 7:7

The richness of the Word of God ought to determine our prayer, not the poverty of our heart.

-Dietrich Bonhoeffer, *Psalms: The Prayer Book of the Bible*

Do not pray for easy lives. Pray to be stronger men! Do not pray for tasks equal to your powers. Pray for powers equal to your tasks!

-Phillips Brooks, "Going Up to Jerusalem", *Twenty Sermons*

The wise man in the storm prays God, not for safety from danger, but for deliverance from fear.

-Ralph Waldo Emerson, *Journals*

Jesus taught that perseverance is the essential element of prayer. Men must be in earnest when they kneel at God's footstool. Too often we get faint-hearted and quit praying at the point when we ought to begin. We let go at the very point where we should hold on strongest. Our prayers are weak because they are not impassioned by an unfailing and resistless will.

-E.M. Bounds, *Purpose in Prayer*

Did not God sometimes withhold in mercy what we ask, we should be ruin'd at our own request.

-Hannah More, "Moses in the Bulrushes", *Sacred Dramas*

Certain thoughts are prayers. There are moments when, whatever the attitude of the body, the soul is on its knees.

-Victor Hugo, *Les Miserables*

Words are but the body, the garment, the outside of prayer; sighs are nearer the heart work. A dumb beggar getteth an alms at Christ's gates, even by making signs, when his tongue cannot plead for him; and the rather, because he is dumb. . . Tears have a tongue, and grammar, and language that our Father knoweth. Babes have no prayer for the breast, but weeping: the mother can read hunger in weeping.

-Samuel Rutherford, *The Trial and Triumph of Faith*

Take time to read - it is the fountain of wisdom.
Take time to think - it is the source of power.
Take time to pray - it is the greatest power on earth.

-Saying

If a son shall ask bread of any of you that is a father, will he give him a stone? or if he ask a fish, will he for a fish give him a serpent? Or if he shall ask an egg, will he offer him a scorpion? If ye then, being evil, know how to give good gifts unto your children: how much more shall your heavenly Father give the Holy Spirit to them that ask him?

-The Bible (*KJV*), Luke 11:11-13

Spread out your petition before God, and then say, "Thy will, not mine, be done." The sweetest lesson I have learned in God's school is to let the Lord choose for me.

-Dwight L. Moody, sermon, "Power in Prayer", 23-24 July 1985

Pray without ceasing.

-The Bible (*KJV*), 1 Thessalonians 5:17

Beware in your prayers, above everything else, of limiting God, not only by unbelief, but by fancying that you know what He can do. Expect unexpected things, above all that we ask or think. Each time, before you intercede, be quiet first, and worship God in His glory. Think of what He can do, and how He delights to hear the prayers of His redeemed people. Think of your place and privilege in Christ, and expect great things.

-Andrew Murray, *The Ministry of Intercession*

Prayer is not monologue but dialogue; God's voice in response to mine is its most essential part.

-Andrew Murray, *With Christ in the School of Prayer*

Father, I want to know Thee, but my coward heart fears to give up its toys. I cannot part with them without inward bleeding, and I do not try to hide from Thee the terror of the parting. I come trembling, but I do come. Please root from my heart all Those things which I have cherished so long and which have become a very part of my living self, so that Thou mayest enter and dwell there without a rival. Then shalt Thou make the place of Thy feet glorious. Then shall my heart have no need of the sun to shine in it, for Thyself wilt be the light of it, and there shall be no night there. In Jesus' name, Amen.

-A.W. Tozer, *The Pursuit of God*

Be careful for nothing; but in everything by prayer and supplication with thanksgiving let your requests be made known unto God.

-The Bible (*KJV*), Philippians 4:6

Many times that which we ask would, if it should be granted, be worse for us, and perhaps tend to our destruction; and then God by denying the particular matter of our prayers doth grant the general matter of them.

-Henry Hammond, *A Practical Catechism*

And when you pray, do not be like the hypocrites, for they love to pray standing in the synagogues and on the street corners to be seen by men.

-The Bible (*NIV*), Matthew 6:5

Pray for your enemy; for if you are good man, you will rejoice to see your enemy become a good man too.

-Owen Felltham, quoted in *Mental Recreation* (1831)

The LORD is near to all who call on him, to all who call on him in truth.

-The Bible (*KJV*), Psalms 145:18

ELEVEN

SALVATION

Strait is the gate, and narrow is the way, which leadeth unto life, and few there be that find it.

-The Bible (*KJV*), Matthew 7:14

Thou hast made us for Thyself, O Lord, and our hearts are restless until they rest in Thee.

-Saint Augustine, *Confessions*

It is as absurd to argue men, as to torture them, into believing.

-John Henry Newman, sermon, "The Usurpations of Reason", 11 December 1831

If in preaching the gospel you substitute your knowledge of the way of salvation for confidence in the power of the gospel, you hinder people from getting to reality.

-Oswald Chambers, *My Utmost for His Highest*

Amazing grace, how sweet the sound
That sav'd a wretch like me!
I once was lost, but now am found,
Was blind, but now I see.

-John Newton, "Amazing Grace"

For to be carnally minded is death; but to be spiritually minded is life and peace.

-The Bible (*KJV*), Romans 8:6

The Christian faith goes mainly to establish these two facts, - the corruption of nature, and the redemption by Jesus Christ.

-Blaise Pascal, *Pensées*

He who conceals his disease cannot expect to be cured.

-Ethiopian Proverb

This is the ministry and its work - not to drill hearts, and minds, and consciences, into right forms of thought and mental postures, but to guide to the living God who speaks.

- Frederick William Robertson, sermon, "The Character of Eli", January 1848

I cannot find in Scripture that anyone ever got to heaven merely by sincerity, or was accepted with God if he was only earnest in maintaining his own views . . . sincerity cannot put away sin.

-J.C. Ryle, *Only One Way*

What can that man fear who takes care to please a Being who is able to crush all his adversaries?

–Joseph Addison, *The Guardian*, 25 July 1713

The nature of Christ's salvation is woefully misrepresented by the present-day "evangelist." He announces a Saviour from Hell rather than a Saviour from sin. And that is why so many are fatally deceived, for there are multitudes who wish to escape the lake of fire who have no desire to be delivered from their carnality and worldliness.

-A.W. Pink, *Studies on Saving Faith*

The same sun that melts the wax hardens the clay.

-Saying

I believe that the root of almost every schism and heresy from which the Christian church has ever suffered, has been the effort of men to earn, rather than to receive, their salvation.

–John Ruskin, *Modern Painters: Of the Imaginative and Theoretic*

TWELVE

Scripture

Nobody ever outgrows Scripture; the book widens and deepens with our years.

-Charles Haddon Spurgeon, sermon, "The Talking Book", 22 October 1871

The devil can cite scripture for his purpose

-William Shakespeare, *The Merchant of Venice*

We pick out a text here and there to make it serve our turn; whereas, if we take it all together, and considered what went before, and what followed after, we should find it meant no such thing.

-John Selden, "The Scriptures", *Table Talk*

Thy word is a lamp unto my feet, and a light unto my path.

-The Bible (*KJV*), Psalms 119:105

It is Christ Himself, not the Bible, who is the true word of God. The Bible, read in the right spirit and with the guidance of good teachers, will bring us to Him.

-C.S. Lewis, letter to Mrs. Ashton, 8 November 1952

Men can make an idol of the Bible.

-Henry Ward Beecher, *Notes From Plymouth Pulpit*

To believe the Gospel when you wish it, and then disbelieve the Gospel when you wish it, is to believe nobody but yourself.

-Saint Augustine, *Reply to Faustus the Manichaean*

The Bible is like a telescope. If a man looks through his telescope, then he sees the worlds beyond; but if he looks at his telescope, then he does not see anything but that. The Bible is a thing to be looked through, to see that which is beyond; but most people only look at it; and so they see only the dead letter.

-Henry Ward Beecher, "The Way of Coming to Christ", *The Sermons*

Doctrinal rightness and rightness of ecclesiastical position are important, but only as a starting point to go on into a living relationship - and not as ends in themselves.

-Francis Schaeffer, letter to a friend, 11 October 1954

THIRTEEN

SIN

No notice is taken of a little evil, but when it increases it strikes the eye.

-Aristotle, *Politics*

One scabby sheep is enough to spoil the whole flock.

-French Proverb

The very heart and root of sin is in an independent spirit. We erect the idol self; and not only wish others to worship, but worship ourselves.

-Richard Cecil, *Remains of the Rev. Richard Cecil*

No one ever reached the climax of vice at one step.

-Juvenal, *Satires*

Destroy the seed of evil, or it will grow up to your ruin.

-Aesop, "The Swallow and the Other Birds", *Fables*

Few love to hear the sins they love to act.

-William Shakespeare, *Pericles, Prince of Tyre*

The sin ye do by two and two ye must pay for one by one!

- Rudyard Kipling, "Tomlinson", *Barrack-room Ballads and Other Verses*

The wise man avoids evil by anticipating it.

-Publilius Syrus, *Moral Sayings*

Sin is never at a stay; if we do not retreat from it, we shall advance in it; and the farther on we go, the more we have to come back.

-Isaac Barrow, “The Danger and Mischief of Delaying Repentance”, *The Works of Isaac Barrow* (1692)

Drunkenness is nothing else but voluntary madness.

-Lucius Annaeus Seneca (the younger), "On The Happy Life", *Moral Essays*

'Tis easier to suppress the first desire, than to satisfy all that follows it.

-Benjamin Franklin, *The Way to Wealth*

Better shun the bait, than struggle in the snare.

-John Dryden, “To My Honoured Kinsman John Driden”

Sin is not hurtful, because it is forbidden;
But it is forbidden, because it is hurtful.

-Benjamin Franklin, *Poor Richard's Almanack*

Sin first is pleasing, then it grows easy, then delightful, then frequent, then habitual, then confirmed; then the man is impenitent, then he is obstinate, then he is resolved never to repent, and then he is ruined.

–Robert Leighton, quoted in *Ballou's Pictorial Drawing-Room Companion*, 3 January 1857

While I see many hoof marks going in, I see none coming out. It is easier to get into the enemy's toils than out again.

-Aesop, "The Lion, The Fox, and The Beasts" *Fables*

It is easier to resist at the beginning than at the end.

-Leonardo da Vinci, *The Notebooks*

A man does not sin by commission only, but often by omission.

-Marcus Aurelius, *Meditations*

Can a man take fire in his bosom and his clothes not be burned?

-The Bible (*KJV*), Proverbs 6:27

Evil enters like a needle and spreads like an oak tree.

-Ethiopian Proverb

Sin will take you further than you ever wanted to go.
It will keep you longer than you ever wanted to stay.
It will cost you more than what you ever wanted to pay!

-Saying

If you think that you can sin, and then by cries avert the consequences of sin, you insult God's character.

-Frederick William Robertson, sermon, "Joseph's Forgiveness of His Brethren", 1 June 1851

There is no man so good, who, were he to submit all his thoughts and actions to the laws, would not deserve hanging ten times in his life.

-Michel de Montaigne, "Of Vanity", *Essays*

Any pleasure which takes and keeps the heart from God is sinful, and unless forsaken, will be fatal to the soul.

-Richard Fuller, "Sinful Pleasures", *Sermons*

It is because of the hasty and superficial conversation with God that the sense of sin is so weak and that no motives have power to help you to hate and flee from sin as you should.

-Andrew Murray, *The Prayer Life*

There is no witness so terrible, no accuser so powerful, as conscience that dwells in the breast of each.

-Polybius, quoted in *Beautiful Thoughts* (1864) by Craufurd Tait Ramage

He that covereth his sins shall not prosper: but whoso confesseth and forsaketh them shall have mercy.

-The Bible (*KJV*), Proverbs 28:13

There is no man suddenly either excellently good or extremely evil.

-Philip Sidney, *The Countess of Pembroke's Arcadia*

Whatever weakens your reason, impairs the tenderness of your conscience, obscures your sense of God, or takes off the relish of spiritual things; in short, whatever increases the strength and authority of your body over your mind, that thing is sin to you, however innocent it may be in itself.

-Susanna Wesley, letter to her son, John Wesley, 8 June 1725

You may be sure that your sin will find you out.

-The Bible (*NIV*), Numbers 32:23

Certain things can only be dealt with by ignoring them; if you face them you increase their power. It is absurd to say, Pray about them; when once a thing is seen to be wrong, don't pray about it, it fixes the mind on it; never for a second brood on it, destroy it by neglect.

-Oswald Chambers, *Biblical Ethics*

All sins are attempts to fill voids.

-Simone Weil, *Notebook*

Righteousness exalteth a nation: but sin is a reproach to any people.

-The Bible (*KJV*), Proverbs 14:34

FOURTEEN

THANKFULNESS

We can be thankful to a friend for a few acres, or a little money: and yet for the freedom and command of the whole earth, and for the great benefits of our being, our life, health, and reason, we look upon ourselves as under no obligation.

-Lucius Annaeus Seneca (the younger), "On Benefits", *Moral Essays*

Only a stomach that rarely feels hunger scorns common things.

-Horace, *Satires, Epistles, and Art of Poetry*

Think of the ills from which you are exempt.

-Joseph Joubert, *Some of the "Thoughts" of Joseph Joubert*

A man should always consider how much more unhappy he might be than he is.

-Joseph Addison, *The Spectator*, 30 July 1714

He is a man of sense who does not grieve for what he has not, but rejoices in what he has.

-Epictetus, “Fragments”, *The Works of Epictetus*

Consider the superior things which you possess, and in gratitude remember how wonderfully you would long after them, if you had them not.

-Marcus Aurelius, *Meditations*

We never know the worth of water till the well is dry.

-English Proverb

Unhappy is the man, though he rule the world, who doesn't consider himself supremely blessed.

-Lucius Annaeus Seneca (the younger), *Moral Letters to Lucilius*

Who does not thank for little will not thank for much.

-Estonian Proverb

Instead of comparing our lot with that of those who are more fortunate than we are, we should compare it with the lot of the great majority of our fellow men. It then appears that we are among the privileged.

-Helen Keller, *We Bereaved*

We are all of us richer than we think we are.

-Michel de Montaigne, "Of Physiognomy", *Essays*

We would often be sorry if our wishes were gratified.

-Aesop, "The Old Man and Death", *Fables*

Ignorant men don't know what good they hold in their hands until they've flung it away.

-Sophocles, *Ajax*

Many a Christian has a thousand reasons for joy which he knows nothing of.

-Charles Haddon Spurgeon, sermon, "The Fruit of the Spirit: Joy", 6 February 1881

It is only when we have lost them that we fully appreciate our blessings.

-Titus Maccius Plautus, *The Captives*

So much has been given to me I have not the time to ponder over that which has been denied.

-Helen Keller, "Helen Keller at 80", *This Week Magazine*, by Ann Carnahan, 19 June 1960

One ungrateful man does an injury to all who are in suffering.

-Publilius Syrus, *Sententiae*

Men are slower to recognize blessings than evils.

-Livy, *History of Rome*

If gratitude is due from children to their earthly parents, how much more is the gratitude of the great family of man due to our Father in heaven?

-Hosea Ballou, quoted in *Ballou's Pictorial Drawing-room Companion* (1853)

I asked of God that He should give success
To the high task I sought for Him to do;
I asked that every hindrance might grow less
And that my hours of weakness might be few;
I asked that far and lofty heights be scaled -
And now I humbly thank Him that I failed.
For with the pain and sorrow came to me
A dower of tenderness in act and thought;
And with the failure came a sympathy,
An insight which success had never brought.
Father, I had been foolish and unblest
If Thou hadst granted me my blind request.

-Unknown Author

PART III

THE SOCIAL LIFE

ONE

Accountability

Many people take no care of their money till they have come nearly to the end of it, and others do just the same with their time.

-Johann Wolfgang von Goethe, quoted in *Treasury of Thought* (1872) by Maturin Ballou

Fool me once, shame on you; fool me twice, shame on me.

-Native American Proverb

God will not look you over for medals, degrees or diplomas, but for scars.

-Elbert Hubbard, *A Thousand and One Epigrams*

A bull does not enjoy fame in two herds.

-Rhodesian Proverb

Everyone is bound to bear patiently the results of his own example.

-Aesop, "The Fox and the Stork", *Fables*

If the master takes no account of his servants, they will make small account of him, and care not what they spend, who are never brought to an audit.

–Thomas Fuller, *The Holy State and the Prophane State*

For unto whomsoever much is given, of him shall be much required.

-The Bible (*KJV*), Luke 12:48

One sword keeps another in the sheath.

-George Herbert, *Jacula Prudentum*

If you can't bite, don't show your teeth.

-Yiddish Proverb

Except the Lord build the house, they labour in vain that build it.

-The Bible (*KJV*), Psalms 127:1

The only true apology is changed behavior.

- J.S. Felts

A fall never hurt anybody; it's the sudden stop that hurts.

-Saying

No man is an island, entire of itself; every man is a piece of the Continent, a part of the main . . . any man's death diminishes me, because I am involved in Mankind;
And therefore never send to know for whom the bell tolls;
It tolls for thee.

-John Donne, *Devotions upon Emergent Occasions*

You are either part of the solution or part of the problem.

-Saying

He who rides the tiger can never dismount.

-Chinese Proverb

Any party which takes credit for the rain must not be surprised if its opponents blame it for the drought.

-Dwight W. Morrow, speech, 10 October 1930

We must reject the idea that every time a law's broken, society is guilty rather than the lawbreaker. It is time to restore the American precept that each individual is accountable for his actions.

-Ronald Reagan, address to the Republican National Convention in Miami, 31 July, 1968

It takes less time to do a thing right, than to explain why you did it wrong.

-Saying

TWO

Admiration

Admiration is a very short-lived passion that immediately decays upon growing familiar with its object, unless it be still fed with fresh discoveries, and kept alive by a new perpetual succession of miracles rising up to its view.

-Joseph Addison, *The Spectator*, 24 December 1711

Admire, but never idolize.

- J.S. Felts

Season your admiration for a while.

-William Shakespeare, *Hamlet*

Admiration and familiarity are strangers.

-George Sand, quoted in *Edge-tools of Speech* (1899) by Maturin Murray Ballou

THREE

Advice

In the multitude of counselors there is safety.

-The Bible (KJV), Proverbs 11:14

We every day and every hour say things of another that we might more properly say of ourselves, could we but apply our observations to our own concerns.

-Michel de Montaigne, "Of the Affections of Fathers to Their Children", *Essays*

The way of a fool seems right to him, but a wise man listens to advice.

-The Bible (*NIV*), Proverbs 12:15

He that will not be counseled cannot be helped.

-Thomas Fuller, *Gnomologia*

Do not open your heart to everyone, but ask counsel of one who is wise and fears God.

-Thomas a' Kempis, *The Imitation of Christ*

Seek ye counsel of the aged for their eyes have looked on the faces of the years and their ears have hardened to the voices of Life. Even if their counsel is displeasing to you, pay heed to them.

–Kahlil Gibran, *The Voice of the Master*

Advice is seldom welcome; and those who want it the most always like it the least.

-Lord Chesterfield, letter to his son, 29 Jan 1748

A man takes contradiction and advice much more easily than people think, only he will not bear it when violently given, even though it be well founded. Hearts are flowers; they remain open to the softly falling dew, but shut up in the violent downpour of rain.

-Jean Paul Richter, quoted in *Other Men's Minds* (1880) by Edwin Davies

He who builds to every man's advice will have a crooked house.

-Danish Proverb

In giving advice seek to help, not to please, your friend.

-Solon, quoted in *Lives and Opinions of Eminent Philosophers* by Diogenes Laertius

Extremely foolish advice is likely to be uttered by those who are looking at the laboring vessel from the land.

-Arthur Helps, *Friends in Council*

Most people, when they come to you for advice, come to have their own opinions strengthened, not corrected.

-Josh Billings, quoted in *Dictionary of Quotations* (1899) by James Wood

To profit from good advice requires more wisdom than to give it.

-John Churton Collins, quoted in *The English Review* – vol. 17 (1914)

What a difficult thing it is to ask someone's advice on a matter without coloring his judgment by the way in which we present our problem.

-Blaise Pascal, *Pensées*

The true secret of giving advice is, after you have honestly given it, to be perfectly indifferent whether it is taken or not and never persist in trying to set people right.

-Hannah Whitall Smith, letter, 3 May 1902

If a man consults whether he is to fight, when he has the power in his own hands, it is certain that his opinion is against fighting.

-Horatio Nelson, letter to Henry Addington, 21 August 1801

It is easy when we are in prosperity to give advice to the afflicted.

-Aeschylus, quoted in *A Dictionary of Thoughts* (1891) by Tryon Edwards

Sometimes the best way to convince a man he is wrong is to let him have his own way.

-Saying

Listen to advice and accept instruction, and in the end you will be wise.

-The Bible (NIV), Proverbs 19:20

A wise man will hear, and will increase learning; and a man of understanding shall attain unto wise counsels.

-The Bible (*KJV*), Proverbs 1:5

FOUR

APPLAUSE

Applause is the spur of noble minds, the end and aim of weak ones.

-Charles Caleb Colton, *Lacon*

People can be induced to swallow anything, provided it is sufficiently seasoned with praise.

-Moliere, *The Miser*

Men often applaud an imitation and hiss the real thing.

-Aesop, "The Buffoon and the Countryman", *Fables*

Appreciate, but never quite believe the applause of the crowd. Jesus once entered a city to triumphant applause, the same city where he was crucified a week later.

- J.S. Felts

He only is a great man who can neglect the applause of the multitude and enjoy himself independent of its favor.

-Joseph Addison, *The Spectator*, 17 September 1711

Anything in any way beautiful derives its beauty from itself and asks nothing beyond itself. Praise is no part of it, for nothing is made worse or better by praise.

-Marcus Aurelius, *Meditations*

Praise makes good men better and bad men worse.

-Thomas Fuller, *Gnomologia*

Better to deserve praise without having it, than to have it without deserving it.

-Ivan Panin, *Thoughts*

Praising all alike, is praising none.

-John Gay, "Epistle to a Lady" (1714)

The applause of a single human being is of great consequence.

-Samuel Johnson, quoted in *Life of Samuel Johnson* (1791) by James Boswell

He who seeks only for applause from without has all his happiness in another's keeping.

-Oliver Goldsmith, *The Good-Natured Man*

In doing what we ought, we deserve no praise, because it is our duty.

-Joseph Addison, *Cato*

Neither human applause nor human censure is to be taken as the test of truth.

-Richard Whately, Essays On Some of the Dangers to Christian Faith

None of us are so much praised or censured as we think; and most men would be thoroughly cured of their self-importance, if they would only rehearse their own funeral, and walk abroad incognito, the very day after that on which they were supposed to have been buried.

-Charles Caleb Colton, *Lacon*

Do not trust that [cheering]; for these very persons would shout as much if you and I were going to be hanged.

-Oliver Cromwell, quoted in *History of My Own Time* (1683) by Gilbert Burnet

FIVE

Appreciation

Wise men appreciate all men, for they see the good in each and know how hard it is to make anything good.

-Baltasar Gracian, *The Art of Worldly Wisdom*

The grateful heart will always find opportunities to show its gratitude.

-Aesop, "The Ant and the Dove", *Fables*

I would rather be able to appreciate things I cannot have than to have things I am not able to appreciate.

-Elbert Hubbard, *The Philistine*, March 1902

The deepest principle of human nature is the craving to be appreciated.

-William James, letter to his Radcliffe College class, 6 April 1896

If we had no winter, the spring would not be so pleasant: if we did not sometimes taste of adversity, prosperity would not be so welcome.

-Anne Bradstreet, *Meditations Divine and Moral*

I would rather be able to appreciate things I cannot have than to have things I am unable to appreciate.

-Elbert Hubbard, *The Note Book*

It is folly to sing twice to a deaf man.

-English Proverb

Ignorant men
Don't know what good they hold in their hands until
They've flung it away.

-Sophocles, *Ajax*

SIX

Argument

The strongest arguments prove nothing so long as the conclusions are not verified by experience.

-Roger Bacon, *Opus Tertium*

No mistake is so commonly made by clever people as that of assuming a cause to be bad because the arguments of its supporters are, to a great extent, nonsensical

-Thomas Henry Huxley, "Emancipation - Black and White ", *The Reader,* 20 May 1865

The aim of argument, or of discussion, should not be victory, but progress.

-Joseph Joubert, Joubert: *A Selection from His Thoughts*

He who knows only his side of the case, knows little of that.

-John Stuart Mill, *On Liberty*

A doctrine capable of being stated only in obscure or involved terms is open to reasonable suspicion of being either crude or erroneous.

-Frederick Pollock, letter to Justice Holmes, 12 February 1920

We must not contradict, but instruct him that contradicts us; for a madman is not cured by another running mad also.

-Antisthenes, quoted in *Select Proverbs of All Nations* (1824) by Thomas Fielding

Hear one side and you will be in the dark. Hear both and all will be clear.

-Chinese Proverb

Don't take the wrong side of an argument just because your opponent took the right side.

-Baltasar Gracian, *The Art of Worldly Wisdom*

An argument derived from the abuse of a thing does not hold good against its use.

-Latin Legal Phrase

Silence is less injurious than a weak reply.

–Charles Caleb Colton, *Lacon*

In a heated argument we lose sight of the truth.

-Publilius Syrus, *Sententiae*

Some in their discourse, desire rather commendation of wit, in being able to hold all arguments, than of judgment, in discerning what is true; as if it were a praise, to know what might be said, and not, what should be thought.

–Francis Bacon, "Of Discourse", *Essays*

He who establishes his argument by noise and command, shows that his reason is weak.

-Michel de Montaigne, "Of Cripples," *Essays*

People's minds are changed through observation and not through argument.

-Will Rogers, *Daily Telegrams*, 16 March 1932

Let thy speech be better than silence, or be silent.

-Dionysius the Elder, *Fragments*

Don't have anything to do with foolish and stupid arguments, because you know they produce quarrels.

-The Bible (*NIV*), 2 Timothy 2:23

A large part of the discussions of disputants come from the want of accurate definition. Let one define his terms and then stick to the definition, and half the differences in philosophy and theology would come to an end, and be seen to have no real foundation.

-Tryon Edwards, *A Dictionary of Thoughts*

A man never tells you anything until you contradict him.

-George Bernard Shaw, letter to Ellen Terry, 28 August 1896

Prepare your proof before you argue.

-Jewish Proverb

There is no arguing with one who denies first principles.

-Latin Legal Phrase

First settle what the case is, before you argue it.

-Robert Wright, spoken at trial of the seven bishops for publishing a libel, June 1688

Persons unmask their evilest qualities when they do quarrel.

-George Herbert, quoted in *Edge-tools of Speech* (1886) by Maturin Murray Ballou

You cannot antagonize and influence people at the same time.

-James Samuel Knox, *The Science and Art of Selling*

Hunting after arguments to make good one side of a question, and wholly to neglect and refuse those which favor the other side. What is this but willfully to misguide the understanding, and is so far from giving truth its due value, that it wholly debases it.

–John Locke, *An Essay Concerning Human Understanding*

Quarrels would not last long if the fault were only on one side.

-Francois de La Rochefoucauld, *Reflections or Sentences and Moral Maxims*

I never make the mistake of arguing with people for whose opinions I have no respect.

-Edward Gibbon, quoted in *The Fra* (1913) by Elbert Hubbard

In all debates, let truth be thy aim, not victory, or an unjust interest.

-William Penn, *Some Fruits of Solitude*

Whenever you're in conflict with someone, there is one factor that can make the difference between damaging your relationship and deepening it. That factor is attitude.

-William James

SEVEN

BREVITY

The most valuable of all talents, that of never using two words where one will do.

-Thomas Jefferson, letter to John Minor, 30 August 1814

If you want to win a case, paint the judge a picture and keep it simple.

-John W. Davis, annual meeting of Scribes, 21 August 1955

It is my ambition to say in ten sentences what other men say in whole books - what other men do not say in whole books.

-Friedrich Nietzsche, *Twilight of the Idols*

One has to try to strike the jugular and let the rest go.

-Oliver Wendell Holmes Jr., address to Massachusetts Supreme Court, 25 November 1899

How many people become abstract in order to appear profound! Most abstract terms are shadows that conceal a void.

-Joseph Joubert, *Pensées of Joubert*

A sentence should contain no unnecessary words, a paragraph no unnecessary sentences, for the same reason that a drawing should have no unnecessary lines and a machine no unnecessary parts.

-William Strunk Jr., *The Elements of Style*

Be brief, be pointed; let your matter stand
Lucid in order, solid, and at hand;
Spend not your words on trifles but condense;
Strike with the mass of thought, not drops of sense;
Press to the close with vigor, once begun,
And leave, (how hard the task!) leave off, when done.

-Joseph Story, "Advice to a Young Lawyer"

If one word does not succeed, ten thousand are of no avail.

-Chinese Proverb

Never be so brief as to become obscure.

-Tryon Edwards, *A Dictionary of Thoughts*

It is simplicity that makes the uneducated more effective than the educated when addressing popular audiences.

-Aristotle, *Rhetoric*

The more you say, the less people remember. The fewer the words, the greater the profit.

-Saint Francis De Sales, quoted in *Short Sayings of Great Men* (1882) by Samuel Arthur Bent

If you would be pungent, be brief; for it is with words as with sunbeams - the more they are condensed, the deeper they burn.

-Robert Southey, quoted in *Many Thoughts of Many Minds* (1862) by Henry Southgate

EIGHT

Candor

Always be ready to speak your mind, and a base man will avoid you.

-William Blake, "Proverbs of Hell", *The Marriage of Heaven and Hell*

A "No" uttered from deepest conviction is better and greater than a "Yes" merely uttered to please, or what is worse, to avoid trouble.

-Mahatma Gandhi, *Young India,* 17 March 1927

He who, when called upon to speak a disagreeable truth, tells it boldly and has done, is both bolder and milder than he who nibbles in a low voice and never ceases nibbling.

-Johann Kaspar Lavater, *Aphorisms on Man*

There is but one way I know of conversing safely with all men; that is, not by concealing what we say or do, but by saying or doing nothing that deserves to be concealed.

-Alexander Pope, letter to H. Cromwell, 28 October, 1720

Many things are lost for want of asking.

-English Proverb

Let us not be ashamed to speak what we shame not to think.

-Michel de Montaigne, "Upon Some Verses of Virgil", *Essays*

Learn to say "No!" It will be of more use to you than to be able to read Latin.

-Charles Haddon Spurgeon, *John Ploughman's Talks*

If people would dare to speak to one another unreservedly, there would be a good deal less sorrow in the world a hundred years hence.

-Samuel Butler (19th Century), *The Way of All Flesh*

The prompter the refusal, the less the disappointment.

-Publilius Syrus, *Sententiae*

There is nothing in the world more difficult than candor and nothing easier than flattery.

-Fyodor Dostoevsky, *Crime and Punishment*

Candor and generosity, which, unless tempered by due moderation, lead to ruin.

-Tacitus, *Histories*

Lack of candor, we find upon examination, is not only the cause of many of our greatest problems, but also the impediment to solving most of our problems.

- J.S. Felts

NINE

CHILDREN

Let thy child's first lesson be obedience, and the second may be what thou wilt.

–Thomas Fuller, *Introduction Ad Prudentiam*

Your children learn what's important, by what you give your attention to.

- J.S. Felts

It is not easy to straighten in the oak the crook that grew in the sapling.

-Gaelic Proverb

Where parents do too much for their children, the children will not do much for themselves.

-Elbert Hubbard, *The Note Book*

That energy which makes a child hard to manage is the energy which afterward makes him a manager of life.

-Henry Ward Beecher, *Proverbs from Plymouth Pulpit*

When a child can be brought to tears, and not from fear of punishment, but from repentance he needs no chastisement.

–Horace Mann, *Thoughts Selected from the Writings of Horace Mann* (1872)

If the mind be curbed and humbled too much in children; if their spirits be abased and broken much by too strict an hand over them; they lose all their vigour and industry, and are in a worse state than the former.

–John Locke, *Some Thoughts Concerning Education*

The most influential of all educational factors is the conversation in a child's home.

-William Temple, *The Hope of a New World*

Parents can only give good advice or put them on the right paths, but the final forming of a person's character lies in their own hands.

-Anne Frank, diary entry, 15 July 1944

Children have more need of models than of critics.

-Joseph Joubert, *Pensées of Joubert*

The most important thing a father can do for his children is to love their mother.

-Theodore Martin Hesburgh

I never hear parents exclaim impatiently, "Children, you must not make so much noise," that I do not think how soon the time may come when, beside the vacant seat, those parents would give all the world, could they hear once more the ringing laughter which once so disturbed them.

–Abbott Eliot Kittredge, quoted in *Dictionary of Burning Words of Brilliant Writers* (1895)

Train up a child in the way he should go: and when he is old he will not depart from it.

-The Bible (*KJV*), Proverbs 22:6

He that will have his son have a respect for him and his orders, must himself have a great reverence for his son.

-John Locke, *Some Thoughts Concerning Education*

As arrows are in the hand of a mighty man; so are children of the youth. Happy is the man that hath his quiver full of them.

-The Bible (*KJV*), Psalms 127:4-5

Teaching children to count is not as important as teaching them what counts.

-Saying

As wax is ready and pliant to receive any kind of figure or print, so is a young child apt to receive any kind of learning.

-Unknown, *Wits Common-wealth* (1674)

In the homes of America are born the children of America, and from them go out into American life, American men and women. They go out with the stamp of these homes upon them; and only as these homes are what they should be, will they be what they should be.

-Josiah Gilbert Holland, "The Institution of Home", *Titcomb's Letters to Young People, Single and Married*

And he said: "Father, don't you weep for me; when I get to heaven I will go straight to Jesus and tell Him that ever since I can remember you have tried to lead me to Him." I would rather have my children say that of me after I am gone; or if they die before me, I would rather they should take that message to the Master than to have a monument over me reaching to the skies.

-Dwight L. Moody, *Heaven*

To understand your parents' love you must raise children yourself.

-Chinese Proverb

And ye fathers, provoke not your children to wrath, but bring them up in the nurture and admonition of the Lord.

-The Bible (*KJV*), Ephesians 6:4

You cannot teach a child to take care of himself unless you will let him take care of himself. He will make mistakes, and out of these mistakes will come his wisdom.

-Henry Ward Beecher, "The Law of Liberty", *Sermons*

There are little eyes upon you
and they're watching night and day;
There are little ears that quickly
take in every word you say;
There are little hands all eager
to do anything you do,
And a little boy who's dreaming
of the day he'll be like you.
You're the little fellow's idol,
you're the wisest of the wise;
In his little mind about you
no suspicions ever rise;
He believes in you devoutly,
holds all you say and do;
He will say and do, in your way
when he's grownup just like you. . .
There's a wide-eyed little fellow
who believes you're always right;
And his eyes are always opened,
and he watches day and night.
You are setting an example
every day in all you do;
For the little boy who's waiting
to grow up to be like you.

-Edgar A. Guest, "His Example", *The Path to Home*

TEN

COMMUNICATION

The eloquent man is he who is no beautiful speaker, but who is inwardly and desperately drunk with a certain belief.

-Ralph Waldo Emerson, "Eloquence", *Society and Solitude*

To be misunderstood even by those whom one loves is the cross and bitterness of life. It is the secret of that sad and melancholy smile on the lips of great men which so few understand; it is the cruelest trial reserved for self-devotion.

-Henri Frederic Amiel, *Journal Intime*, 27 May 1849

You have not converted a man, because you have silenced him.

-John Morley, *On Compromise*

It is better to debate a question without settling it, than to settle it without debate.

-Joseph Joubert, *Pensées of Joubert*

Be humble and gentle in your conversation; of few words, I charge you; but always pertinent when you speak, hearing out before you attempt to answer, and then speaking as if you would persuade, not impose.

–William Penn, quoted in *Memoirs of the Life of William Penn* (1849) by Thomas Clarkson

To a quick question, give a slow answer.

-Italian Proverb

The more the pleasures of the body fade away, the greater to me is the pleasure and charm of conversation.

-Plato, *The Republic*

You never know, till you try to reach them, how accessible men are.

-Henry Ward Beecher, *Royal Truths*

If we are strong, our strength will speak for itself. If we are weak, words will be no help.

-John F. Kennedy, from a prepared, but undelivered speech in Dallas, TX, 22 November 1963

Nature has given to men one tongue, but two ears, that we may hear from others twice as much as we speak.

-Epictetus, *Enchiridion*

There is no such way to ... give defense to strange and absurd doctrines, as to guard them round about with legions of obscure, doubtful, and undefined words.

–John Locke, *An Essay Concerning Human Understanding*

There is always time to add a word, never to withdraw one.

-Baltasar Gracian, *The Art of Worldly Wisdom*

There is but one way I know of conversing safely with all men; that is, not by concealing what we say or do, but by saying or doing nothing that deserves to be concealed.

-Alexander Pope, letter to H. Cromwell, 28 October, 1710

Just because you're friends, doesn't mean you will always agree; also, just because you don't particularly like some-one doesn't mean you have to disagree.

- J.S. Felts

Speak clearly, if you speak at all;
Carve every word before you let it fall.

-Oliver Wendell Holmes Sr., *Urania: A Rhymed Lesson*

Blessed is the man who, having nothing to say, abstains from giving us wordy evidence of the fact.

-George Eliot, "A Man Surprised At His Originality", *Impressions of Theophrastus Such*

A timid question will always receive a confident answer.

-Charles John Darling, "Of Cross-Examination", *Scintillae Juris*

When dealing with people, let us remember we are not dealing with creatures of logic. We are dealing with creatures of emotion.

-Dale Carnegie, *How to Win Friends and Influence People*

One may be confuted and yet not convinced.

-English Proverb

I have often regretted my speech, never my silence.

-Publilius Syrus, *Sententiae*

A verse may find him whom a sermon flies.

–George Herbert, *The Temple*

A man does not know what he is saying until he knows what he is not saying.

-G.K. Chesterton, "About Impenitence", *As I Was Saying*

A soft answer turneth away wrath.

-The Bible (*KJV*), Proverbs 15:1

It is one thing to show a man that he is in an error, and another to put him in possession of truth.

-John Locke, *An Essay Concerning Human Understanding*

He who knows how to flatter also knows how to slander.

-Napoleon Bonaparte, *Napoleon in His Own Words*

Be swift to hear, slow to speak, slow to wrath.

-The Bible (*KJV*), James 1:19

Would you persuade, speak of interest, not of reason.

-Benjamin Franklin, *Poor Richard's Almanack*

Let your speech be always with grace, seasoned with salt.

-The Bible (*KJV*), Colossians 4:6

Teach thy tongue to say "I do not know".

- The *Talmud*

When one by force subdues men, they do not submit to him in heart. They submit, because their strength is not adequate to resist.

-Mencius, *The Life and Works of Mencius*

Answer a fool according to his folly.

-The Bible (*KJV*), Proverbs 26:5

It is one thing, though, to recognize and properly apply a sound principle. It is quite another to run that same sound principle into the ground. It is one thing for a dog to have a tail. It is quite another for the tail to wag the dog.

-Joseph C. Hutcheson Jr., *Deal v. Morrow* (5th Cir. 1952)

Half our troubles in this life can be traced to saying "yes" too quickly and not saying "no" soon enough.

-Saying

A fool's mouth is his destruction.

-The Bible (*KJV*), Proverbs 18:7

To dispute with a drunkard is to debate with an empty house.

-Publilius Syrus, *Sententiae*

How many a debate would have been deflated into a paragraph if the disputants had dared to define their terms!

-Will Durant, *The Story of Philosophy*

He that asketh faintly beggeth a denial.

-English Proverb

Think like a wise man, but express yourself like the common people.

-William Butler Yeats, letter to Dorothy Wellesley, 21 December, 1935

Always look people in the face when you speak to them . . . In order to know people's real sentiments, I trust much more to my eyes than to my ears; for they can say whatever they have a mind I should hear; but they can seldom help looking what they have no intention that I should know.

-Lord Chesterfield, letter to his son, 19 October 1748

When we are in the company of sensible men, we ought to be doubly cautious of talking too much, lest we lose two good things, their good opinion and our own improvement; for what we have to say we know, but what they have to say we know not.

-Charles Caleb Colton, *Lacon*

In language clarity is everything.

-Confucius

A good presence is a letter of recommendation.

-Saying

It is not every question that deserves an answer.

-Publilius Syrus, *Sententiae*

Don't appear so scholarly, pray. Humanize your talk, and speak to be understood. Do you think a Greek name gives more weight to your reasons?

-Moliere, *The Critique of the School for Wives*

Once the subject matter has been provided, words will freely follow.

-Horace, *Epistle to the Pisones*

Words, like glasses, obscure everything which they do not make more clear.

-Joseph Joubert, *Pensées of Joubert*

The first duty of a wise advocate is to convince his opponents, that he understands their arguments, and sympathizes with their just feelings.

-Samuel Taylor Coleridge, *The Friend*

The meanest, most contemptible kind of praise is that which first speaks well of a man, and then qualifies it with a "but".

-Henry Ward Beecher, quoted in *A Dictionary of Thoughts* (1891) by Tryon Edwards

It is good to rub and polish our brain against that of others.

-Michel de Montaigne, *Essays*

Never hold any body by the button, or the hand, in order to be heard out; for, if people are not willing to hear you, you had much better hold your tongue than them.

-Lord Chesterfield, letter to his son, 19 Oct. 1748

One would think that the larger the company is, the greater variety of thoughts and subjects would be started into discourse; but, instead of this we find that conversation is never so much straightened and confined, as in large assemblies.

-Joseph Addison, *The Spectator*, 18 May 1711

Judge a man by his questions, as well as by his answers.

-Charles Haddon Spurgeon, *The Salt-Cellars*

The pith of conversation does not consist in exhibiting your own superior knowledge on matters of small consequence, but in enlarging, improving and correcting the information you possess by the authority of others.

-Walter Scott, *Quentin Durward*

Those who have few affairs to attend to are great speakers. The less men think, the more they talk.

-Charles de Montesquieu, quoted in *The Treasury of Knowledge* (1833) by Edwin Williams

Those who think little, tend to be those who think exactly alike.

- J.S. Felts

He who sedulously attends, pointedly asks, calmly speaks, coolly answers, and ceases when he has no more to say, is in possession of some of the best requisites of man.

-Johann Kaspar Lavater, *Aphorisms on Man*

He that is not open to conviction is not qualified for discussion.

-Richard Whately, Detached Thoughts and Apophthegms

Unanswered questions are less dangerous than unquestioned answers.

-Saying

But words are things, and a small drop of ink,
Falling like dew, upon a thought, produces
That which makes thousands, perhaps millions, think.

-Lord Byron, *Don Juan*

Remember that everyone you meet is afraid of something, loves something, and has lost something.

-Saying

Tears at times have all the weight of speech.

-Ovid, *Epistulae ex Ponto*

To be persuasive, one must be believable.
To be believable, we must be credible.
To be credible, we must be truthful.

-Edward R. Murrow, testimony before a Congressional Committee, May 1963

Learn to respond, and not to react.

-Saying

It is not always by plugging away at a difficulty and sticking at it that one overcomes it; but, rather, often by working on the one next to it. Certain people and certain things require to be approached at an angle.

-Andre Gide, journal entry, 26 October 1924

When you have nothing to say, say nothing; a weak defense strengthens your opponent, and silence is less injurious than a bad reply.

-Charles Caleb Colton, *Lacon*

Just because others are wrong, doesn't make you right.

- J.S. Felts

Much silence makes a powerful noise.

-African Proverb

Ninety percent of all daily friction is caused by tone - mere tone of voice.

-Arnold Bennett, *How to Live*

Conversation enriches the understanding, but solitude is the school of genius.

-Edward Gibbon, *The History of the Decline and Fall of the Roman Empire*

Do you listen or do you just wait for your turn to talk?

-Saying

He who does not understand your silence will probably not understand your words.

-Elbert Hubbard, *A Thousand and One Epigrams*

Let us never negotiate out of fear. But let us never fear to negotiate.

-John F. Kennedy, inaugural address, 20 January 1961

When a man has no design but to speak plain truth, he isn't apt to be talkative.

-George D. Prentice, quoted in *Golden Gleams of Thought* (1881) by Rev. S. Pollock Linn

The eyes of men converse as much as their tongues.

-Ralph Waldo Emerson, "Behaviour", *The Conduct of Life*

In the man whose childhood has known caresses there is always a fiber of memory that can be touched to gentle issues.

-George Eliot, "Janet's Repentance ", *Scenes of Clerical Life*

Be still when you have nothing to say; when genuine passion moves you, say what you've got to say, and say it hot.

-D.H. Lawrence, *Studies in Classic American Literature*

Do not choose to be wrong for the sake of being different.

-Herbert Louis Samuel

A wise man reflects before he speaks; a fool speaks, and then reflects on what he has uttered.

-French Proverb

The best way to show that a stick is crooked is not to argue about it, but to lay a straight stick alongside it.

-Dwight L. Moody

ELEVEN

COURTESY

In courtesy, rather pay a penny too much than too little.

-Saying

Don't flatter yourself that friendship authorizes you to say disagreeable things to your intimates. On the contrary, the nearer you come into relation with a person, the more necessary do tact and courtesy become.

-Oliver Wendell Holmes Sr., *The Autocrat of the Breakfast-table*

There is no outward sign of courtesy that does not rest on a deep moral foundation.

-Johann Wolfgang von Goethe, *Elective Affinities*

Courtesy is as much a mark of a gentleman as courage.

-Theodore Roosevelt, *The Outlook,* 1 April, 1911

Courtesies of a small and trivial character are the ones which strike deepest in the grateful and appreciating heart.

-Henry Clay, quoted in *Golden Deeds in Character Education* (1924) by Massillon Cassidy

Courtesy is due of man to man; not of suit-of-clothes to suit-of-clothes.

-Thomas Carlyle, "Corn-Law Rhymes"

All doors open to courtesy.

-Thomas Fuller, *Gnomologia*

TWELVE

CRITICISM

The fault-finder will find faults even in Paradise.

-Henry David Thoreau, *Walden*

It is better to light a candle than to curse the darkness.

-Chinese Proverb

It is much easier to be critical than to be correct.

-Benjamin Disraeli, speech, 24 January 1860

There is no defense against reproach, but obscurity.

–Jospeh Addison, *The Spectator*, 26 June 1711

Reprove not a scorner, lest he hate thee; rebuke a wise man and he will love thee.

-The Bible (*KJV*), Proverbs 9:8

To escape criticism: do nothing, say nothing, be nothing.

-Elbert Hubbard, *The Philistine*, February 1910

We owe almost all our knowledge, not to those who have agreed, but to those who have differed.

-Charles Caleb Colton, *Lacon*

The strength of criticism lies in the weakness of the thing criticized.

-Henry Wadsworth Longfellow, *Kavanagh*

He can see a louse as far away as China but is unconscious of an elephant on his nose.

-Malay Proverb

The people to fear are not those who disagree with you, but those who disagree with you and are too cowardly to let you know.

-Napoleon Bonaparte

Inventors and men of genius have almost always been regarded as fools at the beginning (and very often at the end) of their careers.

-Fyodor Dostoevsky, *The Idiot*

Made wary by imposters, men look for something wrong even in the righteous.

-The Panchatantra

When an elephant is in trouble, even a frog will kick him.

-Hindu Proverb

Somebody said that it couldn't be done,
But he with a chuckle replied
That "maybe it couldn't," but he would be one
Who wouldn't say so till he'd tried.
So he buckled right in with the trace of a grin
On his face. If he worried he hid it.
He started to sing as he tackled the thing
That couldn't be done, and he did it.
Somebody scoffed: "Oh, you'll never do that;
At least no one ever has done it";
But he took off his coat and he took off his hat,
And the first thing we knew he'd begun it.
With a lift of his chin and a bit of a grin,
Without any doubting or quiddit,
He started to sing as he tackled the thing
That couldn't be done, and he did it.
There are thousands to tell you it cannot be done,
There are thousands to prophesy failure;
There are thousands to point out to you, one by one,
The dangers that wait to assail you.
But just buckle in with a bit of a grin,
Just take off your coat and go to it;
Just start to sing as you tackle the thing
That "cannot be done," and you'll do it.

-Edgar A. Guest, "It Couldn't Be Done", *The Path to Home*

No man can tell another man his faults so as to benefit him unless he loves him.

-Henry Ward Beecher, "Love, The Fulfilling of the Law", *Sermons*

He who rebukes a man will in the end gain more favor than he who has a flattering tongue.

-The Bible (*NIV*), Proverbs 28:23

It is better to hear the rebuke of the wise, than for a man to hear the song of fools.

-The Bible (KJV), Ecclesiastes 7:5

Few persons have sufficient wisdom to prefer censure which is useful to them, to praise which deceives them.

-Francois de La Rochefoucauld, *Reflections or Sentences and Moral Maxims*

Find fault, when you must find fault, in private, if possible; and sometime after the offense, rather than at the time.

-Sydney Smith, quoted in *A Memoir of the Reverend Sydney Smith* (1855) by Lady Holland

Silence is sometimes the severest criticism.

-Charles Buxton, quoted in *A Dictionary of Thoughts* (1891) by Tryon Edwards

The strength of criticism lies in the weakness of the thing criticized.

-Henry Wadsworth Longfellow, *Kavanagh*

Against criticism a man can neither protest nor defend himself; he must act in spite of it, and then it will gradually yield to him.

-Johann Wolfgang von Goethe, *Maxims and Reflections*

What cannot be altered must be borne, not blamed.

-English Proverb

Censure and criticism never hurt anybody. If false, they can't hurt you unless you are wanting in manly character; and if true, they show a man his weak points, and forewarn him against failure and trouble.

-William Gladstone, quoted in *Golden Gleams of Thought* (1881) by Rev. S. Pollock Linn

A man would do nothing, if he waited until he could do it so well that no one would find fault with what he has done.

-John Henry Newman

Don't discourage another's plans unless you have better ones to offer.

-Saying

A bitter jest, when it comes too near the truth, leaves a sharp sting behind it.

-Tacitus, *Annals*

No great advance has ever been made in science, politics, or religion, without controversy.

-Lyman Beecher, *Sermons*

If you limit your actions in life to things that nobody can possibly find fault with, you will not do much.

-Lewis Carroll, letter to his sister Mary, 21 September 1893

Whatever you do, you need courage. Whatever course you decide upon, there is always someone to tell you, you are wrong. There are always difficulties arising which tempt you to believe that your critics are right. To map out a course of action and follow it to an end requires some of the same courage a soldier needs. Peace has its victories, but it takes brave men to win them.

-Ralph Waldo Emerson, quoted in *The Book of Courage* (1924) by Edwin Osgood Grover

Do not free a camel of the burden of his hump. You may be freeing him from being a camel.

-G.K. Chesterton, "The Suicide of Thought", *Orthodoxy*

Praise publicly, when you can, but always correct privately.

- J.S. Felts

THIRTEEN

Encouragement

There is a great man who makes every man feel small. But the real great man is the man who makes every man feel great.

-G.K. Chesterton, *Charles Dickens*

The truest help which one can render to a man who has any of the inevitable burdens of life to carry is not to take his burden off but to call out his best strength that he may be able to bear it.

-Phillips Brooks, "The Preacher in His Work", *Lectures on Preaching*

Treat people as if they were what they ought to be, and you help them become what they are capable of being.

-Johann Wolfgang von Goethe, *Wilhelm Meister's Apprenticeship*

The applause of a single human being is of great consequence.

-Samuel Johnson, quoted in *Life of Samuel Johnson* (1791) by James Boswell

Correction does much but encouragement does more.

-Johann Wolfgang von Goethe, quoted in *Goethe's Opinions* (1853) by Otto von Wenckstern

Praise, like gold and diamonds, owes its value only to its scarcity.

-Samuel Johnson, *The Rambler*, 6 July 1751

A word spoken in due season, how good is it!

-The Bible (*KJV*), Proverbs 15:23

Just as a flower cannot tell what becomes of its fragrance, so no one can tell what becomes of their influence.

-Saying

No man's abilities are so remarkably shining as not to stand in need of a proper opportunity, a patron, and even the praises of a friend to recommend them to the notice of the world.

-Pliny the Younger, *Epistles*

Never discourage anyone who continually makes progress, no matter how slow.

-Plato, *Sophist*

They may forget what you said and they may even forget what you did, but they will never forget how you made them feel.

-Saying

FOURTEEN

FAMILY

He is happiest, be he king or peasant, who finds peace in his home.

-Johann Wolfgang von Goethe, *Iphigenia in Tauris*

The strength of a nation, especially of a republican nation, is in the intelligent and well-ordered homes of the people.

-Lydia Howard Sigourney, "Industry", *Letters to Young Ladies*

All happy families resemble one another; each unhappy family is unhappy in its own way.

-Leo Tolstoy, *Anna Karenina*

Some things are worth dying for, and if they are worth dying for they are worth living for.

-George W. Truett, "Baptists and Religious Liberty", speech in Washington, D.C., 16 May 1920

An old man on the point of death summoned his sons around him to give them some parting advice. He ordered his servants to bring in a faggot of sticks, and said to his eldest son: "Break it." The son strained and strained, but with all his efforts was unable to break the Bundle. The other sons also tried, but none of them was successful. "Untie the faggots," said the father, "and each of you take a stick." When they had done so, he called out to them: "Now, break," and each stick was easily broken. "You see my meaning," said their father.
Union gives strength.

-Aesop, "The Bundle of Sticks", *Fables*

The happiest moments of my life have been the few which I have passed at home in the bosom of my family.

-Thomas Jefferson, letter to Francis Willis, 18 April 1790

Each blade of grass has its spot on earth whence it draws its life, its strength; and so is man rooted to the land from which he draws his faith together with his life.

-Joseph Conrad, *Lord Jim*

One father is more than a hundred schoolmasters.

-George Herbert, *Jacula Prudentum*

The Lord's curse is on the household of the wicked, but He blesses the home of the righteous.

-The Bible (*NIV*), Proverbs 3:33

FIFTEEN

Friendship

True happiness consists not in the multitude of friends, but in the worth and choice.

-Ben Jonson, *Cynthia's Revels*

We cannot tell the precise moment when friendship is formed. As in filling a vessel drop by drop, there is at last a drop which makes it run over; so in a series of kindnesses there is, at last, one which makes the heart run over.

-James Boswell, *The Life of Samuel Johnson*

I hate the prostitution of the name of friendship to signify modish and worldly alliances.

–Ralph Waldo Emerson, "Friendship", *Essays: First Series*

Do not remove a fly from your friend's forehead with a hatchet.

-Chinese Proverb

There are only two people who can tell you the truth about yourself - an enemy who has lost his temper and a friend who loves you dearly.

-Antisthenes

The firmest friendships have been formed in mutual adversity, as iron is most strongly united by the fiercest flame.

-Charles Caleb Colton, *Lacon*

Prosperity makes friends, adversity tries them.

-Publilius Syrus, *Sententiae*

In prosperity our friends know us; in adversity we know our friends.

-John Churton Collins

Faithful are the wounds of a friend, but the kisses of an enemy are deceitful.

-The Bible (*KJV*), Proverbs 27:6

One who's our friend is fond of us; one who's fond of us isn't necessarily our friend.

-Lucius Annaeus Seneca (the younger), *Moral Letters to Lucilius*

Distrust all those who love you extremely upon a very slight acquaintance, and without any visible reason.

-Lord Chesterfield, letter to his son, 15 Jan. 1753

Be courteous to all, but intimate with few; and let those few be well tried before you give them your confidence.

-George Washington, letter to his nephew, Bushrod Washington, 15 January 1783

Associate yourself with men of good quality if you esteem your own reputation, for 'tis better to be alone than in bad company.

-George Washington, "Rules of Civility & Decent Behavior in Company and Conversation"

If you always live with those who are lame, you will yourself learn to limp.

-Latin Proverb

It is better to weep with wise men than to laugh with fools.

-Spanish proverb

Whether you recognize it or not, you tend to become like those you surround yourself with.
Choose wisely!

- J.S. Felts

Greater love hath no man than this, that a man lay down his life for his friends.

-The Bible (*KJV*), John 15:13

Flatterers look like friends, as wolves like dogs.

-George Chapman, *Byron's Conspiracy*

The same man cannot be both friend and flatterer.

-Benjamin Franklin, *Poor Richard's Almanack*

A man, Sir, should keep his friendship in constant repair.

-Samuel Johnson, quoted in *Life of Samuel Johnson* (1791) by James Boswell

If a friend is in trouble, don't annoy him by asking if there is anything you can do. Think up something appropriate and do it.

-Edgar Watson Howe, *Country Town Sayings*

Approve not of him who commends all you say.

-Benjamin Franklin, *Poor Richard's Almanack*

Pay attention to your enemies, for they are the first to discover your mistakes.

-Antisthenes, quoted in *Lives and Opinions of Eminent Philosophers* by Diogenes Laertius

We shall never have friends, if we expect to find them without fault.

-Thomas Fuller, *Gnomologia*

He that lieth down with dogs shall rise up with fleas.

-Benjamin Franklin, *Poor Richard's Almanack*

Meddle not with him that flattereth with his lips.

-The Bible (*KJV*), Proverbs 20:19

It is a general mistake to think the men we like are good for everything; and those we do not, good for nothing.

-George Savile, *A Character of King Charles the Second*

Do not make friends with a hot-tempered man, do not associate with one easily angered, or you may learn his ways and get yourself ensnared.

-The Bible (*NIV*), Proverbs 22:24-25

Reprove your friend in secret and praise him openly.

-Leonardo da Vinci, *The Notebooks*

Bad company corrupts good character.

-The Bible (*NIV*), 1 Corinthians 15:33

Do not open your heart to everyone, but ask counsel of one who is wise and fears God.

-Thomas a' Kempis, *The Imitation of Christ*

If a man is worth knowing at all, he is worth knowing well.

-Alexander Smith, *Dreamthorp*

Seek not the favor of the multitude; it is seldom got by honest and lawful means. But seek the testimony of few; and number not voices, but weigh them.

-Immanuel Kant, quoted in *Treasury of Thought* (1884) by Maturin Murray Ballou

Misfortune shows those who are not really friends.

-Aristotle, *Eudemian Ethics*

A friend is known in time of need.

-German Proverb

We are far more liable to catch the vices than the virtues of our associates.

-Denis Diderot, quoted in *Success* (1897) by Orison Swett Marden

The only way to have a friend is to be one.

-Ralph Waldo Emerson, "Friendship", *Essays*

Take heed of a speedy professing friend. Love is never lasting which flames before it burns.

-Owen Felltham, *Resolves, Divine, Moral and Political*

He that will only have a perfect brother must resign himself to remain brotherless.

-Italian Proverb

Don't flatter yourself that friendship authorizes you to say disagreeable things to your intimates. On the contrary, the nearer you come into relation with a person, the more necessary do tact and courtesy become.

-Oliver Wendell Holmes Sr., *The Autocrat of the Breakfast-table*

Friends are good, - good, if well chosen.

-Daniel Defoe

SIXTEEN

Gossip

The things most people want to know about are usually none of their business.

-George Bernard Shaw

He that covereth a transgression seeketh love; but he that repeateth a matter separateth very friends.

-The Bible (*KJV*), Proverbs 17:9

If people speak ill of you, live so that no one will believe them.

-Saying

Without wood a fire goes out; without a gossip a quarrel dies down.

-The Bible (*NIV*), Proverbs 26:20

What you don't see with your eyes, don't witness with your mouth.

-Jewish Proverb

Whoever gossips to you will gossip of you.

-Spanish Proverb

A man who is always ready to believe what is told him will never do well.

-Petronius, *Satyricon*

A perverse man stirs up dissension, and a gossip separates close friends.

-The Bible (*NIV*), Proverbs 16:28

Gossip is saying behind their back what you would not say to their face. Flattery is saying to their face what you would not say behind their back.

-Unknown

Gossip is always a personal confession either of malice or imbecility, and the young should not only shun it, but by the most thorough culture relieve themselves from all temptation to indulge in it. It is a low, frivolous, and too often a dirty business. There are country neighborhoods in which it rages like a pest. Churches are split in pieces by it. Neighbors are made enemies by it for life. In many persons it degenerates into a chronic disease, which is practically incurable. Let the young cure it while they may.

-Josiah Gilbert Holland, “The Cure for Gossip”, *Every-day Topics*

I lay it down as a fact that if all men knew what others say of them, there would not be four friends in the world.

-Blaise Pascal, *Pensées*

If you reveal your secrets to the wind, you should not blame the wind for revealing them to the trees.

-Khalil Gibran, *Broken Wings*

Rumor travels faster, but it don't stay put as long as Truth.

-Will Rogers, "Politics Getting Ready to Jell", *The Illiterate Digest*

SEVENTEEN

Leadership

Find fault, when you must find fault, in private, if possible; and sometime after the offense, rather than at the time.

-Sydney Smith, quoted in *A Memoir of the Reverend Sydney Smith* (1855) by Lady Holland

A chief is a man who assumes responsibility. He says, "I was beaten." He does not say, "My men were beaten."

-Antoine de Saint-Exupery, *Flight to Arras*

Trust men and they will be true to you; treat them greatly, and they will show themselves great.

-Ralph Waldo Emerson, "Prudence", *Essays*

A leader is a dealer in hope.

-Napoleon Bonaparte, quoted in *Napoleon in His Own Words* (1916) by Jules Bertaut

Example has more followers than reason.

-Christian Nestell Bovee, *Intuitions and Summaries of Thought*

Someone who feels appreciated will do more than someone who is simply being paid.

– J.S. Felts

Example is not the main thing (in influencing others), it is the only thing.

-Albert Schweitzer, interview in *United Nations World* (1952)

The question, "Who ought to be boss?" That is very much like asking: "Who ought to be tenor in the quartet?" Obviously, the man who can sing tenor.

-Henry Ford, *My Life and Work*

A competent leader can get efficient service from poor troops, while on the contrary, an incapable leader can demoralize the best of troops.

-Gen. John J. Pershing, *My Experiences in the World War*

I wonder how far Moses would have gone if he'd taken a poll in Egypt? What would Jesus Christ have preached if he'd taken a poll in Israel? Where would the Reformation have gone if Martin Luther had taken a poll? It isn't polls or public opinion of the moment that counts. It is right and wrong and leadership; men with fortitude, honesty and a belief in the right that makes epochs in the history of the world.

-Harry S. Truman, in memorandum to himself

Wars may be fought with weapons, but they are won by men. It is the spirit of the men who follow, and of the man who leads that gains the victory.

-George S. Patton, *Cavalry Journal*, September 1933

To lead an uninstructed people to war is to throw them away.

-Confucius, *Analects*

He that cannot obey cannot command.

-Benjamin Franklin, *Poor Richard's Almanack*

In time of peril, like the needle to the loadstone, obedience, irrespective of rank, generally flies to him who is best fitted to command.

-Herman Melville, *White-Jacket*

Never tell people how to do things. Tell them what to do and they will surprise you with their ingenuity.

-George S. Patton, *War As I Knew It*

It is better to have a lion at the head of an army of sheep, than a sheep at the head of an army of lions.

-Daniel Defoe, *The Life & Adventures of Mrs. Christian Davies*

Where there is no vision, the people perish.

-The Bible (*KJV*), Proverbs 29:18

The final test of a leader is that he leaves behind him in other men the conviction and the will to carry on.

-Walter Lippmann, "Roosevelt Has Gone", *New York Herald Tribune*, 14 April 1945

He who has never learned to obey cannot be a good commander.

-Aristotle, *Politics*

If you command wisely, you'll be obeyed cheerfully.

-Thomas Fuller, *Gnomologia*

If you suspect a man, don't employ him, and if you employ him, don't suspect him.

-Chinese Proverb

In the multitude of counsellors there is safety.

-The Bible (*KJV*), Proverbs 11:14

Authority without wisdom is like a heavy axe without an edge - fitter to bruise than polish.

-Anne Bradstreet, *Meditations Divine and Moral*

If your actions inspire others to dream more, learn more, do more and become more, you are a leader.

-Unknown

If the blind lead the blind, both shall fall into the ditch.

-The Bible (*KJV*), Matthew 15:14

- ❖ A leader is concerned with purpose, not position.
- ❖ A leader is humbled by the responsibility of leading.
- ❖ A leader is always learning. He understands everyone has something to teach him.
- ❖ A leader is full of praise and gives credit where credit is due.
- ❖ A leader takes action and never asks others to do what he is unwilling to do.
- ❖ A leader isn't afraid of confrontation, especially in defense of those he leads.
- ❖ A leader reveals his mistakes to his subordinates and takes responsibility.
- ❖ A leader is a person of courage, wisdom and integrity, and he inspires the same in others.
- ❖ A leader leads by example, and does not have a double standard.
- ❖ A leader is concerned with doing the right thing, not the popular thing.
- ❖ A leader is able to stand alone, even in the face of overwhelming odds.
- ❖ A leader is a servant. He will fill any position to help those he leads.
- ❖ A leader is specific in what he expects and keeps his subordinates informed.
- ❖ A leader does not expect more from others than he does of himself.
- ❖ A leader listens to input. He understands his ideas are not the only ideas.
- ❖ A leader delegate's authority and does not micromanage.

- ❖ A leader treats those under his command as he would want them to treat him under theirs.
- ❖ A leader is not ruled by his emotions, yet he is not without passion.
- ❖ A leader is not jealous, and he rejoices in the success of his subordinates.
- ❖ A leader has a vision, which he uses to influence others.
- ❖ A leader leads from the front. He is the first into the fray and the last one out.

-J.S. Felts, "21 Principles of Leadership"

Few things help an individual more than to place responsibility upon him, and to let him know that you trust him.

-Booker T. Washington, *Up from Slavery*

There is no limit to what can be accomplished, if it doesn't matter who gets the credit.

-Saying

When in leadership, never fail to follow the same standard you have put in place for others. There is nothing that will undermine leadership more, than having a double-standard.

- J.S. Felts

No man is fit to command another that cannot command himself.

-William Penn, *No Cross, No Crown*

Leadership is based on inspiration, not domination; on cooperation, not intimidation.

-William Arthur Ward

There is a great man who makes every man feel small. But the real great man is the man who makes every man feel great.

-G.K. Chesterton, *Charles Dickens*

A great man shows his greatness by the way he treats little men.

-Thomas Carlyle, quoted in Dale Carnegie's *How to Win Friends and Influence People*

Uneasy lies the head that wears a crown.

-William Shakespeare, *King Henry IV*

The best executive is the one who has sense enough to pick good men to do what he wants done, and self-restraint enough to keep from meddling with them while they do it.

-Theodore Roosevelt

Nothing is politically right which is morally wrong.

-Daniel O'Connell, quoted in a speech by Wendell Phillips, 6 August 1875

Spur not a willing horse.

-Italian Proverb

When the common soldiers are too strong and their officers too weak, the result is insubordination. When the officers are too strong and the common soldiers too weak, the result is collapse.

-Sun Tzu, *The Art of War*

The first method for estimating the intelligence of a ruler is to look at the men he has around him.

-Niccolo Machiavelli, *The Prince*

You will find, if you think for a moment, that the people who influence you are the people who believe in you.

-Henry Drummond, *The Greatest Thing In the World*

The man who is impatient with weakness will be defective in his leadership.

-J. Oswald Sanders, *Spiritual Leadership*

First find the man in yourself if you will inspire manliness in others.

-Amos Bronson Alcott, *Table-Talk*

If a man cannot govern himself, he won't be able to govern others, and if a man cannot govern his own house, trust him not to govern the affairs of the many.

- J.S. Felts

With privilege comes responsibility.

-Saying

Dream no small dreams for they have no power to move the hearts of men.

-Johann Wolfgang Goethe

Everything rises and falls on leadership.

-Saying

Those who insist on the dignity of their office show they have not deserved it.

-Baltasar Gracian, *The Art of Worldly Wisdom*

EIGHTEEN

Loyalty

We must not confuse dissent with disloyalty.

-Edward R. Murrow, "See it Now" broadcast on CBS, 9 March 1954

Loyalty means nothing unless it has at its heart the absolute principle of self-sacrifice.
-Woodrow Wilson, address in Washington, D.C., 13 July 1916

Be slow to fall into friendship, but when thou art in, continue firm and constant.

-Socrates, quoted in *Wits Commonwealth* (1674)

Where you go I will go, and where you stay I will stay. Your people will be my people and your God my God.

-The Bible (*NIV*), Ruth 1:16

NINETEEN

MANNERS

Rudeness is the weak man's imitation of strength.

-Eric Hoffer, *The Passionate State of Mind*

To have a respect for ourselves guides our morals; and to have a deference for others governs our manners.

-Laurence Sterne, "The Koran", *The Works of Laurence Sterne*

Good manners are made up of petty sacrifices.

-Ralph Waldo Emerson, *Letters and Social Aims*

TWENTY

Marriage

It was right for woman to be made from a rib of man. First, to signify the social union of man and woman, for the woman should neither use authority over man, and so she was not made from his head; nor was it right for her to be subject to man's contempt as his slave, and so she was not made from his feet.

-Saint Thomas Aquinas, *Summa Theologica*

No man knows what the wife of his bosom is until he has gone with her through the fiery trials of this world.

-Washington Irving, "The Wife", *The Sketch Book of Geoffrey Crayon*

Marriage must incessantly contend with a monster which devours everything, that is, familiarity.

-Honore de Balzac, *The Physiology of Marriage*

When a wife has a good husband it is easily seen in her face.

-Johann Wolfgang von Goethe, quoted in *Marriage in Epigram* (1903) by Frederick Morton

It's not beauty but fine qualities, my girl, that keep a husband.

-Euripides, *Hecuba*

Choose a wife rather by your ear than your eye.

-English Proverb

In entering into a marriage we should put the question to ourselves: do you believe that you will enjoy conversing with this [person] all the way into old age? Everything else in marriage is transitory, but most of the time together is spent in conversation.

-Friedrich Nietzsche, "Woman and Child", *Human, All Too Human*

Do not spoil what you have by desiring what you have not; but remember that what you now have was once among the things only hoped for.

-Epicurus, "Vatican Sayings"

What therefore God hath joined together, let not man put asunder.

-The Bible (*KJV*), Matthew 19:6

Marriage resembles a pair of shears, so joined that they cannot be separated; often moving in opposite directions, yet always punishing anyone who comes between them.

- Sydney Smith, quoted in *A Memoir of the Reverend Sydney Smith* (1855) by Lady Holland

Those marriages generally abound most with love and constancy that are preceded by a long courtship. The passion should strike root and gather strength before marriage be grafted on it.

-Joseph Addison, *The Spectator*, 29 December 1711

Love one another (John 13:34)
Carry each other's burdens (Gal. 6:2)
Be patient, bearing with one another in love (Eph. 4:2)
Submit to one another (Eph. 5:21)
Be kind and compassionate to one another, forgiving each other (Eph. 4:32)
Serve one another in love (Gal. 5:13)
Honor one another above yourselves (Rom. 12:10)
Encourage one another and build each other up (1 Thess. 5:11)
Accept one another (Rom. 15:7)
Pray for each other (James 5:16)

-J.S. Felts, "Ten Keys to a Successful Marriage"

There is no more lovely, friendly and charming relationship, communion or company than a good marriage.

-Martin Luther, *Table Talk*

Neither sex, without some fertilization of the complimentary characters of the other, is capable of the highest reaches of human endeavor.

-H.L. Mencken, "The Feminine Mind", *In Defense of Women*

In marriage do thou be wise: prefer the person before money, virtue before beauty, the mind before the body; then thou hast a wife, a friend, a companion, a second self.

-William Penn, *Some Fruits of Solitude*

Statistically speaking, you're modeling the marriage your children will have.

- J.S. Felts

A virtuous woman is a crown to her husband.

-The Bible (*KJV*), Proverbs 12:4

Keep your eyes wide open before marriage, and half shut afterwards.

-Benjamin Franklin, *Poor Richard's Almanack*

Who can find a virtuous woman? For her price is far above rubies. The heart of her husband doth safely trust in her.

-The Bible (*KJV*), Proverbs 31:10-11

Beauty captures the attention, but it is personality which captures the heart.

-Saying

If Americans can be divorced for "incompatibility" I cannot conceive why they are not all divorced. I have known many happy marriages, but never a compatible one. The whole aim of marriage is to fight through and survive the instant when incompatibility becomes unquestionable. For a man and a woman, as such, are incompatible.

-G.K. Chesterton, *What's Wrong with the World*

[For a wife,] take the daughter of a good mother.

-Thomas Fuller, *Introduction Ad Prudentiam*

It is not lack of love but lack of friendship that makes unhappy marriages.

-Friedrich Nietzsche

For this reason a man will leave his father and mother and be united to his wife, and the two will become one flesh.

-The Bible (*NIV*), Ephesians 5:31

Hasty marriage seldom proveth well.

-William Shakespeare, *King Henry VI*

So ought men to love their wives as their own bodies. He that loveth his wife loveth himself.

-The Bible (*KJV*), Ephesians 5:28

Be completely humble and gentle; be patient, bearing with one another in love.

-The Bible (*NIV*), Ephesians 4:2

TWENTY-ONE

Obedience

To say that a blind custom of obedience should be a surer obligation than duty taught and understood, it is to affirm, that a blind man may tread surer by a guide than a seeing man by a light.

-Francis Bacon, *The Advancement of Learning*

Let thy child's first lesson be obedience, and the second will be what thou wilt.

-Benjamin Franklin, *Poor Richard's Almanack*

Only he who believes is obedient, and only he who is obedient believes.

-Dietrich Bonhoeffer, *The Cost of Discipleship*

A man's heart deviseth his way, but the Lord directeth his steps.

-The Bible (KJV), Proverbs 16:9

It is a bitter dose to be taught obedience after you have learned to rule.

-Publilius Syrus, *Moral Sayings*

We ought to obey God rather than men.

-The Bible (*KJV*), Acts 5:29

There are two kinds of men who never amount to very much - Those who cannot do what they are told, and those who can do nothing else.

-Cyrus H. K. Curtis

Most of us know perfectly well what we ought to do; our trouble is that we do not want to do it.

-Peter Marshall, opening prayer of U.S. Senate, 26 June, 1947

To obey is better than sacrifice.

-The Bible (*KJV*), 1 Samuel 15:22

It is not hard to obey when we love the one whom we obey.

-Saint Ignatius

Learn to obey before you command.

-Solon, quoted in *Lives and Opinions of Eminent Philosophers* by Diogenes Laertius

TWENTY-TWO

REPUTATION

If I take care of my character, my reputation will take care of itself.

-Dwight L. Moody, quoted in *Methods of Teaching in Country Schools* (1880) by George Lind

We judge ourselves by what we feel capable of doing, while others judge us by what we have already done.

-Henry Wadsworth Longfellow, *Kavanagh*

A good name is more desirable than great riches; to be esteemed is better than silver or gold.

-The Bible (*NIV*) Proverbs 22:1

Outside show is a poor substitute for inner worth.

-Aesop, "The Fox and The Mask", *Fables*

Every cask smells of the wine it contains.

-Spanish proverb

A man's reputation is what other people think of him; his character is what he really is.

-Saying

A friend exaggerates a man's virtues; an enemy inflames his crimes.

–Joseph Addison, *The Spectator*, 7 June 1712

A man is not good or bad for one action.

-Thomas Fuller, *Gnomologia*

Associate yourself with men of good quality if you esteem your own reputation, for 'tis better to be alone than in bad company.

-George Washington, "Rules of Civility & Decent Behaviour in Company and Conversation"

One falsehood spoils a thousand truths.

-African Proverb

There are two modes of establishing our reputation: to be praised by honest men, and to be abused by rogues. It is best, however, to secure the former, because it will invariably be accompanied by the latter.

-Charles Caleb Colton, *Lacon*

A reputation once broken may possibly be repaired, but the world will always keep their eyes on the spot where the crack was.

-Josh Billings, quoted in *Great Thoughts from Master Minds* (1890)

The reputation of a thousand years may be determined by the conduct of one hour.

-Japanese Proverb

A man is what he is, not what men say he is. His character no man can touch. His character is what he is before his God and his judge; and only himself can damage that. His reputation is what men say he is. That can be damaged; but reputation is for time, character is for eternity.

-John B. Gough, quoted in *A Dictionary of Thoughts* (1891) by Tryon Edwards

A man's character was like a tree and reputation like its shadow. The shadow is what we think of it; the tree is the real thing.

-Abraham Lincoln, quoted in "Lincoln's Imagination" in Scribner's Monthly, August, 1879

TWENTY-THREE

RESPECT

A great man shows his greatness by the way he treats little men.

-John Timothy Stone, quoted in *The Christian Workers Magazine*, September 1916

If you want men to respect you, first of all respect yourself.

-Fyodor Dostoevsky, *Injury and Insult*

Perhaps the final test of a gentleman is his attitude toward (those who can be of no value to him).

-William Lyon Phelps, "Human Nature"

Those who insist on the dignity of their office show they have not deserved it.

-Baltasar Gracian, *The Art of Worldly Wisdom*

If Heaven made him, earth can find some use for him.

-Chinese Proverb

There is no king who has not had a slave among his ancestors, and no slave who has not had a king among his.

-Helen Keller, *The Story of My Life*

No race can prosper till it learns that there is as much dignity in tilling a field as in writing a poem.

-Booker T. Washington, Up From Slavery

The fire which enlightens is also the same fire which consumes.

-Henri Frederic Amiel, *Journal Intime*, 6 April 1851

When you are content to be simply yourself and don't compare or compete, everybody will respect you.

-Lao-tzu, *Tao Te Ching*

Every man's affairs, however little, are important to himself.

-Samuel Johnson, letter to Lord Bute, 3 November 1762

Do not despise the bottom rungs in the ascent to greatness.

-Publilius Syrus, *Sententiae*

Familiarity breeds contempt.

-Aesop, "The Fox and The Lion", *Fables*

God hath shewed me [Peter] that I should not call any man common or unclean.

-The Bible (*KJV*), Acts 10:28

Everybody, my friend, everybody lives for something better to come. That's why we want to be considerate of every man - Who knows what's in him, why he was born and what he can do?

-Maxim Gorky, *The Lower Depths*

Respect is what we owe; love what we give.

-Philip James Bailey, *Festus*

Never take a person's dignity: it is worth everything to them, and nothing to you.

-Saying

We must never undervalue any person. The workman loves not that his work should be despised in his presence. Now God is present everywhere, and every person is His work.

-Saint Francis de Sales, *Introduction to the Devout Life*

All men are by nature equal, made, all, of the same earth by the same Creator, and however we deceive ourselves, as dear to God is the poor peasant as the mighty prince.

-Plato, quoted in *Wits Commonwealth* (1674) by Nicholas Ling

Not a day passes over this earth, but men and women of no note do great deeds, speak great words and suffer noble sorrows.

-Charles Reade, *The Cloister and the Hearth*

Self-respect is the fruit of discipline; the sense of dignity grows with the ability to say no to oneself.

-Abraham Heschel, *The Insecurity of Freedom*

Do not rebuke an older man harshly, but exhort him as if he were your father. Treat younger men as brothers, older women as mothers, and younger women as sisters, with absolute purity.

-The Bible (NIV), 1 Timothy 5:1-2

TWENTY-FOUR

Slander

It is honorable to be accused by those who deserve to be accused.

-Latin Proverb

When certain persons abuse us, let us ask ourselves what description of characters it is they admire; we shall often find this a very consolatory question.

-Charles Caleb Colton, *Lacon*

With his mouth the godless man destroys his neighbor, but through knowledge the righteous will be delivered.

-The Bible (*NIV*), Proverbs 11:9

If you're out to beat a dog, you're sure to find a stick.

-Yiddish Proverbs

Whose house is of glass, must not throw stones at another.

-George Herbert, *Jacula Prudentum*

A generous confession disarms slander.

-English Proverb

Let not him who is houseless pull down the house of another, but let him work diligently and build one for himself, thus by example assuring that his own shall be safe from violence when built.

-Abraham Lincoln, reply to New York Workingmen's Assoc., 21 March 1864

When the ox stumbles, all whet their knives.

-Yiddish Proverb

I hate the man who builds his name on ruins of another's fame.

–John Gay, "The Poet and the Rose", *Fables*

Others proclaim the infirmities of a great man with satisfaction and complacence, if they discover none of the like in themselves.

-Joseph Addison, *The Spectator*, 24 December 1711

One man cannot hold another man down in the ditch without remaining down in the ditch with him.

-Booker T. Washington, address before the Republican Club of New York City, 12 Feb 1909

I saw them tear a building down,
A gang of men in a busy town,
With a ho, heave, ho, and a lusty yell,
They swung a beam and the side wall fell.
I asked the foreman, "Are these men skilled
And the kind of men you hire to build?"
And he laughed and answered,
"No indeed, common labor is all I need.
Why, I can easily wreck in a day or two,
What builders have taken years to do."
I thought to myself as I went my way,
Which of these roles have I tried to play?
Am I a builder who works with care,
Shaping my deeds by rule and square?
Or am I a wrecker who walks the town,
Content with the labor of tearing down?

-Unknown

It is not uncommon for ignorant and corrupt men to falsely charge others with doing what they imagine they themselves, in their narrow minds and experience, would have done under the circumstances.

-John H. Clarke, *Valdez v. United States* (1917)

All looks yellow to the Jaundic'd Eye.

-Alexander Pope, *An Essay on Criticism*

Slander cannot destroy an honest man - when the flood recedes the rock is still there.

-Chinese Proverb

There's more danger in a reserved and silent friend, than in a noisy babbling enemy.

-Roger L'Estrange, commentary on "A Country-man and a River", *Fables*

Do not accuse a man for no reason, when he has done you no harm.

-The Bible (NIV), Proverbs 3:30

He who knows how to flatter also knows how to slander.

-Napoleon Bonaparte, *Napoleon in His Own Words*

Even doubtful accusations leave a stain behind them.

-Thomas Fuller, *Gnomologia*

TWENTY-FIVE

TRUST

In order to try whether a vessel be leaky, we first prove it with water, before we trust it with wine.

-Charles Caleb Colton, *Lacon*

Whoever is careless with the truth in small matters cannot be trusted in important affairs.

-Albert Einstein, prepared, but undelivered final statement to the world, April 1955

It is better to trust in the Lord than to put confidence in man.

-The Bible (*KJV*), Psalms 118:8

Love all, trust a few.

–Shakespeare, *All's Well That Ends Well*

Distrust all those who love you extremely upon a very slight acquaintance, and without any visible reason.

-Lord Chesterfield, letter to his son, 15 January 1753

Trial is the school of trust.

-Saying

It is an equal failing to trust everybody, and to trust nobody.

-English Proverb

To be trusted is a greater compliment than being loved.

-George MacDonald, *St. George & St. Michael*

Trust that man in nothing who has not a conscience in everything.

-Laurence Sterne, "The Abuses of Conscience Considered", *Sermons*

Few things help an individual more than to place responsibility upon him, and to let him know that you trust him.

-Booker T. Washington, *Up from Slavery*

If it becomes necessary to employ someone new, always hire a man of character, over a man of knowledge. The later can be taught, not the former.

- J.S. Felts

People are more easily led than driven.

-William Henry Gregory, "Priests: Catholic and Others", *Paddiana*

A brave captain is as a root, out of which (as branches) the courage of his soldiers doth spring.

- Philip Sidney, *Aphorisms of Sir Philip Sidney* (1807)

Even the largest army is nothing without a good general

-Afghan Proverb

Experience, not hope, is what trust is built upon. You may hope someone doesn't fail you, but that is not trust. Trust is believing someone won't fail you because that's what experience has shown.

- J.S. Felts

The highest praise for a person is to give them responsibility.

-Saying

Always to distrust is an error, as well as always to trust.

-Johann Wolfgang von Goethe, quoted in *Dictionary of Quotations* (1893) by Rev. James Wood

To be trusted is a greater compliment than to be loved.

-George MacDonald, *The Marquis of Lossie*

Trust him with little who, without proofs, trusts you with everything; or, when he has proved you, with nothing.

-Johann Kaspar Lavater, *Aphorisms on Man*

TWENTY-SIX

Unity

In necessary things, unity; in uncertain things, liberty; in all things, charity.

-Marco Antonio de Dominis, *De Republica Ecclesiastica*

When bad men combine, the good must associate; else they will fall, one by one, an unpitied sacrifice in a contemptible struggle.

-Edmund Burke, Thoughts on the Cause of the Present Discontents

Have we not all one father? Hath not one God created us?

-The Bible (*KJV*), Malachi 2:10

Even the weak become strong when they are united.

-Friedrich von Schiller, quoted in *Dictionary of Quotations* (1899) by Rev. James Woods

Many ideas grow better when transplanted into another mind than in the one where they sprang up.

-Oliver Wendell Holmes Sr., *The Poet at the Breakfast-Table*

When two men in business always agree, one of them is unnecessary.

-William Wrigley Jr.

In comradeship is danger countered best.

-Johann Wolfgang von Goethe, *Faust*

When the head aches, all the members partake of the pain.

-Miguel de Cervantes, *Don Quixote*

If I have seen further than others, it is by standing on the shoulders of giants.

-Isaac Newton, letter to Robert Hooke, 5 Feb. 1676

If a house be divided against itself, that house cannot stand.

-The Bible (KJV), Mark 3:25

'Tis your own safety that's at stake, when your neighbor's wall is in flames.

-Horace, *Epistles*

We are more inclined to hate one another for points on which we differ, than to love one another for points on which we agree.

-Charles Caleb Colton, *Lacon*

Can two walk together, except they be agreed?

-The Bible (*KJV*), Amos 3:3

Men keep agreements when it is to the advantage of neither to break them.

-Solon

He that is not with me is against me.

-The Bible *(KJV),* Matthew 12:30

Union is strength, even with poor creatures.

-Homer, *The Iliad*

I am not bound to win, but I am bound to be true. I am not bound to succeed, but I am bound to live up to what light I have. I must stand with anybody that stands right, stand with him while he is right and part with him when he is wrong.

-Abraham Lincoln, quoted in *John Marshall and Other Addresses* (1908) by Horace Garvin Platt

Great perils have this beauty, that they bring to light the fraternity of strangers.

-Victor Hugo, *Les Miserables*

Now the body is not made up of one part but of many. If the foot should say, "Because I am not a hand, I do not belong to the body," it would not for that reason cease to be part of the body. And if the ear should say, "Because I am not an eye, I do not belong to the body," it would not for that reason cease to be part of the body. If the whole body were an eye, where would the sense of hearing be? If the whole body were an ear, where would the sense of smell be? But in fact God has arranged the parts in the body, every one of them, just as he wanted them to be. If they were all one part, where would the body be? As it is, there are many parts, but one body.

The eye cannot say to the hand, "I don't need you!" And the head cannot say to the feet, "I don't need you!" On the contrary, those parts of the body that seem to be weaker are indispensable, and the parts that we think are less honorable we treat with special honor. And the parts that are unpresentable are treated with special modesty, while our presentable parts need no special treatment. But God has combined the members of the body and has given greater honor to the parts that lacked it, so that there should be no division in the body, but that its parts should have equal concern for each other. If one part suffers, every part suffers with it; if one part is honored, every part rejoices with it.

-The Bible (*NIV*), 1 Corinthians 12:14-26

All for one, and one for all.

-Alexandre Dumas, *The Three Musketeers*

It is evident that many great and useful objects can be attained in this world only by cooperation. It is equally evident that there cannot be efficient cooperation if men proceed on the principle that they must not cooperate for one object unless they agree about other objects.

-Thomas Babington Macaulay, "Gladstone on Church and State", *Critical and Miscellaneous Essays*

Light is the task when many share the toil.

-Homer, *The Iliad*

United we stand, divided we fall.

-Aesop, "The Four Oxen and the Lion", *Fables*

Unity of freedom has never relied on uniformity of opinion.

-John F. Kennedy, State of the Union address, 14 January 1963

Recompense to no man evil for evil. Provide things honest in the sight of all men. If it be possible, as much as lieth in you, live peaceably with all men.

-The Bible (*KJV*), Romans 12:17-18

Grief knits two hearts in closer bonds than happiness ever can; and common sufferings are far stronger links than common joys.

-Alphonse de Lamartine, *Raphael*

Has it ever occurred to you that one hundred pianos all tuned to the same fork are automatically tuned to each other? They are of one accord by being tuned, not to each other, but to another standard to which each one must individually bow. So one hundred worshippers meeting together, each one looking away to Christ, are in heart nearer to each other than they could possibly be were they to become "unity" conscious and turn their eyes away from God to strive for closer fellowship. Social religion is perfected when private religion is purified. The body becomes stronger as its members become healthier. The whole church of God gains when the members that compose it begin to seek a better and a higher life.

-A.W. Tozer, *The Pursuit of God*

The lack of brotherhood among believers themselves has paralyzed the church in front of the skepticism and immorality of the world; but when we go back, in simple faith, to the one great fact of our redemption, we shall both be brought into closer fellowship with each other, and stimulated to more tender regard for the salvation of men.

-William M. Taylor, *Moses the Law-giver*

I never yet have known the Spirit of God to work where the Lord's people were divided.

-Dwight L. Moody, *Secret Power*

Division has done more to hide Christ from the view of men than all the infidelity that has ever been spoken.

-George MacDonald, *Paul Faber, Surgeon*

A chain is only as strong as its weakest link.

-Saying

Perseverance is more prevailing than violence; and many things which cannot be overcome when they are together, yield themselves up when taken little by little.

-Quintus Sertorius, *Plutarch's Lives*

We find not in the Gospel, that Christ hath anywhere provided for the uniformity of churches, but only for their unity.

-Roger Williams, *The Bloudy Tenent of Persecution*

PART IV

THE INTELLECTUAL IDEAS

ONE

Appearances

What we do see depends mainly on what we look for.

-John Lubbock, *The Beauties of Nature*

A wise man may look ridiculous in the company of fools.

-Thomas Fuller, *Gnomologia*

The first appearance deceives many.

-Phaedrus, "The Weasel and the Mice", *The Fables of Phaedrus*

Stop judging by mere appearances, and make a right judgment.

-The Bible (*NIV*), John 7:24

Conceal a flaw, and the world will imagine the worst.

-Martial, *Epigrams*

All that glisters is not gold.

-William Shakespeare, *The Merchant of Venice*

It is in knowledge as in swimming; he who flounders and splashes on the surface, makes more noise, and attracts more attention, than the pearl diver who quietly dives in the quest of treasures to the bottom.

-Washington Irving, *A History of New York*

Beware, as long as you live, of judging people by appearances.

-Jean de La Fontaine, *Fables*

Too many spend money they don’t have, to buy things they don't want, to impress people that they don't like.

-Unknown

When the oak-tree is felled, the whole forest echoes with it; but a hundred acorns are planted silently by some unnoticed breeze.

-Thomas Carlyle, "On History", *Critical and Miscellaneous Essays*

Appearances often are deceiving.

-Aesop, "The Wolf in Sheep's Clothing", *Fables*

People that seem so glorious are all show; underneath they’re like anybody else.

-Euripides, *Andromache*

Too many people spend time worrying about what the people, who never think about them, think about them.

- J.S. Felts

Ten persons crying out make more noise than thousand who are silent.

-Napoleon Bonaparte, quoted in *The British and Foreign Evangelical Review*, January 1876

Because half a dozen grasshoppers under a fern make the field ring with their importunate chink . . . do not imagine that those who make the noise are the only inhabitants of the field.

-Edmund Burke, *Reflections on the Revolution in France*

Outside show is a poor substitute for inner worth.

-Aesop, "The Fox and The Mask", *Fables*

The man with a toothache thinks everyone happy whose teeth are sound. The poverty-stricken man makes the same mistake about the rich man.

-George Bernard Shaw, *Man and Superman*

The Lord does not look at the things man looks at. Man looks at the outward appearance, but the Lord looks at the heart.

-The Bible (*NIV*), 1 Samuel 16:7

They are not all saints who use holy water.

-English Proverb

Every cloud engenders not a storm.

-William Shakespeare, *King Henry VI*

A long habit of not thinking a thing wrong, gives it a superficial appearance of being right, and raises at first a formidable outcry in defense of custom.

-Thomas Paine, *Common Sense*

Things are not always what they seem.

-Phaedrus, "The Weasel and the Mice", *Fables*

The fire which seems extinguished often slumbers beneath the ashes.

-Pierre Corneille, *Rodogune*

You can't wake a person who is pretending to be asleep.

-Native American Proverb

Abstain from all appearance of evil.

-The Bible (*KJV*), 1 Thessalonians 5:22

There are wicked people who would be much less dangerous if they were wholly without goodness.

-Francois de La Rochefoucauld, *Reflections or Sentences and Moral Maxims*

Do not think you are on the right road just because it is a well beaten path.

-Saying

One may smile, and smile, and be a villain!

-William Shakespeare, *Hamlet*

Rough diamonds are sometimes mistaken for worthless pebbles.

-Thomas Browne, *Christian Morals*

Think not that all is well within when all is well without, or that thy being pleased is a sign that God is pleased.

-Jeremy Taylor, *The Golden Grove*

Do not judge men from mere appearances; for the light laughter that bubbles on the lip often mantles over the depths of sadness, and the serious look may be the sober veil that covers a divine peace and joy. The bosom can ache beneath diamond brooches; and many a blithe heart dances under coarse wool.

-Edwin Hubbel Chapin, *Humanity in the City*

As those who believe in the visibility of ghosts can easily see them, so it is always easy to see repulsive qualities in those we despise and hate.

-Frederick Douglass, "The Color Line", published in *The North American Review*, June 1881

You must look into people, as well as at them.

-Lord Chesterfield, letter to his son, 4 October 1746

As blushing will sometimes make a whore pass for a virtuous woman, so modesty may make a fool seem a man of sense.

-Jonathan Swift, *Thoughts on Various Subjects*

Take nothing on its looks; take everything on evidence. There's no better rule.

-Charles Dickens, *Great Expectations*

A turtle lays thousands of eggs without anyone knowing, but when the hen lays an egg, the whole country is informed.

-Malay Proverb

For the great majority of mankind are satisfied with appearances, as though they were realities, and are often more influenced by the things that seem than by those that are.

-Niccolo Machiavelli, *Discourses on Livy*

TWO

Attitude

The greatest discovery of my generation is that man can alter his life simply by altering his attitude.

-Unknown

We are all in the gutter, but some of us are looking at the stars.

-Oscar Wilde, Lady Windermere's Fan

If you are distressed by anything external, the pain is not due to the thing itself but to your own estimate of it, and this you have the power to revoke at any moment.

-Marcus Aurelius, *Meditations*

Now if you are going to win any battle you have to do one thing. You have to make the mind run the body. Never let the body tell the mind what to do. The body will always give up.

-George Patton

It is not so wretched to be blind, as it is not to be capable of enduring blindness.

-John Milton, *Second Defense of the English People*

Murmur at nothing: if our ills are reparable, it is ungrateful; if remediless, it is in vain.

–Charles Caleb Colton, *Lacon*

The meaning of things lies not in the things themselves but in our attitude towards them.

-Antoine de Saint-Exupery, *The Wisdom of Sands*

Life is a grindstone, and whether it grinds a man down or polishes him up depends on the stuff he is made of.

-Thomas Holcroft

The burden becomes light by being well borne.

-Henry Fielding, *Amelia*

The world is a looking glass, and gives back to every man the reflection of his own face. Frown at it, and it will in turn look sourly upon you; laugh at it and with it, and it is a jolly, kind companion.

-William Makepeace Thackeray, *Vanity Fair*

Do everything without complaining or arguing.

-The Bible (NIV), Philippians 2:14

Whenever you're in conflict with someone, there is one factor that can make the difference between damaging your relationship and deepening it. That factor is attitude.

-William James

THREE

CURIOSITY

The whole art of teaching is only the art of awakening the natural curiosity of young minds for the purpose of satisfying it afterwards.

-Anatole France, *The Crime of Sylvestre Bonnard*

Steady and undissipated attention to one object, is a sure mark of a superior genius.

-Lord Chesterfield, letter to his son, 14 April 1747

Every now and then a man's mind is stretched by a new idea or sensation, and never shrinks back to its former dimensions.

-Oliver Wendell Holmes Sr., *The Autocrat of the Breakfast Table*

Imagination is more important than knowledge. For knowledge is limited.

-Albert Einstein, interview in *Saturday Evening Post*, 26 October, 1929

Were I to wish for anything, I should not wish for wealth and power, but for the passionate sense of the potential, for the eye which, ever young and ardent, sees the possible . . . what wine is so sparkling, so fragrant, so intoxicating!

-Soren Kierkegaard, *Either/Or*

The world will never starve for want of wonders; but only for want of wonder.

-G.K. Chesterton, *Tremendous Trifles*

Curiosity is one of the permanent and certain characteristics of a vigorous intellect.

-Samuel Johnson, *The Rambler*, 12 March 1751

Familiar things happen, and mankind does not bother about them. It requires a very unusual mind to undertake the analysis of the obvious.

-Alfred North Whitehead, Science and the Modern World

There is no such thing on earth as an uninteresting subject; the only thing that can exist is an uninterested person.

-G.K. Chesterton, "On Mr. Rudyard Kipling", *Heretics*

Curiosity is as much the parent of attention, as attention is of memory.

-Richard Whately, Miscellaneous Remains

Men give me credit for some genius. When I have a subject in hand, I study it profoundly. Day and night it is before me. I explore it in all its bearings. My mind becomes pervaded with it. Then the effort which I have made is what people are pleased to call the fruit of genius. It is the fruit of labor and thought.

-Alexander Hamilton, quoted in *Other Men's Minds* (1800) by Edwin Davies

Do not hover always on the surface of things, nor take up suddenly with mere appearances; but penetrate into the depth of matters, as far as your time and circumstances allow, especially in those things which relate to your profession.

-Isaac Watts, The Improvement of the Mind

Nobody is bored when he is trying to make something that is beautiful, or discover something that is true.

-William Ralph Inge, *Our Present Discontents*

They are ill discoverers that think there is no land, when they see nothing but sea.

-Francis Bacon, *The Advancement of Learning*

The only true voyage...would be not to visit strange lands but to possess other eyes.

-Marcel Proust, *The Captive*

FOUR

Determination

Always bear in mind that your own resolution to succeed, is more important than any other one thing.

-Abraham Lincoln, letter to Isham Reavis, 5 November 1855

The fixed determination to have acquired the warrior soul, to either conquer or perish with honor, is the secret of victory.

-George S. Patton

Where there is a will there is a way.

-Saying

If at first you don't succeed, try, try again.

-William Edward Hickson, "Try Again"

Everyone has a dream, but those whose dreams become reality lies in determination.

- J.S. Felts

Nothing in this world can take the place of persistence. Talent will not; nothing is more common than unsuccessful people with talent. Genius will not; unrewarded genius is almost a proverb. Education will not; the world is full of educated derelicts. Persistence and determination alone are omnipotent. The slogan "press on" has solved and always will solve the problems of the human race.

-Unknown

A strong will, a settled purpose, an invincible determination, can accomplish almost anything; and in this lies the distinction between great men and little men.

-Thomas Fuller, quoted in *The World's Laconics* (1871) by Tryon Edwards

He who would learn to fly one day must first learn to stand and walk and run and climb and dance: one cannot fly into flying.

-Friedrich Nietzsche, *Thus Spoke Zarathustra*

FIVE

EDUCATION

There is a precious instruction to be got by finding that we were wrong.

-Thomas Carlyle, letter to unknown young man, 13 March 1843

Every man who rises above the common level has received two educations: the first from his teachers; the second, more personal and important, from himself.

–Edward Gibbon, *The Autobiography of Edward Gibbon*

The aim of education should be to teach us rather how to think, than what to think.

-James Beattie, *Essays on the Nature and Immutability of Truth*

A teacher who is attempting to teach without inspiring the pupil with a desire to learn is hammering cold iron.

-Horace Mann, quoted in the *Journal of Education*, December 1901

Those who cannot remember the past are condemned to repeat it.

-George Santayana, *The Life of Reason*

To make your children capable of honesty is the beginning of education.

-John Ruskin, *Time and Tide*

Much learning does not teach understanding.

-Heraclitus, *Fragments*

An education which does not cultivate the will is an education that depraves the mind.

-Anatole France, *The Crime of Sylvestre Bonnard*

Very few men are wise by their own counsel, or learned by their own teaching. For he that was only taught by himself had a fool for his master.

-Ben Jonson, *Discoveries*

Learn to see in another's calamity the ills which you should avoid.

-Publilius Syrus, *Sententiae*

One great reason why many children abandon themselves wholly to silly sports, and trifle away all their time insipidly, is, because they have found their curiosity baulked, and their inquiries neglected.

–John Locke, *Some Thoughts Concerning Education*

A mind all logic is like a knife all blade. It makes the hand bleed that uses it.

-Rabindranath Tagore, *Stray Birds*

If a man will begin with certainties, he shall end in doubts, but if he will be content to begin with doubts, he shall end in certainties.

-Francis Bacon, *The Advancement of Learning*

Knowledge which is acquired under compulsion obtains no hold on the mind.

-Plato, *The Republic*

A teacher affects eternity; he can never tell where his influence stops.

-Henry Adams, *The Education of Henry Adams*

A little philosophy inclineth man's mind to atheism, but depth in philosophy bringeth men's mind about to religion.

-Francis Bacon, "Of Atheism", *Essays*

To spend too much time in studies is sloth; to use them too much for ornament, is affectation; to make judgment wholly by their rules, is the humor of a scholar.

-Francis Bacon, "Of Studies", *Essays*

The ignorant classes are the dangerous classes. Ignorance is the womb of monsters.

-Henry Ward Beecher, *Proverbs from Plymouth Pulpit*

When you know a thing, to recognize that you know it; and when you do not know a thing, and when you do not know a thing, to recognize that you do not know it. That is knowledge.

-Confucius, *Analects*

He, who will not reason, is a bigot; he who cannot is a fool; and he who dares not is a slave.

-William Drummond, *Academical Questions*

Seek information from the experienced.

-Marcus Tullius Cicero

Whoever acquires knowledge and does not practice it, resembles him, who ploughs his land, and leaves it unsown.

-Sa'di, *Gulistan*

Every now and then a man's mind is stretched by a new idea or sensation, and never shrinks back to its former dimensions.

-Oliver Wendell Holmes Sr., *The Autocrat of the Breakfast-table*

Tell me and I will forget. Show me, and I may not remember. Involve me, and I will understand.

-Saying

The things taught in colleges and schools are not an education, but the means of an education.

-Ralph Waldo Emerson, *Journals*

Education is not the filling of a pail, but the lighting of a fire.

-William Butler Yeats

Knowledge is of two kinds; we know a subject ourselves, or we know where we can find information upon it.

-Samuel Johnson, quoted in *Life of Samuel Johnson* (1791) by James Boswell

Give a man a fish and you feed him for a day. Teach man to fish and you feed him for a lifetime.

-Chinese Proverb

He can best avoid a snare who knows how to set one.

-Publilius Syrus, *Sententiae*

As land is improved by sowing it with various seeds, so is the mind by exercising it with different studies.

-Pliny the Elder, "Letter to Tuscus", *Letters of Pliny* (1810)

A little learning is a dangerous thing;
Drink deep, or taste not the Pierian spring:
There shallow draughts intoxicate the brain,
And drinking largely sobers us again.

-Alexander Pope, *An Essay on Criticism*

A single conversation across the table with a wise man is better than ten years mere study of books.

-Henry Wadsworth Longfellow, *Hyperion*

Consciousness of a fact is not knowing it: if it were, the fish would know more of the sea than the geographers.

-George Bernard Shaw, *Back to Methuselah*

Education makes a people easy to lead, but difficult to drive; easy to govern, but impossible to enslave.

-Henry Brougham, speech to the House of Commons, 29 January 1828

He who asks a question is a fool for five minutes; he who does not ask a question remains a fool forever.

-Chinese Proverb

Wear your learning, like your watch, in a private pocket; and do not pull it out, and strike it, merely to show that you have one.

-Lord Chesterfield, letter to his son, 22 Feb. 1748

The fatal tendency of mankind to leave off thinking about a thing when it is no longer doubtful is the cause of half their errors.

-John Stuart Mill, *On Liberty*

The only people who achieve much are those who want knowledge so badly that they seek it while the conditions are still unfavorable. Favorable conditions never come.

-C.S. Lewis, "The Weight of Glory", address at Oxford University Church, 8 June 1941

Where there is much desire to learn, there of necessity will be much arguing, much writing, many opinions; for opinion in good men is but knowledge in the making.

-John Milton, *Areopagitica*

Meek young men grow up in libraries, believing it their duty to accept the views which Cicero, which Locke, which Bacon, have given; forgetful that Cicero, Locke and Bacon were only young men in libraries, when they wrote these books.

-Ralph Waldo Emerson, "The American Scholar", address at Cambridge, August 1837

The mind is not a vessel that needs filling, but wood that needs igniting.

-Plutarch, “On Listening to Lectures”, *Moralia*

To be conscious that you are ignorant is a great step to knowledge.

-Benjamin Disraeli, *Sybil*

Poor is the pupil who does not surpass his master.

-Leonardo Da Vinci, *The Notebooks*

Sit down before a fact as a little child; be prepared to give up every preconceived notion; follow humbly wherever and to whatever abyss nature leads or you shall learn nothing.

-Thomas Henry Huxley, letter to Charles Kingsley, 23 September 1860

In a free system, literacy is as imperative as ignorance is necessary in a slave system.

-Horace Mann Bond, *The Education of the Negro in the American Social Order*

A free curiosity is more effective in learning than a discipline based on fear.

-Saint Augustine, *Confessions*

There are three schoolmasters that are always at hand . . . eyes to see with, and ears to hear with, and a tongue to ask questions with.

-Henry Ward Beecher, "Practical Ethics for the Young", *Sermons*

Since we cannot... know all that is to be known of everything, we ought to know a little about everything.

-Blaise Pascal, *Pensées*

Observation more than books, experience more than persons, are the prime educators.

-Amos Bronson Alcott, *Table-Talk*

Learning is not attained by chance; it must be sought for with ardor and attended to with diligence.

-Abigail Adams, letter to her son, John Quincy Adams, 8 May 1780

I am always ready to learn, although I do not always like being taught.

-Winston Churchill, speech to House of Commons, 4 November 1952

I have never met a man so ignorant that I couldn't learn something from him.

-William Sullivan, quoted at his funeral by John T. Sargent, 15 September 1839

Most of our so-called reasoning consists in finding arguments for going on believing as we already do.

-James Harvey Robinson, *The Mind in the Making*

As turning the logs will make a dull fire burn, so change of studies a dull brain.

-Henry Wadsworth Longfellow, "Driftwood", *Table-Talk*

The whole art of teaching is only the art of awakening the natural curiosity of young minds for the purpose of satisfying it afterwards.

-Anatole France, *The Crime of Sylvestre Bonnard*

It is impossible for a man to learn that which he thinks he already knows.

-Epictetus, *Discourses*

Inconsistency with past views or conduct may be but a mark of increasing knowledge and wisdom.

-Tryon Edwards, *A Dictionary of Thoughts*

All knowledge is of itself of some value. There is nothing so minute or inconsiderable, that I would not rather know it than not.

-Samuel Johnson, quoted in *Life of Samuel Johnson* (1791) by James Boswell

Histories make men wise; poets witty; the mathematics subtile; natural philosophy deep; moral grave; logic and rhetoric able to contend.

-Francis Bacon, "Of Studies", *Essays*

The most learning and knowledge that we have, is the least part of what we are ignorant of.

-Plato, quoted in *Wits Common-wealth* (1722) by Nicholas Ling

To train the mind shall be the first object, and to stock it only the second.

-William Gladstone, *Gleanings of Past Years*

You know everybody is ignorant, only on different subjects.

-Will Rogers, “From Nuts to the Soup”, published in *New York Times*, 31 August, 1924

Real education must ultimately be limited to men who INSIST on knowing, the rest is mere sheep-herding.

-Ezra Pound, "The Instructor", *ABC of Reading*

It is absurd to hold that a man ought to be ashamed of being unable to defend himself with his limbs but not of being unable to defend himself with speech and reason, when the use of reason is more distinctive of a human being than the use of his limbs.

-Aristotle, *Rhetoric*

All men who have turned out worth anything have had the chief hand in their own education.

-Walter Scott, letter to J.G. Lockhart, June 1830

Education is only a ladder to gather fruit from the tree of knowledge, not the fruit itself.

-Austin O'Malley, *Keystones of Thought*

The great end of education is to discipline rather than to furnish the mind; to train it to the use of its own powers, rather than fill it with the accumulations of others.

-Tryon Edwards, *A Dictionary of Thoughts*

The most influential of all educational factors is the conversation in a child's home.

-William Temple, *The Hope of a New World*

SIX

ENTHUSIASM

What counts is not necessarily the size of the dog in the fight - it's the size of the fight in the dog.

-Dwight D. Eisenhower, address to Republican National Committee, 31 Jan. 1958

No man is sane who does not know how to be insane on proper occasions.

-Henry Ward Beecher, *Star Papers*

Passion, though a bad regulator, is a powerful spring.

-Ralph Waldo Emerson, "Considerations by the Way", *The Conduct of Life*

Success is going from failure to failure without loss of enthusiasm.

-Unknown

He did it with all his heart, and prospered.

-The Bible (*KJV*), 2 Chronicles 31:21

Let a man in a garret but burn with enough intensity, and he will set fire to the whole world.

-Antoine de Saint-Exupery, *Wind, Sand and Stars*

A rock pile ceases to be a rock pile the moment a single man contemplates it, bearing within him the image of a cathedral.

-Antoine de Saint-Exupery, *Flight to Arras*

One can never consent to creep when one feels an impulse to soar.

-Helen Keller, *The Story of My Life*

I am in earnest. I will not equivocate - I will not excuse - I will not retreat a single inch - and I will be heard.

-William Lloyd Garrison, *The Liberator*, 1 January 1831

It is always with the best intentions that the worst work is done.

-Oscar Wilde, "The Critic as Artist", *Intentions*

Martyrdom has always been a proof of the intensity, never of the correctness of a belief.

-Arthur Schnitzler, *Buch der Sprüche und Bedenken*

If you're possessed by a thought, then you find it expressed everywhere; you can even smell it.

-Thomas Mann, *Tonio Kroger*

Zeal without knowledge is fire without light.

-Thomas Fuller, *Gnomologia*

Nothing great was ever achieved without enthusiasm.

-Ralph Waldo Emerson, "Circles", *Essays*

I make bold to say that some men have been styled eccentric because they are really in earnest, and earnestness defies rules. I do not believe that it is possible for a man in downright earnest to be always "proper".

-Charles Haddon Spurgeon, *Eccentric Preachers*

A burning heart will soon find for itself a flaming tongue.

-Charles Haddon Spurgeon, *Lectures to My Students*

I will be as harsh as truth and as uncompromising as justice. On this subject I do not wish to think, or speak, or write, with moderation. No! No! Tell a man whose house is on fire to give a moderate alarm; tell him to moderately rescue his wife from the hands of the ravisher; tell the mother to gradually extricate her babe from the fire into which it has fallen; but urge me not to use moderation.

-William Lloyd Garrison, *The Liberator*, 1 January 1831

People who are unable to motivate themselves must be content with mediocrity, no matter how impressive their other talents.

-Andrew Carnegie

In things pertaining to enthusiasm, no man is sane who does not know how to be insane on proper occasions.

-Henry Ward Beecher, *Proverbs from Plymouth Pulpit*

Give me the love that leads the way,
The faith that nothing can dismay,
The hope no disappointments tire,
The passion that will burn like fire,
Let me not sink to be a clod:
Make me Thy fuel, Flame of God.

-Amy Carmichael, "Flame of God"

One contented with what he has done will never become famous for what he will do. He has lain down to die.

-Christian Nestell Bovee, *Intuitions and Summaries of Thought*

If you want to build a ship, don't drum up people to collect wood and don't assign them tasks and work, but rather teach them to long for the endless immensity of the sea.

-Antoine de Saint-Exupery

Enthusiasm begets enthusiasm.

-Henry Wadsworth Longfellow, *Hyperion: A Romance*

Whatsoever thy hand findeth to do, do it with thy might.

-The Bible (*KJV*), Ecclesiastes 9:10

We act as though comfort and luxury were the chief requirements of life, when all that we need to make us really happy is something to be enthusiastic about.

-Anonymous, quoted in *The Smart Set*, August 1914

SEVEN

EXPERIENCE

You don't set a fox to watching the chickens just because he has a lot of experience in the hen house.

-Harry S. Truman, speech, 30 October, 1960

The true art of memory is the art of attention.

-Samuel Johnson, *The Idler*, 15 September 1759

Many people know so little about what is beyond their short range of experience. They look within themselves - and find nothing! Therefore they conclude that there is nothing outside themselves, either.

-Helen Keller, *The World I Live In*

The condition of all progress is experience; we must go wrong a thousand times before we find the right.

-Felix Adler, *Creed and Deed*

He can best avoid a snare who knows how to set one.

-Publilius Syrus, *Sententiae*

A gram of experience is worth a ton of theory.

-Robert Gascoyne-Cecil, *Saturday Review* (1859)

If you do what you've always done, you'll get what you've always gotten.

-Saying

Natural abilities are like natural plants, that need pruning by study; and studies themselves do give forth directions too much at large, except they be bounded in by experience.

-Francis Bacon, "Of Studies", *Essays*

Experience comprises illusions lost, rather than wisdom gained.

-Joseph Roux, *Meditations of a Parish Priest*

Experience does not err; your judgments err by expecting from her what is not in her power.

-Leonardo Da Vinci, *Notebooks*

I have but one lamp by which my feet are guided, and that is the lamp of experience. I know of no way of judging the future but by the past.

-Patrick Henry, speech in Virginia Convention, 23 March 1775

He who is shipwrecked twice is foolish to blame the sea.

-Publilius Syrus

One thorn of experience is worth a whole wilderness of warning.

-James Russell Lowell, "Shakespeare Once More", *Among My Books*

You know more of a road by having travelled it than by all the conjectures and descriptions in the world.

-William Hazlitt, "On the Conduct of Life", *Table-Talk*

I know not anything more pleasant, or more instructive than to compare experience with expectation, or to register from time to time the difference between idea and reality. It is by this kind of observation that we grow daily less liable to be disappointed.

-Samuel Johnson, letter to Bennet Langton, 27 June 1758

Although it rains, throw not away your watering pot.

-English Proverb

Nothing is a waste of time if you use the experience wisely.

-Auguste Rodin

The strongest arguments prove nothing so long as the conclusions are not verified by experience.

-Roger Bacon, *Opus Tertium*

The years teach much which the days never know.

-Ralph Waldo Emerson, "Experience", *Essays*

If a man cheat me once, shame on him; if he cheat me twice, shame on me.

-Scottish Proverb

EIGHT

Facts

Facts are stubborn things, and whatever may be our wishes, our inclinations, or the dictates of our passion, they cannot alter the state of facts and evidence.

-John Adams, argument in defense of British soldiers in the Boston Massacre trials, Dec. 1770

A thousand probabilities do not make one fact.

-Italian Proverb

Facts do not cease to exist because they are ignored.

-Aldous Huxley, "A Note on Dogma", *Proper Studies*

Facts are many, but the truth is one.

-Rabindranath Tagore, *Sadhana: The Realization of Life*

You'll find the fewer the facts, the stronger the opinions.

- J.S. Felts

Sit down before fact as a little child, be prepared to give up every preconceived notion, follow humbly wherever and to whatever abysses nature leads, or you shall learn nothing.

-Thomas Henry Huxley, letter to Charles Kingsley, 23 September 1860

Feelings don't change facts.

-Saying

The sky is not less blue because the blind man does not see it.

-Danish Proverb

If a man will kick a fact out of the window, when he comes back he finds it again in the chimney corner.

-Ralph Waldo Emerson, *Journals*

Consciousness of a fact is not knowing it; if it were, the fish would know more of the sea than the sea than the geographers and the naturalists.

-George Bernard Shaw, *Back to Methuselah*

Facts are not truths, they are not conclusions; they are not even premises... the Truth depends on, and is only arrived at by, a legitimate deduction from all the facts which are truly material.

-Samuel Taylor Coleridge, *Table Talk*, 27 December 1831

NINE

Goals

Our plans miscarry because they have no aim. When a man does not know what harbour he is making for, no wind is the right wind.

-Lucius Annaeus Seneca (the younger), *Moral Letters to Lucilius*

Obstacles are those frightful things you see when you take your eyes off the goal.

-Hannah More

Aim at perfection in everything, though in most things it is unattainable; however, they who aim at it, and persevere, will come much nearer to it than those whose laziness and despondency make them give it up as unattainable.

-Lord Chesterfield, letter to his son, 24 May 1750

A horse never runs so fast as when he has other horses to catch up and outpace.

-Ovid, *The Art of Love*

One contented with what he has done will never become famous for what he will do. He has lain down to die.

-Christian Nestell Bovee, *Intuitions and Summaries of Thought*

If you tell [count] every step, you will make a long journey of it.

-Thomas Fuller, *Gnomologia*

It is not enough to take steps which may some day lead to a goal; each step must be itself a goal and a step likewise.

-Johann Wolfgang von Goethe, quoted in *Conversations with Goethe* (1850) by Johann Eckermann

Dream no small dreams for they have no power to move the hearts of men.

-Johann Wolfgang von Goethe

In everything you do, consider the end.

-Solon, quoted in *The History of Greece* (1848) by William Hendry Stowell

Slight not what's near though aiming at what's far.

-Euripides, *Rhesus*

It is common to overlook what is near by keeping the eye fixed on something remote.

-Samuel Johnson, *The Idler*, 12 January 1760

The true worth of a man is to be measured by the objects he pursues.

-Marcus Aurelius, *Meditations*

No wind serves him who addresses his voyage to no certain port.

-Michel de Montaigne, "Of the Inconstancy of Our Actions", *Essays*

One of the most important factors, not only in military matters but in life as a whole, is the power of execution, the ability to direct one's whole energies towards the fulfillment of a particular task.

-Erwin Rommel

Who begins too much accomplishes little.

-German Proverb

If you run after two hares, you will catch neither.

-Thomas Fuller, *Gnomologia*

Victories that are cheap, are cheap. Those only are worth having which come as the result of hard fighting.

-Henry Ward Beecher, *Royal Truths*

One principal reason why men are so often useless is, that they neglect their own profession, and divide and shift their attention among a multitude of objects and pursuits.

-Nathanael Emmons, sermon in Oxford, 13 April 1791

One may as much miss the mark, by aiming too high, as too low.

-Thomas Fuller, *Gnomologia*

It is by attempting to reach the top at a single leap that so much misery is produced in the world.

-William Cobbett, *Cottage Economy*

The mightiest rivers lose their force when split up into several streams.

-Ovid, *Love's Cure*

It is time we steered by the stars, not by the lights of each passing ship.

-Omar Bradley, speech, 31 May 1948

In the long run men hit only what they aim at.

-Henry David Thoreau, *Walden*

Four steps to achievement:
Plan purposefully.
Prepare prayerfully.
Proceed positively.
Pursue persistently.

-Saying

Delight yourself in the LORD and he will give you the desires of your heart.

-The Bible (*NIV*), Psalms 37:4

He who considers too much will accomplish little.

-Friedrich Schiller, *William Tell*

TEN

JUDGMENT

Before we set our hearts too much upon anything, let us examine how happy they are who already possess it.

-Francois de La Rochefoucauld

O Lord, help me not to despise or oppose what I do not understand.

-William Penn

The strength of a man's virtue should not be measured by his special exertions, but by his habitual acts.

-Blaise Pascal

While you can count the number of seeds in an apple, you can never count the number of apples in a seed.

-Proverb

Men always love what is good or what they find good; it is in judging what is good that they go wrong.

-Jean-Jacques Rousseau, *The Social Contract*

Statistics are no substitute for judgment.

-Henry Clay

One series of consequences will not serve the turn, but many different and opposite deductions must be examined, and laid together, before a man can come to make a right judgment of the point in question.

–John Locke, quoted in *A Dictionary of the English Language* (1785) by Samuel Johnson

Just because something doesn't do what you planned it to do, doesn't mean it's useless.

-Thomas A. Edison

The most powerful cause of error is the war existing between the senses and reason.

-Blaise Pascal, *Pensées*

The fly that doesn't want to be swatted is most secure when it lights on the fly-swatter.

-Georg Christoph Lichtenberg

The drunkard smells of whiskey, but so does the bartender.

-Jewish Proverb

An idealist is one who, on noticing that a rose smells better than a cabbage, concludes that it will also make a better soup.

-H. L. Mencken, "Sententiae", *A Book of Burlesques*

It isn't that they can't see the solution; it's that they can't see the problem.

-G.K. Chesterton, *The Scandal of Father Brown*

Men willingly believe what they wish.

-Julius Caesar, *The Gallic War*

All men, who deliberate on controversial matters, should be free from hatred, love, anger, and pity.

-Julius Caesar, quoted in Sallust's *The Conspiracy of Catiline*

The judge should not be young; he should have learned to know evil, not from his own soul, but from late and long observation of the nature of evil in others.

-Plato, *The Republic*

There is only one way of seeing things rightly, and that is, seeing the whole of them.

-John Ruskin, "The Unity of Art", speech at Manchester, 22 February 1859

Drink nothing without seeing it; sign nothing without reading it.

-Spanish proverb

Beware the fury of a patient man.

-John Dryden, *Absalom and Achitophel*

Don't judge any man until you have walked two moons in his moccasins.

-Native American Proverb

You shall judge of a man by his foes as well as by his friends.

-Joseph Conrad, *Lord Jim*

God, when he makes the prophet, does not unmake the man.

-John Locke, *An Essay Concerning Human Understanding*

People only see what they are prepared to see.

-Ralph Waldo Emerson, *Journals*

When the mouse laughs at the cat there's a hole nearby.

-Nigerian Proverb

Do not count your chickens before they are hatched.

-Aesop, "The Milkmaid and Her Pail", *Fables*

Dig the well before you are thirsty.

-Chinese Proverb

You don't set a fox to watching the chickens just because he has a lot of experience in the hen house.

-Harry S. Truman, speech, 30 October, 1960

By their fruits ye shall know them.

-The Bible (*KJV*), Matthew 7:20

Mighty rivers can easily be leaped at their source.

-Publilius Syrus, *Sententiae*

The drowning man is not troubled by rain.

-Persian Proverb

By the husk you may guess at the nut.

-English Proverb

An ox with long horns, even if he does not butt, will be accused of butting.

-Malay Proverb

It is folly to sing twice to a deaf man.

-English Proverb

Better to measure ten times and cut once, than measure once and cut ten times.

-Saying

Burn not your house, to fright away the mice.

-Thomas Fuller, *Gnomologia*

The one being carried does not realize how far away the town is.

-Nigerian Proverb

By a small sample we may judge of the whole piece.

-Miguel de Cervantes, *Don Quixote*

Never confuse reputation for character.
Never confuse management with leadership.
Never confuse fame for success.
Never confuse knowledge with wisdom.
Never confuse lust for love.
Never confuse flattery for friendship.
Never confuse perception with reality.
Never confuse dissent for disloyalty.
Never confuse opinions with facts.
Never confuse pleasure for happiness.
Never confuse defeat with failure.
Never confuse honesty for truth.
Never confuse hearing with listening.
Never confuse courage for fearlessness.
Never confuse faith with feelings.
Never confuse age for maturity.
Never confuse contentment with satisfaction.
Never confuse liberty with license.
Never confuse unity for uniformity.
Never confuse change with progress.

-J.S. Felts, "Never Confuse"

Every heart has its secret sorrows which the world knows not, and oftentimes we call a man cold, when he is only sad.

-Henry Wadsworth Longfellow, *Hyperion: A Romance*

What the sober man has in his heart, the drunken man has on his lips.

-Danish Proverb

He is not good himself who speaks well of everybody alike.

-Thomas Fuller, *Gnomologia*

Why beholdest thou the mote that is in thy brother's eye, but considerest not the beam that is in thine own eye?

-The Bible (KJV), Matthew 7:3

The enthusiasm of the cause may sometimes warp judgment.

-William Howard Taft, address in Ocean Grove, N.J., 15 August 1911

From a drop of water, a logician could infer the possibility of an Atlantic or a Niagara without having seen or heard of one or the other.

-Arthur Conan Doyle, *A Study In Scarlet*

Stop judging by mere appearances, and make a right judgment.

-The Bible (*NIV*), John 7:24

By the work one knows the workman.

-Jean de La Fontaine, "The Hornets and The Bees", *Fables*

Judge a man not by the words of his mother, but from the comments of his neighbors.

-Jewish Proverb

Only judge when you have heard all.

-Greek Proverb

Beware, as long as you live, of judging people by appearances.

-Jean de La Fontaine, *Fables*

Judge a man only by his own deeds and words; the opinions of others can be false.

-The *Talmud*

If the root is holy, so are the branches.

-The Bible (*NIV*), Romans 11:16

The wolf will hire himself out very cheaply as a shepherd.

-Russian Proverb

When the people of the world all know beauty as beauty,
There arises the recognition of ugliness.
When they all know the good as good,
There arises the recognition of evil.

-Lao-tzu, *Tao Te Ching*

A thief believes everybody steals.

-Edgar Watson Howe, *Country Town Sayings*

Ponder the path of thy feet, and let all thy ways be established.

-The Bible (*KJV*), Proverbs 4:26

That should be long considered which can be decided but once.

-Latin Proverb

As I grow older, I pay less attention to what men say. I just watch what they do.

-Andrew Carnegie

Tempt not a desperate man.

-William Shakespeare, *Romeo and Juliet*

Judge a tree from its fruit; not from the leaves.

-Euripides

Our duty is to believe that for which we have sufficient evidence, and to suspend our judgment when we have not.

-John Lubbock, *The Use of Life*

Don't throw away the old bucket until you know whether the new one holds water.

-Swedish Proverb

Nor is the people's judgment always true;
The most may err as grossly as the few.

-John Dryden, *Absalom and Achitophel*

If it ain't broke, don't fix it.

-Saying

Show me the man you honor; I know by that symptom, better than any other, what kind of man you yourself are.

-Thomas Carlyle, "Hudson's Statue", *Latter-day Pamphlets*

The best way to show that a stick is crooked is not to argue about it or to spend time denouncing it, but to lay a straight stick alongside it.

-Dwight L. Moody

Deliberate with caution, but act with decision; and yield with graciousness, or oppose with firmness.

-Charles Caleb Colton, *Lacon*

Examine what is said, not him who speaks.

-Arab Proverb

We should not judge of a man's merits by his great qualities, but by the use he makes of them.

-Francois de La Rochefoucauld, *Reflections or Sentences and Moral Maxims*

Not every dog that barks bites.

-French Proverb

As those who believe in the visibility of ghosts can easily see them, so it is always easy to see repulsive qualities in those we despise and hate.

-Frederick Douglass, "The Color Line", published in *The North American Review*, June 1881

A man with one watch will always knows the time.
A man with two watches will always be in doubt.

-Saying

If we all worked on the assumption that what is accepted as true is really true, there would be little hope of advance.

-Orville Wright, letter to George Spratt, 7 June 1903

Don't judge each day by the harvest you reap, but by the seeds you plant.

-Robert Louis Stevenson, *Admiral Guinea*

You are young, my son, and, as the years go by, time will change and even reverse many of your present opinions. Refrain therefore awhile from setting yourself up as a judge of the highest matters.

-Plato, *Laws*

Don't find fault; find a remedy.

-Henry Ford

Everything that irritates us about others can lead us to an understanding of ourselves.

-Carl Gustav Jung

Look beneath the surface; let not the intrinsic quality of a thing nor its worth escape you.

-Marcus Aurelius, *Meditations*

Take nothing on its looks; take everything on evidence. There's no better rule.

-Charles Dickens, *Great Expectations*

Fools rush in where angels fear to tread.

-Alexander Pope, *An Essay on Criticism*

There is a precious instruction to be got by finding that we were wrong.

-Thomas Carlyle, letter to unknown young man, 13 March 1843

Examine everything carefully; hold fast to that which is good.

-The Bible (NASB), 1 Thessalonians 5:21

Where there's smoke, there's fire.

-Saying

If thou art a master, be sometimes blind; if a servant, sometimes deaf.

-Thomas Fuller, *Introductio Ad Prudentiam*

Search men's governing principles, and consider the wisest, what they shun and what they cleave to.

-Marcus Aurelius, *Meditations*

Where there is no choice, we do well to make no difficulty.

-George MacDonald, *Sir Gibbie*

In everything you do, consider the end.

-Saying

No man can lose what he never had.

-Izaak Walton, *The Compleat Angler*

You pity a man who is lame or blind; but you never pity him for being a fool, which is often a much greater misfortune.

-Sydney Smith, quoted in *A Memoir of the Reverend Sydney Smith* (1855) by Lady Holland

Be careful what you wish for.

-Saying

Don't fall victim to believing something is completely wrong because you found an error contained therein. In the same way, don't believe something to be right because it contains a single truth.

- J.S. Felts

He that steals an egg will steal an ox.

-George Herbert, *Jacula Prudentum*

There are none more abusive to others than they that lie most open to it themselves.

-Lucius Annaeus Seneca (the younger), "On Anger", *Moral Essays*

No process is so fatal as that which would cast all men in one mould. Every human being is intended to have a character of his own, to be what no other is, to do what no other can do.

-William Ellery Channing, "Remarks on Associations", *Remarks on the Character and Writings of Fenelon*

ELEVEN

Opinion

Those who never retract their opinions love themselves more than they love truth.

-Joseph Joubert, *Pensées of Joubert*

I could never divide myself from any man upon the difference of an opinion, or be angry with his judgment for not agreeing with me in that from which perhaps within a few days I should dissent myself.

-Thomas Browne, *Religio Medici*

Judge a man only by his own deeds and words; the opinions of others can be false.

-The *Talmud*

There never were, in the world, two opinions alike, no more than two hairs, or two grains: their most universal quality is diversity.

-Michel de Montaigne, "Of the Resemblance of Children to Their Fathers", *Essays*

Some people will never learn anything, for this reason, that they understand everything too soon.

-Alexander Pope, *Thoughts on Various Subjects*

The fact that an opinion has been widely held is no evidence whatever that it is not utterly absurd; indeed in view of the silliness of the majority of mankind, a widespread belief is more likely to be foolish than sensible.

-Bertrand Russell, *Marriage and Morals*

Every horse thinks his own pack heaviest.

-English Proverb

Wars of opinion, as they have been the most destructive, are also the most disgraceful of conflicts, being appeals from right to might and from argument to artillery.

-Charles Caleb Colton, *Lacon*

Error of opinion may be tolerated where reason is left free to combat it.

-Thomas Jefferson, first inaugural address, 4 March 1801

New opinions are always suspected, and usually opposed, without any other reason but because they are not already common.

-John Locke, *An Essay Concerning Human Understanding*

The man who never alters his opinion is like standing water, and breeds reptiles of the mind.

-William Blake, "A Memorable Fancy", *The Marriage of Heaven and Hell*

If a man would register all his opinions upon love, politics, religion, learning, etc., beginning from his youth, and so go to old age, what a bundle of inconsistencies and contradictions would appear at last!

-Jonathan Swift, *Thoughts on Various Subjects*

Christians have burnt each other, quite persuaded
That all the Apostles would have done as they did.

-Lord Byron, *Don Juan*

A prophet is not without honour, save in his own country.

-The Bible (*KJV*), Matthew 13:57

Away with this hurrah of masses, and let us have the considerate vote of single men.

-Ralph Waldo Emerson, "Considerations by the Way", *The Conduct of Life*

Too often we . . . enjoy the comfort of opinion without the discomfort of thought.

-John F. Kennedy, speech at Yale University, 11 June 1962

The best rules to form a young man are: to talk little, to hear much, to reflect alone upon what has passed in company, to distrust one's own opinions, and value others that deserve it.

-William Temple, *The Works of Sir William Temple* (1814)

I beseech you, in the bowels of Christ, think it possible you may be mistaken.

-Oliver Cromwell, letter to general assembly of the Church of Scotland, 3 August 1650

Greater things are believed of those who are absent.

-Tacitus, *Histories*

Nothing is so uncertain or as incalculable as the feelings of a crowd.

-Livy, *Ab urbe condita*

Great men lose somewhat of their greatness by being near us; ordinary men gain much.

-Walter Savage Landor, "Aeschines and Phocion", *Imaginary Conversations*

We often contradict an opinion, while actually it is only the tone with which it has been presented that we find disagreeable.

-Friedrich Nietzsche, "Man In Society", *Human, All Too Human*

There is nothing that makes more cowards and feeble men than public opinion.

-Henry Ward Beecher, *Proverbs from Plymouth Pulpit*

Man goes into the noisy crowd to drown his own clamor of silence.

-Rabindranath Tagore, *Stray Birds*

But the peculiar evil of silencing the expression of an opinion is, that it is robbing the human race; posterity as well as the existing generation; those who dissent from the opinion, still more than those who hold it. If the opinion is right, they are deprived of the opportunity of exchanging error for truth: if wrong, they lose, what is almost as great a benefit, the clearer perception and livelier impression of truth, produced by its collision with error.

-John Stuart Mill, *On Liberty*

The strength of our persuasions is no evidence at all of their own rectitude: crooked things may be as stiff and inflexible as straight: and men may be as positive and peremptory in error as in truth.

-John Locke, *An Essay Concerning Human Understanding*

I have no more right to object to a man for holding a different opinion from mine than I have to differ with a man because he wears a wig and I wear my own hair; but if he takes his wig off and shakes the powder in my eyes, I shall consider it my duty to get rid of him as soon as possible.

-John Wesley, *Journal*, 14 May 1765

Never believe anything bad about anybody, unless you positively know it to be true. Never tell even that, unless you feel that it is absolutely necessary, and that God is listening while you tell it.

-Henry Van Dyke, "A Song From a Cave", *The Story of the Psalms*

Do not think of knocking out another person's brains because he differs in opinion from you. It will be as rational to knock yourself on the head because you differ from yourself ten years ago.

-James Burgh, *The Dignity of Human Nature*

To maintain an opinion because it is thine, and not because it is true, is to prefer thyself above the truth.

-Joseph Henshaw, *Meditations*

The sole fact you have an opinion is not evidence you obtained it from thought.

- J.S. Felts

The shepherd drives the wolf from the sheep's throat, for which the sheep thanks the shepherd as a liberator, while the wolf denounces him for the same act as the destroyer of liberty.

-Abraham Lincoln, speech in Baltimore, Maryland, 18 April 1864

The fashion of this world passeth away.

-The Bible (KJV), 1 Corinthians 7:31

Most of the change we think we see in life
Is due to truths being in and out of favour.

-Robert Frost, "The Black Cottage", *North of Boston*

He that complies against his will,
Is of his own opinion still.

-Samuel Butler (17th century), *Hudibras*

TWELVE

Perfection

Until you realize perfection is an ideal and not a reality, you will never have self-confidence.

- J.S. Felts

Striving to better, oft we mar what's well.

-William Shakespeare, *King Lear*

Perfection does not exist; to comprehend it is the triumph of human intelligence; to desire to possess it, the most dangerous of follies.

-Alfred de Musset, A Confession of a Child of the Century

Aim at perfection in everything, though in most things it is unattainable; however, they who aim at it, and persevere, will come much nearer to it than those whose laziness and despondency make them give it up as unattainable.

-Lord Chesterfield, letter to his son, 24 May 1750

Trying to have everything will often leave you with nothing.

- J.S. Felts

The maxim "Nothing avails but perfection" may be spelt shorter "Paralysis."

-Winston Churchill, note to General Ismay, 6 December, 1942

A man would do nothing, if he waited until he could do it so well that no one would find fault with what he has done.

-John Henry Newman

Desire to have things done quickly prevents their being done thoroughly.

-Confucius, *Analects*

The best may err.

-Joseph Addison, *Cato*

THIRTEEN

READING

Reading furnishes the mind only with materials of knowledge; it is thinking that makes what we read ours.

-John Locke, An Essay Concerning Human Understanding

Some read to think, these are rare; some to write, these are common; and some read to talk, and these form the great majority.

-Charles Caleb Colton, *Lacon*

Without meditation reading is a waste of time.

-Charles Haddon Spurgeon, *The Treasury of David*

Many books require no thought from those who read them, and for a very simple reason: they made no such demand upon those who wrote them.

-Charles Caleb Colton, *Lacon*

The man who does not read good books has no advantage over the man who can't read.

-Saying

A man ought to read just as inclination leads him, for what he reads as a task will do him little good.

-Samuel Johnson, quoted in *Life of Samuel Johnson* (1791) by James Boswell

If we encounter a man of rare intellect, we should ask him what books he reads.

-Ralph Waldo Emerson, quoted in *Perfect Jewels* (1884) by William Ralston Balch

Some books are to be tasted, others to be swallowed, and some few to be chewed and digested: that is, some books are to be read only in parts, others to be read, but not curiously, and some few to be read wholly, and with diligence and attention.

-Francis Bacon, "Of Studies", *Essays*

It is chiefly through books that we enjoy intercourse with superior minds. . . In the best books, great men talk to us, give us their most precious thoughts, and pour their souls into ours.

-William Ellery Channing, "Self-Culture", address in Boston, Sept 1838

The reading of all good books is like conversation with the finest men of past centuries.

-Rene Descartes, *Discourse on the Method*

Once you learn to read, you will be forever free.

-Frederick Douglass

Books are standing counselors and preachers, always at hand, and always disinterested; having this advantage over oral instructors, that they are ready to repeat their lessons as often as we please.

-Robert Chambers, quoted in *The Young Men's Magazine*, May 1858

To read without reflecting is like eating without digesting.

-Edmund Burke, quoted in *Many Thoughts of Many Minds* (1863) by Henry Southgate

Read not to contradict and confute; nor to believe and take for granted; nor to find talk and discourse; but to weigh and consider.

-Francis Bacon, "Of Studies", *Essays*

Reading is to the mind what exercise is to the body.

-Joseph Addison, *The Tatler*, 18 March 1709

The man who never reads will never be read; he who never quotes will never be quoted. He, who will not use the thoughts of other men's brains, proves that he has no brains of his own.

-Charles Haddon Spurgeon, sermon, "Paul - His Cloak and His Books", 29 November 1863

Reading maketh a full man; conference a ready man; and writing an exact man.

-Francis Bacon, "Of Studies", *Essays*

The books which help you most are those which make you think the most.

-Theodore Parker, *Lessons from the World of Matter and the World of Men*

The greatest education to be had can be found in a library full of books. There, we can meet with those who are no longer alive, visit faraway places, relive history from a front row seat, listen to many of the greatest minds who have even lived, take advice from the greatest of counselors, and learn from many of the world's greatest teachers; all in a lonely aisle flanked with some dusty old books.

– J.S. Felts

FOURTEEN

Self-Confidence

Believe that you can whip the enemy, and you have won half the battle.

-J.E.B. Stuart, The Life and Campaigns of Major-General J. E. B. Stuart

Self-confidence is the first requisite to great undertakings.

-Samuel Johnson, "Pope", *Lives of the English Poets*

If confidence is contagious, doubt is also contagious.

-Charles William Gerstenberg, "Selling", *Principles of Business*

Immense power is acquired by assuring yourself in your secret reveries that you were born to control affairs.

-Andrew Carnegie, speech at Curry Commercial College in Pittsburg, 23 June 1885

The way to develop self-confidence is to do the thing you fear to do, and get a record of successful experiences behind you.

-William Jennings Bryan

Self-trust is the essence of heroism.

-Ralph Waldo Emerson, "Heroism", *Essays*

Confidence is a plant of slow growth.

-English Proverb

Self-trust is the first secret of success.

-Ralph Waldo Emerson, "Success", *Society and Solitude*

To wish you were someone else is to waste the person you are.

-Saying

FIFTEEN

SELF-RELIANCE

Insist on yourself. Never imitate.

-Ralph Waldo Emerson, "Self-Reliance", *Essays*

That man is best prepared for life, who makes all that concerns his welfare depend upon himself, or nearly so, instead of hanging his hopes on other men.

-Plato, *Menexenus*

Not in the clamor of the crowded street,
Not in the shouts and plaudits of the throng.
But in ourselves, are triumph and defeat.

-Henry Wadsworth Longfellow, "The Poets", *Poetical Works*

You've got to do your own growing, no matter how tall your grandfather was.

-Irish Proverb

For both ruin and recovery are from within.

-Epictetus, *Discourses*

Either find a way, or make one.

-Latin Proverb

To be obliged to beg our daily happiness from others bespeaks a more lamentable poverty than that of him who begs his daily bread.

-Charles Caleb Colton, *Lacon*

To know what you prefer, instead of humbly saying amen to what the world tells you that you ought to prefer, is to have kept your soul alive.

-Robert Louis Stevenson, *An Inland Voyage*

It is a painful thing
To look at your own trouble and know
That you yourself and no one else has made it.

-Sophocles, *Ajax*

Destiny is not a matter of chance, it is a matter of choice; it is not a thing to be waited for, it is a thing to be achieved.

-William Jennings Bryan, "America's Mission", speech to Virginia Democratic Association, 22 February 1899

Where the old tracks are lost, new country is revealed with its wonders.

-Rabindranath Tagore, *Gitanjali*

It is necessary to the happiness of man that he be mentally faithful to himself.

-Thomas Paine, *The Age of Reason*

Shallow men believe in luck . . . strong men in cause and effect.

-Ralph Waldo Emerson, "Worship", *The Conduct of Life*

No great man ever complains of want of opportunity.

-Ralph Waldo Emerson, *Journals*

Most of the luxuries, and many of the so called comforts of life, are not only indispensable, but positive hindrances to the elevation of mankind.

-Henry David Thoreau, *Walden*

Be able to be alone. Lose not the advantage of solitude, and the society of thyself.

-Thomas Browne, *Christian Morals*

If a man does not keep pace with his companions, perhaps it is because he hears a different drummer. Let him step to the music which he hears, however measured or far away.

-Henry David Thoreau, *Walden*

What I must do is all that concerns me, not what the people think. This rule, equally arduous in actual and in intellectual life, may serve for the whole distinction between greatness and meanness. It is the harder, because you will always find those who think they know what is your duty better than you know it. It is easy in the world to live after the world's opinion; it is easy in solitude to live after your own; but the great man is he who in the midst of the crowd keeps with perfect sweetness the independence of solitude.

-Ralph Waldo Emerson, "Self Reliance", *Essays*

Imitation is suicide.

-Ralph Waldo Emerson, "Self Reliance", *Essays*

I don't know who my grandfather was, and am more concerned to know what his grandson will be.

-Abraham Lincoln, quoted in *The Early Life of Abraham Lincoln* (1896) by Ida Tarbell

If a little tree grows in the shade of a larger tree, it will die small.

-Senegalese Proverb

He only is a great man who can neglect the applause of the multitude and enjoy himself independent of its favor.

-Joseph Addison, *The Spectator*, 17 September 1711

Those who depend on the merits of their ancestors may be said to search in the root of the tree for those fruits which the branches ought to produce.

-Unknown French author

I never saw a wild thing sorry for itself.
A small bird will drop frozen dead from a bough
without ever having felt sorry for itself

-D.H. Lawrence, "Self-Pity", *Pansies*

He who seeks only for applause from without has all his happiness in another's keeping.

-Oliver Goldsmith, *The Good-Natured Man*

Some of the roads most used lead nowhere.

-Saying

The greatest works that have been done have been accomplished by the ones. The hundreds do not often effect much; the companies never do; it is the units, just the single individuals, that after all, are the power and the might . . . Individual effort is, after all, the grand thing.

-Charles Haddon Spurgeon, *Spurgeon's Gems*

How much time he gains, who does not look to see what his neighbor says or does or thinks, but only at what he does himself, to make it just and holy.

-Marcus Aurelius, *Meditations*

It is a common habit to blame life upon the environment. Environment modifies life but does not govern life. The soul is stronger than its surroundings.

-William James

The wisest man could ask no more of Fate
Than to be simple, modest, manly, true,
Safe from the many, honored by the few;
To count as naught in world, or church, or state;
But inwardly in secret to be great.

-James Russell Lowell, "Jeffries Wyman", *Heartsease and Rue*

Know then that the world exists for you. . . . All that Adam had, all that Caesar could, you have and can do. Adam called his house heaven and earth; Caesar called his house Rome; you perhaps call yours a cobbler's trade, a hundred acres of ploughed land, or a scholar's garret. Yet line for line and point for point your dominion is as great as theirs, though without fine names. Build, therefore, your own world.

-Ralph Waldo Emerson, "Prospects", *Nature*

SIXTEEN

THOUGHT

A man who does not think for himself does not think at all.

-Oscar Wilde, "The Soul of Man Under Socialism"

We sow a thought and reap an act,
We sow an act and reap a habit,
We sow a habit and reap a character,
We sow a character and reap a destiny.

-Saying

I will govern my life and my thoughts as if the whole world were to see the one, and to read the other; for "what does it signify to make anything a secret to my neighbor, when to God (who is the searcher of our hearts) all our privacies are open."

-Lucius Annaeus Seneca (the younger), "On The Happy Life", *Moral Essays*

If you are possessed by an idea, you find it expressed everywhere; you even smell it.

-Thomas Mann, "Tonio Kroger", *Death in Venice*

Learning without thought is labour lost; thought without learning is perilous.

-Confucius, *Analects*

Too often we ... enjoy the comfort of opinion without the discomfort of thought.

-John F. Kennedy, speech at Yale University, 11 June 1962

You cannot put a rope around the neck of an idea: you cannot put an idea up against a barrack-square wall and riddle it with bullets: you cannot confine it in the strongest prison cell that your slaves could ever build.

-Sean O'Casey, *Death of Thomas Ashe*

Reading furnishes the mind only with materials of knowledge; it is thinking that makes what we read ours.

-John Locke, *An Essay Concerning Human Understanding*

A man is not idle, because he is absorbed in thought. There is a visible labor and there is an invisible labor.

-Victor Hugo, *Les Misérables*

I have always thought the actions of men the best interpreters of their thoughts.

-John Locke, *An Essay Concerning Human Understanding*

To think justly, we must understand what others mean: to know the value of our thoughts, we must try their effect on other minds.

-William Hazlitt, "On People of Sense", *The Plain Speaker*

We think in generalities, but we live in detail.

-Alfred North Whitehead, "The Education of an Englishman", *Essays in Science and Philosophy*

Men give me credit for some genius. All the genius I have lies in this: When I have a subject in hand, I study it profoundly. Day and night it is before me. I explore it in all its bearings. My mind becomes pervaded with it. Then the effort which I have made is what people are pleased to call the fruit of genius. It is the fruit of labor and thoughts.

-Alexander Hamilton

There are a thousand thoughts lying within a man that he does not know till he takes up a pen to write.

-William Makepeace Thackeray, *The History of Henry Esmond*

All that a man does outwardly is but the expression and completion of his inward thought. To work effectually, he must think clearly. To act nobly, he must think nobly.

-William Ellery Channing, "On the Elevation of the Laboring Classes"

It is the mark of an educated mind to be able to entertain a thought without accepting it.

-Unknown

A simple man believes anything, but a prudent man gives thought to his steps.

-The Bible (*NIV*), Proverbs 14:15

Finally, brothers, whatever is true, whatever is noble, whatever is right, whatever is pure, whatever is lovely, whatever is admirable if anything is excellent or praise-worthy think about such things.

-The Bible (*NIV*), Philippians 4:8

A man would do well to carry a pencil in his pocket, and write down the thoughts of the moment. Those that come unsought for are commonly the most valuable, and should be secured, because they seldom return.

-Francis Bacon, quoted in *Cooper's Journal* (1850) by Thomas Cooper

The ancestor of every action is a thought.

-Ralph Waldo Emerson, "Spiritual Laws", *Essays*

SEVENTEEN

Wisdom

A wise man will desire no more than what he may get justly, use soberly, distribute cheerfully, and leave contently.

-Benjamin Franklin, *Poor Richard's Almanack*

Call unto me, and I will answer thee, and show thee great and mighty things, which thou knowest not.

-The Bible (*KJV*), Jeremiah 33:3

The wise man corrects his own errors by observing those of others.

-Publilius Syrus, *Sententiae*

Wisdom is not knowledge and we must not confound the two. Wisdom is the right use of knowledge.

-Charles Hadden Spurgeon, "Christ – The Power and Wisdom of God", *Sermons*

A wise man will make more opportunities than he finds.

-Francis Bacon, *The Advancement of Learning*

Better be wise by the misfortunes of others than by your own.

-Aesop, "The Lion, The Ass and The Fox", *Fables*

The fear of the Lord is the beginning of knowledge: but fools despise wisdom and instruction.

-The Bible (*KJV*), Proverbs 1:7

A blind man who sees is better than a seeing man who is blind.

-Persian Proverb

You will seek me and find me when you seek me with all your heart.

-The Bible (*NIV*), Jeremiah 29:13

Truly wise men are never above asking questions.

-Charles Hadden Spurgeon, *Christ's Incarnation*

Cleverness is not wisdom.

-Euripides, *Bacchae*

Knowledge is proud that he has learned so much; Wisdom is humble that he knows no more.

-William Cowper, "The Winter Walk at Noon", *The Task*

Solomon made a book of proverbs, but a book of proverbs never made a Solomon!

-English Proverb

Smooth runs the water where the brook is deep.

-William Shakespeare, *King Henry VI*

Wisdom is the principal thing; therefore get wisdom.

-The Bible (*KJV*), Proverbs 4:7

To see things in the seed, that is genius.

-Lao-tzu

The words of a man's mouth are deep waters, but the fountain of wisdom is a bubbling brook.

-The Bible (*KJV*), Proverbs 18:4

He who knows not, and knows not that he knows not, is a fool - avoid him.

He who knows not, and knows that he knows not, is simple - teach him.

He who knows, and knows not that he knows, is asleep - wake him.

He who knows, and knows that he knows, is wise man - follow him.

-Arab Proverb

If we would guide by the light of reason, we must let our minds be bold.

-Louis D. Brandeis, dissenting opinion in *New York State Ice Co. v. Liebmann* (1932)

Deep calleth unto deep.

-The Bible (*KJV*), Psalms 42:7

A wise man reflects before he speaks; a fool speaks, and then reflects on what he has uttered.

-French Proverb

[Wisdom] is more precious than rubies, and all the things thou canst desire are not to be compared unto her.

-The Bible (*KJV*), Proverbs 3:15

The fool wonders, the wise man asks.

-Benjamin Disraeli, *The Tragedy of Count Alarcos*

Wisdom is not communicable. The wisdom which a wise man tries to communicate always sounds foolish . . . Knowledge can be communicated, but not wisdom. One can find it, live it, be fortified by it, do wonders through it, but one cannot communicate and teach it.

-Hermann Hesse, *Siddhartha*

Wisdom is only found in truth.

-Johann Wolfgang von Goethe, *Proverbs in Prose*

Man who know little say much.
Man who know much say little.

-Saying

If any of you lack wisdom, let him ask of God, that giveth to all men liberally, and upbraideth not; and it shall be given him.

-The Bible (*KJV*), James 1:5

A fool may be known by six things: anger without cause; speech without profit; change without progress; inquiry without object; putting trust in a stranger; and mistaking foes for friends.

-Arab Proverb

PART V

The Ethical Choice

ONE

CHARACTER

Our deeds determine us, as much as we determine our deeds.

-George Eliot, *Adam Bede*

Peace hath higher tests of manhood than battle ever knew.
-John Greenleaf Whittier, "The Hero", *Poetical Works*

It is only an error of judgment to make a mistake, but it shows an infirmity of character to adhere to it when discovered.

-Christian Nestell Bovee, *Intuitions and Summaries of Thought*

"When wealth is lost, nothing is lost;
when health is lost, something is lost;
when character is lost, all is lost."

–Saying

True gold does not fear the test of fire.

-Chinese Proverb

In great matters men show themselves, as they wish to be seen; in small matters, as they are.

-Nicolas Chamfort, *Maxims and Thoughts*

Sir, I would rather be right, than be President.

-Henry Clay, reply to Senator Preston, in U.S. Senate (1850)

The superior man thinks of virtue; the small man thinks of comfort.

-Confucius, *Analects*

When we are planning for posterity, we ought to remember that virtue is not hereditary.

-Thomas Paine, *Common Sense*

Nor is it always in the most distinguished achievements that men's virtues or vices may be best discerned; but often an action of small note, a short saying, or a jest, may distinguish a person's real character more than the greatest sieges or the most important battles.

-Plutarch, "Life of Alexander", *Parallel Lives*

What you are stands over you the while, and thunders so that I cannot hear what you say to the contrary

-Ralph Waldo Emerson, "Social Aims"

There is nothing in which people more betray their character than in what they find to laugh at.

-Johann Wolfgang von Goethe, *Elective Affinities*

There is no pillow as soft as a clear conscience.

-French Proverb

What thou art, that thou art; neither by words canst thou be made greater than what thou art in the sight of God.

-Thomas a' Kempis, *The Imitation of Christ*

Character is like a tree and reputation like its shadow. The shadow is what we think of it; the tree is the real thing.

-Abraham Lincoln, quoted in *Elementary Composition Exercises* (1890) by Irene Hardy

Talents are best nurtured in solitude: character is best formed in the stormy billows of the world.

-Johann Wolfgang von Goethe, *Torquato Tasso*

To enjoy the things we ought and to hate the things we ought has the greatest bearing on virtue of character.

-Aristotle, *Nicomachean Ethics*

If I take care of my character, my reputation will take care of itself.

-Dwight L. Moody, quoted in *Methods of Teaching in Country Schools* (1880) by George Lind

Woe unto you, when all men shall speak well of you!

-The Bible (*KJV*), Luke 6:26

Let men see, let them know, a real man who lives as he was meant to live.

-Marcus Aurelius, *Meditations*

A man who lives right has more power in his silence than another has by his words.

-Unknown

Character is what you are in the dark.

-Dwight L. Moody, quoted in *The Pew and the Pupil* (1914) by Robinson P. D. Bennett

God give us men! A time like this demands
Strong minds, great hearts, true faith and ready hands;
Men whom the lust of office does not kill;
Men whom the spills of office cannot buy;
Men who possess opinions and a will;
Men who have honor, men who will not lie;
Men who can stand before a demagogue,
And damn his treacherous flatteries without winking!
Tall men, sun-crowned, who live above the fog
In public duty and in private thinking;
For while the rabble, with their thumb-worn creeds,
Their large professions and their little deeds,
Mingle in selfish strife; lo! Freedom weeps,
Wrong rules the land, and waiting justice sleeps!

-Josiah Gilbert Holland, "Wanted", *Garnered Sheaves*

If you want to find out what a man is to the bottom, give him power. Any man can stand adversity - only a great man can stand prosperity.

-Robert Ingersoll, speech in Washington, D.C., 16 January, 1883

A wise man associating with the vicious becomes an idiot; a dog traveling with good men becomes a rational being.

-Arab Proverb

No change of circumstances can repair a defect of character.

–Ralph Waldo Emerson, "Character", *Essays: Second Series*

The conduct of our lives is the true mirror of our doctrine.

-Michel de Montaigne, "The Education of Children", *Essays*

Character is much easier kept than recovered.

-Thomas Paine, *The American Crisis*

Happiness is not the end of life; character is.

-Henry Ward Beecher, *Life Thoughts*

There is no odor so bad as that which arises from goodness tainted.

-Henry David Thoreau, *Walden*

We need someone, I say, on whom our character may mould itself: you'll never make the crooked straight without a ruler.

-Lucius Annaeus Seneca (the younger), *Moral Letters to Lucilius*

The wicked flee when no man pursueth; but the righteous are bold as a lion.

-The Bible (*KJV*), Proverbs 28:1

It is not what he has, nor even what he does, which directly expresses the worth of a man, but what he is.

-Henri Frederic Amiel, *Journal Intime*, 15 December 1859

You can construct the character of a man not only from what he does and says, but from what he fails to say and do.

-George Norman Douglas, *South Wind*

We sow a thought and reap an act,
We sow an act and reap a habit,
We sow a habit and reap a character,
We sow a character and reap a destiny.

-William Makepeace Thackeray, quoted in *The New Acts of the Apostles* (1894) by Arthur Pierson

Resolved, never to do anything, which I should be afraid to do if it were the last hour of my life.

-Jonathan Edwards, "Seventy Resolutions"

It is in the character of very few men to honor without envy a friend who has prospered.

-Aeschylus, *Agamemnon*

I prefer to be true to myself, even at the hazard of incurring the ridicule of others, rather than to be false, and incur my own abhorrence.

-Frederick Douglass, *Narrative of the Life of Frederick Douglass, an American Slave*

There is in many, if not in all men, a constant inward struggle between the principles of good and evil; and because a man has grossly fallen, and at the time of his fall added the guilt of hypocrisy to another sort of immorality, it is not necessary, therefore, to believe that his whole life has been false, or that all the good which he ever professed was insincere or unreal.

-Roundell Palmer, *Symington v. Symington* (1875)

I will stay in jail to the end of my days before I make a butchery of my conscience.

-John Bunyan, paraphrase of a quote from Bunyan's *A Confession of My Faith*

There is no such test of a man's superiority of character as in the well-conducting of an unavoidable quarrel.

-Henry Taylor, *The Statesman*

Character may be manifested in the great moments, but it is made in the small ones.

-Alexander MacLaren, “The Eagle and It’s Brood”, *Triumphant Certainties and Other Sermons*

Oh, young man, character is worth more than money, character is worth more than anything else in this wide world.

-Dwight L. Moody, sermon, "On Daniel and The Value of Character", 21 January 1880

You can easily judge the character of a man by the way he treats those who can do nothing for him.

-Saying

Not education but character is man's greatest need and man's greatest safeguard.

-Herbert Spencer, quoted in *A Dictionary of Thoughts* (1891) by Tryon Edwards

To do an evil act is base. To do a good one without incurring danger is common enough. But it is part of a good man to do great and noble deeds though he risks everything in doing them.

-Plutarch, quoted in *A Dictionary of Thoughts* (1908) by Tryon Edwards

A man's character is the reality of himself;
His reputation, the opinion others have formed about him;
Character resides in him, reputation in other people;
That is the substance, this is the shadow.

-Henry Ward Beecher, quoted in *Treasury of Thought* (1872) by Maturin Murray Ballou

The great hope of society is in individual character.

-William Ellery Channing, "Remarks on the Life and Character of Napoleon", Discourses, *Reviews and Miscellanies*

Keep a broad distinction between character and reputation, for one may be destroyed by slander, while the other can never be harmed, except by its possessor . . . Reputation is in no man's keeping. You and I cannot determine what other men shall think and say about us. We can only determine what they ought to think of us and say about us.

-Josiah Gilbert Holland, *Gold-foil: Hammered from Popular Proverbs*

I will govern my life and my thoughts as if the whole world were to see the one, and to read the other; for "what does it signify to make anything a secret to my neighbor, when to God (who is the searcher of our hearts) all our privacies are open."

-Lucius Annaeus Seneca (the younger), "On the Happy Life", *Moral Essays*

The man that makes a character makes foes.

-Edward Young, "Epistles to Mr. Pope", *The Poetical Works*

Not armies, not nations, have advanced the race; but here and there, in the course of ages, an individual has stood up and cast his shadow over the world.

-Edwin Hubbel Chapin, sermon, "The Relation of the Individual to the Republic", 3 Jan. 1844

When the character of a man is not clear to you, look at his friends.

-Japanese Proverb

For out of the abundance of the heart the mouth speaketh.

-The Bible (*KJV*), Matthew 12:34

A noble man compares and estimates himself by an idea which is higher than himself, and a mean man by one which is lower than himself. The one produces aspiration; the other, ambition. Ambition is the way in which a vulgar man aspires.

-Henry Ward Beecher, *Life Thoughts*

Be your character what it will, it will be known; and nobody will take it upon your word.

-Lord Chesterfield, letter to his son, 19 October 1748

He, who in questions of right, virtue, or duty, sets himself above all ridicule, is truly great, and shall laugh in the end with truer mirth than ever he was laughed at.

-Johann Kaspar Lavater, *Aphorisms on Man*

What is it to be a gentleman? Is it to be honest, to be gentle, to be generous, to be brave, to be wise, and, possessing all these qualities, to exercise them in the most graceful outward manner? Ought a gentleman to be a loyal son, a true husband, an honest father? Ought his life to be decent, his bills to be paid, his taste to be high and elegant, his aims in life lofty and noble?

-William Makepeace Thackeray, *The Book of Snobs*

You cannot dream yourself into a character; you must hammer and forge yourself one.

-James Anthony Froude, *The Nemesis of Faith*

I am delighted to have you play football. I believe in rough, manly sports. But I do not believe in them if they degenerate into the sole end of any one's existence. I don't want you to sacrifice standing well in your studies to any over-athleticism; and I need not tell you that character counts for a great deal more than either intellect or body in winning success in life. Athletic proficiency is a mighty good servant, and like so many other good servants, a mighty bad master.

-Theodore Roosevelt, letter to his son, Ted, 4 October 1903

Be not anxious about what you have, but about what you are.

-Saint Gregory I, *Homilies on the Gospel*

A man should be upright, not kept upright.

-Marcus Aurelius, *Meditations*

He who is void of virtuous attachments in private life, is, or very soon will be void of all regard for his country. There is seldom an instance of a man guilty of betraying his country, who had not before lost the feeling of moral obligations in his private connections.

-Samuel Adams, letter to James Warren, 4 November 1775

A good conscience is a continual feast.

-Lucius Annaeus Seneca (the younger), "On the Happy Life", *Moral Essays*

A man's action is only a picture book of his creed.

-Ralph Waldo Emerson, "Poetry and Imagination", *Works*

Better a diamond with a flaw than a pebble without.

-Chinese Proverb

A man is what he is, not what men say he is. His character no man can touch. His character is what he is before his God and his judge; and only he can damage that. His reputation is what men say he is. That can be damaged; but reputation is for time, character is for eternity.

-John B. Gough, quoted in *A Dictionary of Thoughts* (1891) by Tryon Edwards

Be such a man, live such a life, that if every man were such as you, and every life a life like yours, this earth would be paradise.

-Phillips Brooks, quoted in *The World Beautiful: Second Series* (1896) by Lilian Whiting

TWO

COMPROMISE

Much rain wears the marble.

-William Shakespeare, King Henry VI

The time to guard against corruption and tyranny is before they shall have gotten hold of us. It is better to keep the wolf out of the fold, than to trust to drawing his teeth and claws after he shall have entered.

-Thomas Jefferson, *Notes on the State of Virginia*

When people once begin to deviate, they do not know where to stop.

-King George III, quoted in *The Friend* -vol.15 (1842)

Show us a person who is not an extremist about some things, who is a "middle-of-the-roader" in everything, and I will show you someone who is insecure.

-George Aiken Taylor

Through clever and constant application of propaganda, people can be made to see paradise as hell, and also the other way round, to consider the most wretched sort of life as paradise.

-Adolf Hitler, *Mein Kampf*

Moderation in temper is always a virtue, but moderation in principle is always a vice.

-Thomas Paine, *The Rights of Man*

Nothing that is not a real crime makes a man appear so contemptible and little in the eyes of the world as inconsistency.

-Joseph Addison, *The Spectator*, 5 September 1711

If the camel once gets his nose in the tent, his body will soon follow.

-Arab proverb

No notice is taken of a little evil, but when it increases it strikes the eye.

-Aristotle, *Politics*

Men, like nails, lose their usefulness when they lose direction and begin to bend.

-Walter Savage Landor, "Cromwell and Noble", *Imaginary Conversations*

Give us clear vision that we may know where to stand and what to stand for, because unless we stand for something, we shall fall for anything.

-Peter Marshall, *Mr. Jones, Meet the Master*

Woe unto them that call evil good, and good evil.

-The Bible (*KJV*), Isaiah 5:20

In matters of principle, stand like a rock; in matters of taste, swim with the current.

-Unknown

Men trip not on mountains, they stumble on stones.

-Hindu proverb

Fame has also this great drawback, that if we pursue it, we must direct our lives in such a way as to please the fancy of men.

-Baruch Spinoza, *On the Improvement of the Understanding*

There is nothing more corrupting than compromise. One step in that direction calls for another, makes it necessary and compelling, and soon it swamps you with the force of a rolling snowball become a landslide.

-Alexander Berkman, *What Is Communist Anarchism*

Compromise is but the sacrifice of one right or good in the hope of retaining another – too often ending in the loss of both.

-Tryon Edwards, *A Dictionary of Thoughts*

Vice is a monster of so frightful mien,
As, to be hated, needs but to be seen;
Yet seen too oft, familiar with her face,
We first endure, then pity, then embrace.

-Alexander Pope, *An Essay on Man*

And be not conformed to this world: but be ye transformed by the renewing of your mind, that ye may prove what is that good, and acceptable, and perfect, will of God.

-The Bible *(KJV)*, Romans 12:2

Following the path of least resistance is what makes both men and rivers crooked.

-Saying

Yield to all and you will soon have nothing to yield.

-Aesop, "The Man and His Two Wives", *Fables*

THREE

Conformity

The reasonable man adapts himself to the world: the unreasonable one persists in trying to adapt the world to himself. Therefore all progress depends on the unreasonable man.

-George Bernard Shaw, *Man and Superman*

Insist on yourself. Never imitate.

-Ralph Waldo Emerson, "Self-Reliance", *Essays*

Be who you are and say what you feel, because those who mind don't matter, and those who matter don't mind.

-Saying

A man must consider what a rich realm he abdicates when he becomes a conformist.

-Ralph Waldo Emerson, *Journals*

The young are too apt to believe what a great man says, especially if he be an authority in the profession they follow.

-George W. Keeton, quoted in *Hints on Advocacy* (1906) by Richard Harris

Ten thousand things there are which we believe merely upon the authority or credit of those who have spoken or written them.

–Isaac Watts, Logic

Whenever you find yourself on the side of the majority, it is time to pause and reflect.

-Mark Twain, *Notebook*

In the moment of our creation we receive the stamp of our individuality; and much of life is spent in rubbing off or defacing the impression.

-Julius Charles Hare, *Guesses at Truth*

Sometimes you'll find yourself needing to conform for the simple reason the conformists are right.

– J.S. Felts

One dog barks at something, and a hundred bark at the bark.

-Chinese Proverb

Imitation is suicide.

-Ralph Waldo Emerson, "Self Reliance", *Essays*

It is better to fail in originality than to succeed in imitation. He who has never failed somewhere, that man cannot be great. Failure is the true test of greatness.

-Herman Melville, "Hawthorne and His Mosses", in *The Literary World*, 17 August 1850

Do not think you are on the right road just because it is a well beaten path.

-Saying

We cannot help conforming ourselves to what we love.

-Saint Francis de Sales, *Treatise on the Love of God*

A man of honour should never forget what he is because he sees what others are.

-Baltasar Gracian, *The Art of Worldly Wisdom*

The great majority of men grow up and grow old in seeming and following.

-Ralph Waldo Emerson, *Journals*

FOUR

COURAGE

So will I go in unto the king, even though it is against the law. And if I perish, I perish.

-The Bible (*NIV*), Esther 4:16

We could never learn to be brave and patient, if there were only joy in the world.

-Helen Keller, *The Story of My Life*

Cowards die many times before their deaths;
The valiant never taste of death but once.

-William Shakespeare, *Julius Caesar*

If you knew how cowardly your enemy is, you would slap him. Bravery is knowledge of the cowardice in the enemy.

-Edgar Watson Howe, *Country Town Sayings*

Wealth lost - something lost; Honor lost - much lost; Courage lost - all lost.

-German proverb

Familiarity with danger makes a brave man braver, but less daring.

-Herman Melville, *White-Jacket*

God grant me the courage not to give up on what I think is right, even though I think it is hopeless.

-Chester W. Nimitz, *Soldier's and Sailors' Prayer Book* (1944)

Physical courage, which despises all danger, will make a man brave in one way; and moral courage, which despises all opinion, will make a man brave in another. The former would seem most necessary for the camp, the latter for the council; but to constitute a great man, both are necessary.

-Charles Caleb Colton, *Lacon*

Whatever course you decide upon, there is always someone to tell you that you are wrong. There are always difficulties arising which tempt you to believe that your critics are right. To map out a course of action and follow it to an end requires some of the same courage a soldier needs. Peace has its victories, but it takes brave men and women to win them.

-Ralph Waldo Emerson, quoted in *The Book of Courage* (1924) by Edwin Osgood Grover

Tender-handed stroke a nettle,
And it stings you for your pains;
Grasp it like a man of mettle,
And it soft as silk remains.

-Aaron Hill, quoted in *The Poetical Farrago* (1794)

The greatest test of courage on earth is to bear defeat without losing heart.

-Robert G. Ingersoll, speech on 100th anniversary of Declaration of Independence in Peoria, IL, 4 July 1876

To see what is right and not do it, is want of courage.

-Confucius, *Analects*

-Courage is the thing. All goes if courage goes.

-James M. Barrie, *Courage*

Courage is resistance to fear, mastery of fear - not absence of fear.

-Mark Twain, *Pudd'nhead Wilson*

The direct foe of courage is the fear itself, not the object of it.

–George MacDonald, quoted in *Edge-tools of Speech* (1899) by Maturin Murray Ballou

Audacity augments courage; hesitation, fear.

-Publilius Syrus, *Sententiae*

True bravery is shown by performing without witness what we may be capable of doing with the whole world looking on.

-Francois de La Rochefoucauld, quoted in *Other Men's Minds* (1800) by Edwin Davies

Courage is a quality so necessary for maintaining virtue that it is always respected even when it is associated with vice.

-Samuel Johnson, quoted in *Life of Samuel Johnson* (1791) by James Boswell

I love the man that can smile in trouble that can gather strength from distress, and grow brave by reflection.

-Thomas Paine, *Common Sense*

I would define true courage to be a perfect sensibility of the measure of danger, and a mental willingness to incur it.

-William T. Sherman, *Memoirs of Gen. W.T. Sherman*

It is easy to be brave from a safe distance.

-Aesop, "The Wolf and The Kid", *Fables*

Courage enlarges, cowardice diminishes resources. In desperate straits the fears of the timid aggravate the dangers that imperil the brave.

-Christian Nestell Bovee, *Intuitions and Summaries of Thought*

It requires more courage to suffer than to die.

-Napoleon Bonaparte, quote in *The Saint Helena Journal* (1899) by Gaspard Gourgaud

Whatever your sex or position, life is a battle in which you are to show your pluck, and woe be to the coward. Whether passed on a bed of sickness or a tented field, it is ever the same fair play and admits no foolish distinction. Despair and postponement are cowardice and defeat. Men were born to succeed, not to fail.

-Henry David Thoreau, *Journal*

To do anything in this world worth doing, we must not stand shivering on the bank and thinking of the cold and danger, but jump in, and scramble through as well as we can.

-Sydney Smith, lecture “On the Conduct of the Understanding” at Royal Institution

The world has no room for cowards. We must all be ready somehow to toil, to suffer, to die. And yours is not the less noble because no drum beats before you when you go out into your daily battlefields, and no crowds shout about your coming when you return from your daily victory or defeat.

-Robert Louis Stevenson, letter to his editor, Pate Hamilton

Courage is like love; it must have hope for nourishment.

-Napoleon Bonaparte, *Napoleon in His Own Words*

No man can be brave who considers pain the greatest evil of life; or temperate, who regards pleasure as the highest good.

-Marcus Tullius Cicero, quoted in *A Dictionary of Thoughts* (1908) by Tryon Edwards

A great deal of talent is lost in the world for want of a little courage. Every day sends to their graves a number of obscure men, who have only remained obscure because their timidity has prevented them from making a first effort.

-Sydney Smith, lecture "On the Conduct of the Understanding" at Royal Institution

All are brave when the enemy flies.

-Italian Proverb

A man with backbone is a tonic, and courage is contagious.

-Charles Phelps Cushing, "The Business Man with Nerves", in *The World's Work*, September 1916

FIVE

DISCIPLINE

Self-respect is the fruit of discipline; the sense of dignity grows with the ability to say no to oneself.

-Abraham Heschel, *The Insecurity of Freedom*

Self-discipline is that which, next to virtue, truly and essentially raises one man above another.

-Joseph Addison, *The Guardian* (1713)

The great end of education is to discipline rather than to furnish the mind; to train it to the use of its own powers, rather than fill it with the accumulations of others.

-Tryon Edwards, *A Dictionary of Thoughts*

What we do upon a great occasion will probably depend upon what we already are; what we are will be the result of previous years of self-discipline.

-Henry Parry Liddon, "The Curse on Meroz", *Sermons Preached Before the University of Oxford*

Whom the Lord loveth he chasteneth.

-The Bible (KJV), Hebrews 12:6

Discipline is the soul of an army. It makes small numbers formidable; procures success to the weak, and esteem to all.

-George Washington, general orders, 29 July 1757

With self-discipline most anything is possible.

-Theodore Roosevelt

Just as the twig is bent, the tree is inclined!

-Alexander Pope, *The Works of Alexander Pope*

He that would be superior to external influences must first become superior to his passions.

-Samuel Johnson, *The Idler*

My son, despise not the chastening of the Lord; neither be weary of his correction: for whom the Lord loveth he correcteth; even as a father the son in whom he delighteth.

-The Bible (*KJV*), Proverbs 3:11-12

SIX

Dishonesty

Unfaithfulness in the keeping of an appointment is an act of clear dishonesty. You may as well borrow a person's money as his time.

-Horace Mann, quoted in *Excellent Quotations for Home and School* (1890) by Julia B. Hoitt

Dishonesty is a forsaking of permanent for temporary advantages.

-Christian Nestell Bovee, *Intuitions and Summaries of Thought*

It is a trick among the dishonest to offer sacrifices that are not needed or not possible, to avoid making those that are required.

-Ivan Goncharov, *Oblomov*

Who purposely cheats his friend, would cheat his God.

-Johann Kaspar Lavater, *Aphorisms on Man*

That which is won ill, will never wear well, for there is a curse attends it, which will waste it; and the same corrupt dispositions which incline men to the sinful ways of getting, will incline them to the like sinful ways of spending.

-Matthew Henry, *An Exposition of the Old Testament*

If you want to ruin the truth, stretch it.

-Saying

No man has a good enough memory to be a successful liar.

-Abraham Lincoln, quoted in *The Texas Outlook* (1916)

A lie faces God and shrinks from man.

-Francis Bacon, "Of Truth", *Essays*

One deceit needs many others, and so the whole house is built in the air and must soon come to the ground.

-Baltasar Gracian, *The Art of Worldly Wisdom*

A liar will not be believed, even when he speaks the truth.

-Aesop, "The Shepherd's Boy", *Fables*

Repetition does not transform a lie into a truth.

-Franklin Delano Roosevelt, radio address, 26 Oct. 1939

It is easy to tell a lie, hard to tell but one lie.

-Thomas Fuller (2), *Good Thoughts in Bad Times*

If it be well weighed, to say that a man lieth, is as much to say, as that he is brave towards God and a coward towards men.

-Michel de Montaigne, "Of Giving the Lie", *Essays*

The least initial deviation from the truth is multiplied later a thousand fold.

-Aristotle, *On the Heavens*

He who permits himself to tell a lie once, finds it much easier to do it a second and third time, till at length it becomes habitual; he tells lies without attending to it, and truths without the world's believing him. This falsehood of the tongue leads to that of the heart, and in time depraves all its good dispositions.

-Thomas Jefferson, letter to Peter Carr, 19 Aug. 1785

Oh, what a tangled web we weave,
When first we practice to deceive!

-Walter Scott, *Marmion*

You can fool some of the people all of the time, and all of the people some of the time, but you can't fool all of the people all of the time.

-Abraham Lincoln, speech in Bloomington, Illinois, 29 May 1856

Exaggeration is a branch of lying.

-Baltasar Gracian, *The Art of Worldly Wisdom*

Who lies for you will lie against you.

-Bosnian Proverb

A little lie is like a little pregnancy; it doesn't take long before everyone knows.

-Unknown

To tell a falsehood is like the cut of a saber; for though the wound may heal, the scar of it will remain.

-Sa'di, *The Gulistan*

Lying to ourselves is more deeply ingrained than lying to others.

-Fyodor Dostoevsky

There is no such thing as a white lie; a lie is as black as a coal-pit, and twice as foul.

-Henry Ward Beecher, quoted in *Excellent Quotations for Home and School* (1890) by Julia B. Hoitt

A lie is a coward's way of getting out of trouble.

-Saying

Seldom are lies told without some hint of truth in them. People rarely tell things which are completely false because they don't think anyone would believe them.

- J.S. Felts

SEVEN

FALSEHOOD

The most useful piece of learning for the uses of life is to unlearn what is untrue.

-Antisthenes, quoted in *The International Library of Famous Literature* (1898) by Andrew Lang

It ain't ignorance that makes so much trouble; it's so many people knowing too many things that ain't so.

-Josh Billings

An error is the more dangerous in proportion to the degree of truth which it contains.

-Henri Frederic Amiel, *Journal Intime*, 26 December 1852

Old custom, without truth, is but an old error.

-Thomas Fuller, *Gnomologia*

Falsehoods not only disagree with truths, but usually quarrel among themselves.

-Daniel Webster, argument in Knapp's trial, 6 April 1830

Falsehood is cowardice; Truth is courage.

-Hosea Ballou, quoted in *Treasury of Thought* (1872) by Maturin Murray Ballou

Error flies from mouth to mouth, from pen to pen, and to destroy it takes ages.

-Voltaire, "Assassin", *Philosophical Dictionary*

Whoever has even once become notorious by base fraud, even if he speaks the truth, gains no belief.

-Phaedrus, *Fables*

It is natural for the mind to believe and for the will to love; so that, for want of true objects, they must attach themselves to false.

-Blaise Pascal, *Pensées*

It is more from carelessness about truth, than from intentional lying, that there is so much falsehood in the world.

-Samuel Johnson, quoted in *Life of Samuel Johnson* (1791) by James Boswell

Falsehood is never so successful as when she baits her hook with truth, and no opinions so fatally mislead us, as those that are not wholly wrong.

-Charles Caleb Colton, *Lacon*

It is often said it is no matter what a man believes if he is only sincere. . . But let a man sincerely believe that seed planted without plowing is as good with, that January is as favorable for seed sowing as April, and that cockle seed will produce as good a harvest as wheat, and is it so?

-Henry Ward Beecher, *Life Thoughts*

We see every day that our imaginations are so strong and our reason so weak, the charms of wealth and power are so enchanting, and the belief of future punishments so faint, that men find ways to persuade themselves to believe any absurdity, to submit to any prostitution, rather than forego their wishes and desires. Their reason becomes at last an eloquent advocate on the side of their passions, and bring themselves to believe that black is white, that vice is virtue, that folly is wisdom, and eternity a moment.

-John Adams, diary entry, 9 February 1772

Whatever is only almost true is quite false, and among the most dangerous of errors, because being so near truth, it is the more likely to lead astray.

-Henry Ward Beecher, quoted in *A Dictionary of Thoughts* (1891) by Tryon Edwards

It is error only, and not truth, that shrinks from inquiry.

-Thomas Paine, Address to the Addressers

What is earnest is not always true; on the contrary, error is often more earnest than truth.

-Benjamin Disraeli, letter to Queen Victoria, 4 November 1868

A lie should be trampled on and extinguished wherever found. I am for fumigating the atmosphere when I suspect that falsehood, like pestilence, breathes around me.

–Thomas Carlyle, quoted in *A Commonplace Book of Thoughts* (1855) by Anna Jameson

It is more from carelessness about truth than from intentionally lying that there is so much falsehood in the world.

–Samuel Johnson, quoted in *The Life of Samuel Johnson* (1791) by James Boswell

EIGHT

HABIT

We become just by performing just actions, temperate by performing temperate actions, brave by performing brave actions.

-Aristotle, *Nicomachean Ethics*

One must change one's tactics every ten years if one wishes to maintain one's superiority.

-Napoleon Bonaparte

A wolf may lose his teeth, but he never loses his inclination.

-Spanish Proverb

The despotism of custom is everywhere the standing hindrance to human advancement.

-John Stuart Mill, *On Liberty*

To say that a blind custom of obedience should be a surer obligation than duty taught and understood, it is to affirm, that a blind man may tread surer by a guide than a seeing man by a light.

-Francis Bacon, *The Advancement of Learning*

Habituation is a falling asleep or fatiguing of the sense of time, which explains why young years pass slowly, while later life flings itself faster and faster upon its course.

-Thomas Mann, *The Magic Mountain*

The diminutive chains of habit are scarcely ever heavy enough to be felt, till they are too strong to be broken.

-Samuel Johnson, attributed in *Forester* by Maria Edgeworth

It is difficult to free fools from the chains they revere.

-Voltaire, *The Dinner at Count Boulainvillier's*

The heart errs like the head; its errors are not any the less fatal, and we have more trouble getting free of them because of their sweetness.

-Anatole France, *Little Pierre*

A rose too often smelled loses its fragrance.

-Spanish Proverb

If you do what you always did, you will get what you always got.

-Saying

We naturally like what we have been accustomed to . . . This is likewise one of the causes which prevent men from finding truth.

-Moses Maimonides, *The Guide for the Perplexed*

A single bad habit will mar an otherwise faultless character, as an ink drop soileth the pure white page.

-Hosea Ballou, quoted in *Treasury of Thought* (1872) by Maturin Murray Ballou

Habits are at first cobwebs, then cables.

-Spanish Proverb

Ill habits gather by unseen degrees,
As brooks make rivers, rivers run to seas.

–John Dryden, “Absalom and Achitophel”

Habit maketh no monk; no wearing of gilt spurs maketh no knight.

-Thomas Usk, *The Testament of Love*

Habits are soon assumed; but when we strive
To strip them off, 'tis being flayed alive.

-William Cowper, "The Progress of Error", *Poems*

Chaos often breeds life, when order breeds habit.

-Henry Adams, *The Education of Henry Adams*

Infinite toil would not enable you to sweep away a mist; but, by ascending a little, you may often look over it altogether. So it is with our moral improvement; we wrestle fiercely with a vicious habit, which could have no hold upon us if we ascended to a higher moral atmosphere.

-Arthur Helps, "On Self-Discipline", *Essays Written in the Intervals of Business*

It is easier to resist at the beginning than at the end.

-Leonardo Da Vinci, *The Notebooks*

NINE

HEROISM

Calculation never made a hero.

-John Henry Newman, *An Essay on the Development of Christian Doctrine*

Every man is scared in his first battle. If he says he's not, he's a liar! Some men are cowards but they fight the same as the brave men or they get the hell slammed out of them watching men fight who are just as scared as they are. The real hero is the man who fights even though he is scared.

-George S. Patton, speech to the Third Army before invasion of France, June 1944

The world's battlefields have been in the heart chiefly. More heroism has there been displayed in the household and in the closet, than on the most memorable military battlefields of history.

-Henry Ward Beecher, *Royal Truths*

Heroism is the brilliant triumph of the soul over the flesh - that is to say, over fear: fear of poverty, of suffering, of calumny, of sickness, of isolation, and of death. There is no serious piety without heroism. Heroism is the dazzling and glorious concentration of courage.

-Henri Frederic Amiel, *Journal Intime*, 1 October 1849

Heroes are people who do what has to be done when it needs to be done, regardless of the consequences.

-Unknown

Self-trust is the essence of heroism.

-Ralph Waldo Emerson, "Heroism", *Essays*

TEN

Honesty

He who does not bellow the truth when he knows it, makes himself the accomplice of liars and forgers.

-Charles Peguy, *Basic Verities*

Dishonest money dwindles away, but he who gathers money little by little makes it grow.

-The Bible (*NIV*), Proverbs 13:11

Men are alike in their promises. It is only in their deeds that they differ.

-Moliere, *The Miser*

The thing from which [the world] suffers just now more than from any other evil is not the assertion of falsehoods, but the endless and irrepressible repetition of half-truths.

-G.K. Chesterton, *G.F. Watts*

That a lie which is half a truth is ever the blackest of lies,
That a lie which is all a lie may be met and fought with outright,
But a lie which is part a truth is a harder matter to fight.

-Alfred Tennyson, "The Grandmother's Apology", *Poetical Works*

He who is most slow in making a promise is usually the most faithful in the performance of it.

-Jean-Jacques Rousseau, quoted in *The Treasury of Knowledge* (1833)

What you don't see with your eyes, don't invent with your tongue.

-Jewish Proverb

We are never deceived; we deceive ourselves.

-Johann Wolfgang von Goethe, *Maxims and Reflections*

Never make a promise in haste.

-Mahatma Gandhi, note he wrote inside young woman's book

To exaggerate is to weaken.

-Jean-Francois de La Harpe, *Melanie*

To go beyond is as wrong as to fall short.

-Confucius, *Analects*

Better break your word, than do wrong in keeping it.

-Thomas Fuller, *Gnomologia*

A false balance is an abomination to the Lord: but a just weight is his delight.

-The Bible (*KJV*), Proverbs 11:1

To believe all men honest would be folly. To believe none so, is something worse.

-John Quincy Adams, letter to Secretary of War, William Eustis, 22 June 1809

You have no business with consequences; you are to tell the truth.

-Samuel Johnson, quoted in *Life of Samuel Johnson* (1791) by James Boswell

I'm not upset that you lied to me, I'm upset that from now on I can't believe you.

-Friedrich Nietzsche

We must not promise what we ought not, lest we be called on to perform what we cannot.

-Abraham Lincoln, speech at Illinois Republican State Convention, 29 May 1856

Magnificent promises are always to be suspected.

-Theodore Parker, quoted in *Treasury of Thought* (1894) by Maturin Murray Ballou

A truth that's told with bad intent
Beats all the lies you can invent.

-William Blake, "Auguries of Innocence"

In an age of universal deceit, telling the truth is a revolutionary act.

-Unknown

The Lord detests lying lips, but he delights in men who are truthful.

-The Bible (*NIV*), Proverbs 12:22

ELEVEN

Honor

The louder he talked of his honour, the faster we counted our spoons.

-Ralph Waldo Emerson, "Worship", *The Conduct of Life*

We make men without chests and expect of them virtue and enterprise. We laugh at honor and are shocked to find traitors in our midst.

-C.S. Lewis, *The Abolition of Man*

Rather fail with honor than succeed by fraud.

-Sophocles

It is better to deserve honors and not have them than to have them and not deserve them.

-Mark Twain, *Notebook*

Honour and shame from no condition rise;
Act well your part, there all the honour lies.

-Alexander Pope, *An Essay on Man*

Honor and profit do not always lie in the same sack.

-George Herbert, quoted in *Character* (1883) by Samuel Smiles

A man of honour should never forget what he is because he sees what others are.

-Baltasar Gracian, *The Art of Worldly Wisdom*

For titles do not reflect honor on men, but rather men on their titles.

-Niccolo Machiavelli, *Discourses on Livy*

Before honour is humility.

-The Bible (*KJV*), Proverbs 15:33

He has honor if he holds himself to an ideal of conduct though it is inconvenient, unprofitable, or dangerous to do so.

-Walter Lippmann, *A Preface to Morals*

A prophet is not without honor except in his own town and in his own home.

-The Bible (NIV), Matthew 13:57

TWELVE

Hypocrisy

Every man alone is sincere. At the entrance of a second person, hypocrisy begins.

-Ralph Waldo Emerson, "Friendship", *Essays*

Men will wrangle for religion, write for it, fight for it, die for it, anything but live for it.

-Charles Caleb Colton, *Lacon*

Woe to you, teachers of the law and Pharisees, you hypocrites! You clean the outside of the cup and dish, but inside they are full of greed and self-indulgence.

-The Bible (*NIV*), Matthew 23:25

No man, for any considerable period, can wear one face to himself, and another to the multitude, without finally getting bewildered as to which may be the true.

-Nathaniel Hawthorne, *The Scarlet Letter*

Since we are all naturally prone to hypocrisy, any empty semblance of righteousness is quite enough to satisfy us instead of righteousness itself.

-John Calvin, *Institutes of the Christian Religion*

We are so accustomed to disguise ourselves to others, that at last we become disguised even to ourselves.

-Francois de La Rochefoucauld, *Reflections or Sentences and Moral Maxims*

A life lived is a much better gauge of someone's belief, than what they say.

- J.S. Felts

I detest that man, who hides one thing in the depths of his heart, and speaks forth another.

-Homer, *Iliad*

Though there is antipathy in the human heart to the gospel of Christ, yet when Christians make their good work shine, all admire them. It is when great disparity exists between profession and practice that we secure the scorn of mankind.

-David Livingstone, *Journal*, 17 January 1866

Great hypocrites are the true atheists.

-Francis Bacon, "Superstition", *Essays*

You admit there is a God; yet you offer Him no homage; you never worship Him. You admit that you are a sinner; yet you exercise no repentance; you make no effort to become holy; you make no use of the means to secure pardon, and to avoid the wrath to come. You admit that you can be saved only by the merits of the Lord Jesus Christ; yet you are not seeking to obtain an interest in His blood. You profess to believe that there is a heaven; yet you are making no efforts to secure it; a hell, yet you make no efforts to avoid it.

-Albert Barnes, *Scenes and Incidents in the Life of the Apostle Paul*

The true hypocrite is the one who ceases to perceive his deception, the one who lies with sincerity.

-Andre Gide, *The Counterfeiters*

What we are alone, that alone we are ... judgment upon ourselves will be much more likely to be correct, if we examine our hidden life than if we measure ourselves by that which is seen of men.

-Charles Hadden Spurgeon, *Flowers from a Puritan's Garden*

Hypocrisy in anything whatever may deceive the cleverest and most penetrating man, but the least wide-awake of children recognizes it, and is revolted by it, however ingeniously it may be disguised.

-Leo Tolstoy, *Anna Karenina*

We are never so easily deceived as when we imagine we are deceiving others.

-Francois de La Rochefoucauld, *Reflections or Sentences and Moral Maxims*

Most people have seen worse things in private than they pretend to be shocked at in public.

-Edgar Watson Howe, *Country Town Sayings*

If the world despises hypocrites, what must be the estimate of them in heaven?

-Madame Roland, quoted in *Edge-tools of Speech* (1899) by Maturin Murray Ballou

THIRTEEN

INTEGRITY

Better is the poor that walketh in his uprightness, than he that is perverse in his ways, though he be rich.

-The Bible (*KJV*), Proverbs 28:6

The integrity of men is to be measured by their conduct, not by their professions.

-Junius, *The Beauties and Maxims of Junius*

The man of integrity walks securely, but he who takes crooked paths will be found out.

-The Bible (NIV), Proverbs 10:9

The true test of integrity doesn't come when your enemies laugh at you, but when your friends do.

- J.S. Felts

Men should utter nothing for which they would not willingly be responsible through time and in eternity.

-Abraham Lincoln, annual message to Congress, 1 December 1862

Do not repeat anything you would not be willing to sign your name to.

-Saying

A righteous man who walks in his integrity.
How blessed are his sons after him.

-The Bible (KJV), Proverbs 20:7

If we are ever in doubt about what to do, it is a good rule to ask ourselves what we shall wish on the morrow that we had done.

-John Lubbock, *The Pleasures of Life*

I prefer to be true to myself, even at the hazard of incurring the ridicule of others, rather than to be false, and to incur my own abhorrence.

-Frederick Douglass, *Narrative of the Life of Frederick Douglass, an American Slave*

God grant me the courage not to give up on what I think is right, even though I think it is hopeless.

-Chester W. Nimitz, *Soldier's and Sailors' Prayer Book* (1944)

FOURTEEN

LAZINESS

Idleness and pride tax with a heavier hand than kings and parliaments.

-Benjamin Franklin, letter to Charles Thomson, 11 July 1765

In doing nothing men learn to do evil.

-Cato the Elder

Shun idleness. The life of man resembles iron, which being wrought into instruments and used, becomes bright and shining; left unwrought the rust eats and consumes it.

-Archibald Campbell, *Instructions to a Son*

Lazy hands make a man poor, but diligent hands bring wealth.

-The Bible (*NIV*), Proverbs 10:4

Laziness grows on people; it begins in cobwebs, and ends in iron chains.

-Matthew Hale, quoted in *The Monthly Traveller* (1833)

By too much sitting still the body becomes unhealthy; and soon the mind.

-Henry Wadsworth Longfellow, *Hyperion*

All hard work brings a profit, but mere talk leads only to poverty.

-The Bible (*NIV*), Proverb 14:23

Laziness travels so slowly that poverty soon overtakes him.

-Benjamin Franklin, *Poor Richard's Almanack*

FIFTEEN

Modesty

Modesty is not only an ornament, but also a guard to virtue.

-Joseph Addison, *The Spectator*, 24 November 1711

Your beauty should not come from outward adornment, such as braided hair and the wearing of gold jewelry and fine clothes. Instead, it should be that of your inner self, the unfading beauty of a gentle and quiet spirit, which is of great worth in God's sight.

-The Bible (*NIV*), 1 Peter 3:3-4

A great man is always willing to be little.

-Ralph Waldo Emerson, "Compensation", *Essays*

Nothing is more amiable than true modesty, and nothing is more contemptible than the false.

-Joseph Addison, *The Spectator*, 15 August 1712

Modesty is bred of self-reverence.

-Amos Bronson Alcott, *Tablets*

Modesty isn't about whether something is seen, but rather whether something is flaunted.

– J.S. Felts

True modesty does not consist in an ignorance of our merits, but in a due estimate of them.

-Julius Charles Hare, *Guesses at Truth*

SIXTEEN

PRIORITIES

Better say, "This one thing I do," than to say, "These fifty things I dabble in."

-Dwight L. Moody, *Notes from My Bible*

Quit saying you don't have the time, and simply admit it's not a priority.

- J.S. Felts

Riches, no more than glory or health, have no more beauty or pleasure, than their possessor is pleased to lend them.

-Michel de Montaigne, "Good and Evil Depend Upon Opinion", *Essays*

Changing your life, is as simple as changing your priorities.

-Unknown

What shall it profit a man, if he shall gain the whole world, and lose his own soul?

-The Bible (*KJV*), Mark 8:36

What is wealth? Money - or what's worth money? Would you take a million dollars for your health, or your eyesight, or your wife and child? Certainly not! Well, then, what do you mean by complaining of having too little? Good heavens, man, you're a millionaire!

-Channing Pollock, *The Adventures of a Happy Man*

For where your treasure is, there will your heart be also.

-The Bible *(KJV)*, Matthew 6:21

If everything is important, then nothing is important.

-Saying

He that sips of many arts, drinks of none.

-Thomas Fuller (2), *The Holy and Profane States*

Actions express priorities.

-Saying

It is a mistake to look too far ahead. Only one link of the chain of destiny can be handled at a time.

-Winston Churchill, speech in the House of Commons, 27 February 1945

SEVENTEEN

Responsibility

The highest praise for a person is to give them responsibility.

-Saying

God hath entrusted me with myself.

-Epictetus, “On Attention”, *The Discourses*

What it is our duty to do we must do because it is right, not because any one can demand it of us.
-William Whewell, The Elements of Morality

The present is the living sum-total of the whole past.

-Thomas Carlyle, "Characteristics", *Critical and Miscellaneous Essays*

Whatsoever a man soweth, that shall he also reap.

-The Bible (*KJV*), Galatians 6:7

The opportunity that God sends does not wake up him who is asleep.

-Senegalese Proverb

He that is faithful in that which is least is faithful also in much; and he that is unjust in the least is unjust also in much.

-The Bible (*KJV*), Luke 16:10

A man who is good for making excuses is good for nothing else.

-Benjamin Franklin, quoted in *Theory and Practice of Teaching* (1847) by David Page

You cannot bring about prosperity by discouraging thrift.
You cannot help small men by tearing down big men.
You cannot strengthen the weak by weakening the strong.
You cannot lift the wage earner by pulling down the wage payer.
You cannot help the poor man by destroying the rich.
You cannot keep out of trouble by spending more than your income.
You cannot further the brotherhood of man by inciting class hatred.
You cannot establish security on borrowed money.
You cannot build character and courage by taking away man's initiative and independence.
You cannot help men permanently by doing for them what they could and should do for themselves.

-William John Henry Boetcker, "The Ten Cannots"

The number of malefactors authorizes not the crime.

-Thomas Fuller, *Gnomologia*

The time to repair the roof is when the sun is shining.

-John F. Kennedy, State of the Union address, 11 Jan. 1962

Better is it that thou shouldest not vow, than that thou shouldest vow and not pay.

-The Bible (*KJV*), Ecclesiastes 5:5

Hold yourself responsible for a higher standard than anyone else expects of you.

-Henry Ward Beecher, letter to his son, Herbert, 18 October 1878

There are no precedents: You are the first you that ever was.

-Christopher Morley, *Inward Ho!*

If we believe a thing to be bad, and if we have a right to prevent it, it is our duty to try to prevent it, and damn the consequences.

-Alfred Milner, speech in Glasgow, 26 November 1909

Do your duty, and leave the rest to heaven.

-Pierre Corneille, *Horace*

Do not follow the crowd in doing wrong.

-The Bible (*NIV*), Exodus 23:2

War is an ugly thing, but not the ugliest of things: the decayed and degraded state of moral and patriotic feeling which thinks nothing worth a war is worse. When a people are used as mere human instruments for firing cannon or thrusting bayonets, in the service and for the selfish purposes of a master, such war degrades a people. A war to protect other human beings against tyrannical injustice; a war to give victory to their own ideas of right and good, and which is their own war, carried on for an honest purpose by their free choice, is often the means of their regeneration. A man who has nothing which he is willing to fight for, nothing which he cares more about than he does about his personal safety, is a miserable creature who has no chance of being free, unless made and kept so by the exertions of better men than himself. As long as justice and injustice have not terminated their ever-renewing fight for ascendancy in the affairs of mankind, human beings must be willing, when need is, to do battle for the one against the other.

-John Stuart Mill, The Contest in America

Trust me, no tortures which the poets feign,
Can match the fierce, the unutterable pain,
He feels, who night and day, devoid of rest,
Carries his own accuser in his breast.

-Juvenal, *Satires*

Like a bad tooth or a lame foot is reliance on the unfaithful in times of trouble.

-The Bible (*NIV*), Proverbs 25:19

Men should utter nothing for which they would not willingly be responsible through time and in eternity.

-Abraham Lincoln, annual message to Congress, 1 December 1862

If everyone will sweep before his own door, the street will be clean.

-Proverb

Duty is ours: consequences are God's.

-Stonewall Jackson, *Memoirs of Stonewall Jackson*

I wear the chain I forged in life.

-Charles Dickens, *A Christmas Carol*

A new position of responsibility will usually show a man to be a far stronger creature than was supposed.

-William James, "The Energies of Men", *Memories and Studies*

The price of greatness is responsibility.

-Winston Churchill, speech at Harvard University, 6 September 1943

Let every man shovel out his own snow and the whole city will be passable.

-Ralph Waldo Emerson, *Journals*

Man must cease attributing his problems to his environment, and learn again to exercise his will - his personal responsibility.

-Albert Schweitzer, quoted in Time magazine, 25 June, 1949 v

A man, as a general rule, owes very little to what he is born with. A man is what he makes of himself.

-Alexander Graham Bell, interview in *How They Succeeded* (1901) by Orison Swett Marden

You are not only responsible for what you say, but also for what you do not say.

-Martin Luther

About the only thing you should ever assume is responsibility.

- J.S. Felts

Be not as those who spend the day in complaining of headache, and the night in drinking the wine that gives the headache.

-Johann Wolfgang von Goethe, quoted in *The Life of Goethe* (1864) by George Henry Lewes

Unstringing the bow does not cure the wound.

-French Proverb

To persevere in one's duty and be silent, is the best answer to calumny.

-George Washington, letter to Governor William Livingston, 7 December 1779

Nothing strengthens the judgment and quickens the conscience like individual responsibility.

-Elisabeth Cady Stanton, "The Solitude of Self", speech in United States Congress, 18 January 1892

It is easy to dodge our responsibilities, but we cannot dodge the consequences of dodging our responsibilities.

-Josiah Stamp, quoted in *Labor Digest* (1928)

For it is our own past which has made us what we are. We are the children of our own deeds.

-James Oswald Dykes, sermon, "The New Self", in *The Congregationalist*, January, 1873

"Do the duty which lies nearest thee", which thou knowest to be a duty. Thy second duty will already have become clear.

-Thomas Carlyle, *Sartor Resartus*

EIGHTEEN

SELF-CONTROL

The taste for emotion may, however, become a dangerous taste; and we should be very cautious how we attempt to squeeze out of human life, more ecstasy and paroxysm than it can well afford.

-Sydney Smith, lecture "On the Passions" at Royal Institution

What we do upon a great occasion will probably depend upon what we already are; what we are will be the result of previous years of self-discipline.

-Henry Parry Liddon, "The Curse on Meroz", *Sermons Preached Before the University of Oxford*

Until you learn to control your emotions, you will never control your life.

- J.S. Felts

He is happy, whose circumstances suit his temper; but he is more excellent, who can suit his temper to any circumstances.

-David Hume, *Moral Philosophy*

He who requires much from himself and little from others, will keep himself from being the object of resentment.

-Confucius, *Analects*

In vain do they talk of happiness who never subdued an impulse in obedience to a principle. He who never sacrificed a present to a future good, or a personal to a general one, can speak of happiness only as the blind do of colors.

-Horace Mann, *The Common School Journal,* 2 January, 1843

When the fight begins within himself,
A man's worth something.

-Robert Browning, "Bishop Blougram's Apology", *Men and Women*

Where it is in our power to do a thing, it is equally in our power to abstain from doing it.

-Aristotle, *Nicomachean Ethics*

The lust for comfort, that stealthy thing that enters the house a guest, and then becomes a host, and then a master.

-Khalil Gibran, "Houses", *The Prophet*

Rule your desires lest your desires rule you.

-Publilius Syrus, *Sententiae*

Like a city whose walls are broken through is a person who lacks self-control.

-The Bible (*NIV*), Proverbs 25:28

Total abstinence is easier than perfect moderation.

-Saint Augustine, *"On the Good of Marriage"*

Nothing in excess.

-Aristotle, *Rhetoric*

A fool uttereth all his mind.

-The Bible (*KJV*), Proverbs 29:11

It is easier to abstain than to restrain.

-French Proverb

Everything is permissible for me - but not everything is beneficial. Everything is permissible for me - but I will not be mastered by anything.

-The Bible (*NIV*), 1 Corinthians 6:12

Therefore, prepare your minds for action; be self-controlled; set your hope fully on the grace to be given you when Jesus Christ is revealed.

-The Bible (*NIV*), 1 Peter 1:13

He that has not a mastery over his inclinations, he that knows not how to resist the importunity of present pleasure or pain, for the sake of what reason tells him is fit to be done, wants the true principle of virtue and industry, and is in danger never to be good for anything.

-John Locke, *Some Thoughts Concerning Education*

I count him braver who conquers his desires than him who conquers his enemies; for the hardest victory is the victory over self.

-Aristotle, quoted in *Dictionary of Quotations* (1897) by Thomas Benfield Harbottle

Beware of desperate steps. The darkest day, / Lived till tomorrow, will have passed away.

-William Cowper, "The Needless Alarm", *Poems*

The wise old soldier is never in haste to strike a blow.

-Pietro Metastasio, *Adriano in Siria*

Do not bite at the bait of pleasure, till you know there is no hook beneath it.

-Thomas Jefferson, letter to Mrs. Cosway, 12 October 1786

I beat my body and make it my slave so that after I have preached to others, I myself will not be disqualified for the prize.

-The Bible (*NIV*), 1 Corinthians 9:27

NINETEEN

SELFISHNESS

It is well to remember that the entire universe, with one trifling exception, is composed of others.

-John Andrew Holmes, *Wisdom in Small Doses*

For where you have envy and selfish ambition, there you find disorder and every evil practice.

-The Bible (*NIV*), James 3:16

Selfishness isn't looking to your own interest, but doing so at the expense or neglect of others.

- J.S. Felts

The selfish man suffers more from his selfishness than he from whom that selfishness withholds some important benefit.

-Ralph Waldo Emerson, lecture "New England Reformers" in Amory Hall, 3 March 1844

Selfishness is not living as one wishes to live, it is asking others to live as one wishes to live.

-Oscar Wilde, The Soul of Man Under Socialism

The very heart and root of sin is in an independent spirit. We erect the idol self; and not only wish others to worship, but worship ourselves.

-Richard Cecil, *Remains of the Rev. Richard Cecil*

We are too much haunted by ourselves; we project the central shadow of ourselves on every thing around us. And then comes in the gospel to rescue us from this selfishness. Redemption is this, to forget self in God.

-Frederick William Robertson, "Christianity and Hindooism", *Sermons*

Thorough selfishness destroys or paralyzes enjoyment.

-Henry Ward Beecher, *Lectures to Young Men*

Great crimes come never singly; they are linked
To sins that went before.

-Jean Racine, *Phaedra*

TWENTY

Tolerance

I have no more right to object to a man for holding a different opinion from mine than I have to differ with a man because he wears a wig and I wear my own hair; but if he takes his wig off and shakes the powder in my eyes, I shall consider it my duty to get rid of him as soon as possible.

-John Wesley, *Journal*, 14 May 1765

There is a limit at which forbearance ceases to be a virtue.

-Edmund Burke, *Observations on a Late Publication on the Present State of the Nation*

Resolve to be tender with the young, compassionate with the aged, sympathetic with the striving, and tolerant of the weak and the wrong. Sometime in life you will have been all of these.

-Lloyd Shearer, *Parade* magazine, 30 December, 1973

Toleration, as it is now widely preached, may be a very one-sided bargain. It will not do to let falsehood and moral idiocy say to truth and honesty, "I will tolerate you if you will tolerate me."

-Coventry Patmore, *The Rod, the Root, and the Flower*

Toleration is the prerogative of humanity; we are all full of weaknesses and mistakes; let us reciprocally forgive ourselves. It is the first law of nature.

-Voltaire, *Treatise on Tolerance*

TWENTY-ONE

TRUTH

The thing from which [the world] suffers just now more than from any other evil is not the assertion of falsehoods, but the endless and irrepressible repetition of half-truths.

-G.K. Chesterton, *G.F. Watts*

Truth is hate to those who hate truth.

-Saying

Martyrdom has always been a proof of the intensity, never of the correctness of a belief.

-Arthur Schnitzler

It is one thing to show a man that he is in an error, and another to put him in possession of truth.

-John Locke, *An Essay Concerning Human Understanding*

Repetition does not transform a lie into a truth.

-Franklin Delano Roosevelt, radio address, 26 Oct. 1939

We naturally like what we have been accustomed to . . . This is likewise one of the causes which prevent men from finding truth.

-Moses Maimonides, *The Guide for the Perplexed*

Convictions are more dangerous enemies of truth than lies.

-Friedrich Nietzsche, "Man Alone With Himself", *Human, All Too Human*

We should not be so taken up in the search for truth, as to neglect the needful duties of active life ; for it is only action that gives a true value and commendation to virtue.

-Marcus Tullius Cicero, quoted in *A Dictionary of Thoughts* (1891) by Tryon Edwards

You do not thoroughly know any truth till you can put it before a child so that he can see it.

-Charles Hadden Spurgeon, *Come Ye Children*

Contradiction is not a sign of falsity, nor the lack of contradiction a sign of truth.

-Blaise Pascal, *Pensées*

A belief is not true because it is useful.

-Henri Frederic Amiel, *Journal Intime*, 15 November 1876

Truth is not only violated by falsehood; it may equally be outraged by silence.

-Henri Frederic Amiel, *Journal Intime*, 17 December 1856

What is truth? said jesting Pilate; and would not stay for an answer.

-Francis Bacon, "Of Truth", *Essays*

It is proof of a base and low mind for one to wish to think with the masses or majority, merely because the majority is the majority. Truth does not change because it is, or is not, believed by a majority of the people.

-Giordano Bruno, debate at College of Cambray, 25 May 1588

But whoever is a genuine follower of truth keeps his eye steady upon his guide, indifferent whither he is led, provided that she is the leader.

-Edmund Burke, *A Vindication of Natural Society*

They who know the truth are not equal to those who love it, and they who love it are not equal to those who find delight in it.

-Confucius, *Analects*

If you would be a real seeker after truth, it is necessary that at least once in your life you doubt, as far as possible, all things.

-Rene Descartes, *Principles of Philosophy*

No man thoroughly understands a truth until he has contended against it.

-Ralph Waldo Emerson, "Compensation", *Essays*

And one may say boldly that no man has a right perception of any truth who has not been reacted on by it so as to be ready to be its martyr.

-Ralph Waldo Emerson, "Fate", *The Conduct of Life*

He who does not bellow the truth when he knows it, makes himself the accomplice of liars and forgers.

-Charles Peguy, *Basic Verities*

Many errors, of a truth, consist merely in the application of the wrong names to things.

-Baruch Spinoza, "The Nature and Origin of the Mind", *The Ethics*

An error is none the better for being common, nor truth the worse for having lain neglected.

-John Locke, *An Essay Concerning Human Understanding*

Two and two continue to make four, in spite of the whine of the amateur for three, or the cry of the critic for five.

-James McNeill Whistler, *Whistler v. Ruskin* (1878)

A thing is not necessarily true because it is eloquently expressed, nor false because it is badly uttered.

-Saint Augustine, *Confessions*

Pure truth, like pure gold, has been found unfit for circulation, because men have discovered that it is far more convenient to adulterate the truth, than to refine themselves.

-Charles Caleb Colton, *Lacon*

Beware lest you lose the substance by grasping at the shadow.

-Aesop, "The Dog and The Shadow", *Fables*

It is by doubting that we come to investigate and by investigating that we recognize the truth.

-Peter Abelard, *Yes and No*

If a man will kick a fact out of the window, when he comes back he finds it again in the chimney corner.

-Ralph Waldo Emerson, *Journals*

You cannot leave out that part of the truth which is so dark and so solemn without weakening the force of all the other truths you preach . . . Brethren, leave out nothing. Be bold enough to preach unpalatable and unpopular truth.

-Charles Haddon Spurgeon, *The Greatest Fight in the World*

Ye knights of truth, charge home! Spare not, but slay; let error die before you, until truth, and truth alone, shall sit king over the whole world!

-Charles Haddon Spurgeon, "A Solemn Warning for All Churches", sermon, 24 February 1856

Truth is truth, whether from the lips of Jesus or Balaam.

-George MacDonald, "The New Name", *Unspoken Sermons*

Truth never yet fell dead in the streets; it has such affinity with the soul of man, the seed however broadcast will catch somewhere and produce its hundredfold.

-Theodore Parker, *A Discourse of Matters Pertaining to Religion*

Every man is fully satisfied that there is such a thing as truth, or he would not ask any question.

-Charles Sanders Peirce, "Pragmatism", lecture at Harvard (1903)

Truth often suffers more by the heat of its defenders, than from the arguments of its opposers.

-William Penn, *Some Fruits of Solitude*

Though all the winds of doctrine were let loose to play upon the earth, so Truth be in the field, we do injuriously, by licensing and prohibiting, to misdoubt her strength. Let her and Falsehood grapple; who ever knew Truth put to the worse, in a free and open encounter?

-John Milton, *Areopagitica*

Right is right, even if everybody is against it, and wrong is wrong, even if everyone is for it.

-William Penn

Our great problem is the problem of trafficking in unlived truth. We try to communicate what we've never experienced in our own lives.

-Dwight L. Moody

[Johnson said] striking his foot with mighty force against a large stone, till he rebounded from it, "I refute it thus."

-James Boswell, quoted in *Life of Samuel Johnson* (1791) by James Boswell

God give me strength to face a fact though it slay me.

-Thomas Henry Huxley

The first and last thing that is demanded of genius is love of truth.

-Johann Wolfgang von Goethe, *Proverbs in Prose*

Truth is often eclipsed but never extinguished.

-Livy, *The History of Rome*

A half truth is a whole lie.

-Yiddish Proverb

Be not so bigoted to any custom as to worship it at the expense of truth.

-Johann Georg von Zimmermann, quoted in *Laconics* (1829) by John Timbs

Peace is such a precious jewel that I would give anything for it but truth.

-Matthew Henry, *Exposition of the Old and New Testament*

Truth, like the sun, submits to be obscured; but, like the sun, only for a time.

-Christian Nestell Bovee, *Intuitions and Summaries of Thought*

We swallow greedily any lie that flatters us, but we sip only little by little at a truth we find bitter.

-Denis Diderot, *Rameau's Nephew*

Peace, if possible, but truth at any rate.

-Martin Luther, quoted in *A Dictionary of Thoughts* (1891) by Tryon Edwards

It is far more difficult, I assure you, to live for the truth than to die for it.

-Horace Mann, "Miracles", *Twelve Sermons*

Every truth passes through three stages before it is recognized. In the first stage it is ridiculed, in the second stage it is opposed, in the third stage it is regarded as self-evident.

-Arthur Schopenhauer

There are no new truths, only discoveries of which we were once ignorant.

- J.S. Felts

Truth is incontrovertible. Panic may resent it; ignorance may deride it; malice may distort it; but there it is.

-Winston Churchill, speech to House of Commons, 17 May 1916

Never be guilty of sacrificing any portion of truth upon the altar of peace.

-J.C. Ryle, "St. Peter at Antioch", *Home Truths*

If you add to the truth, you subtract from it.

-The *Talmud*

Truth is outraged by silence.

-Saying

Neither human applause nor human censure is to be taken as the test of truth.

-Richard Whately, Essays On Some of the Dangers to Christian Faith

I make it my rule to lay hold of light and embrace it, wherever I see it, though held forth by a child or an enemy.

-Jonathan Edwards, *Some Thoughts Concerning the Present Revival of Religion*

Lovers of truth sometimes have to stand beside those, who bring no pleasure in standing beside.

- J.S. Felts

Deviation from either truth or duty is a downward path, and none can say where the descent will end.

-Tryon Edwards, A Dictionary of Thoughts

It is one thing to wish to have Truth on our side, and another thing to wish to be on the side of Truth.

-Richard Whately, Essays: On some of the Difficulties in the Writings of St Paul

Keep one thing forever in view, the truth; and if you do this, though it may seem to lead you away from the opinions of men, it will assuredly conduct you to the throne of God.

-Horace Mann, letter to a young man, 16 June 1851

The only way to shine, even in this false world, is to be modest and unassuming. Falsehood may be a thick crust, but, in the course of time, truth will find a place to break through.

-William Cullen Bryant, letter to young man

Truth is tough. It will not break, like a bubble, at the touch; nay, you may kick it about all day, like a football, and it will be round and full at evening.

-Oliver Wendell Holmes Sr., *The Professor at the Breakfast-table*

People have become so accustomed to lies they no longer have a stomach for truth.

-Unknown

There is nothing so strong or safe, in any emergency of life, as simple truth.

-Charles Dickens, quoted in *Golden Gleams of Thought* (1881) by Rev. S. Pollock Linn

The searching-out and thorough investigation of truth ought to be the primary study of man.

-Marcus Tullius Cicero, quoted in *Excellent Quotations for Home and School* (1890) by Julia Hoitt

To die for an idea; it is unquestionably noble. But how much nobler it would be if men died for ideas that were true!

-H.L. Mencken, *Prejudices: Fifth Series*

Ye shall know the truth, and the truth shall make you free.

-The Bible (KJV), John 8:32

If you want to ruin the truth, stretch it.

-Saying

He that speaks truth must have one foot in the stirrup.

-Turkish Proverb

Accuracy of statement is one of the first elements of truth; inaccuracy is a near kin to falsehood.

-Tryon Edwards, *A Dictionary of Thoughts*

Religious controversy does only harm. It destroys the humble inquiry after truth; it throws all the energies into an attempt to prove ourselves right . . . in that despairing spirit no man gets at truth.

-Frederick William Robertson, sermon, "The Scepticism of Pilate", 7 November 1852

Facts are many, but the truth is one.

-Rabindranath Tagore, *Sadhana: The Realization of Life*

When the light of the sun shines through a prism it is broken into beautiful colors, and when the prism is shattered, still the light remains.

-Felix Adler, *Life and Destiny*

Error does not become truth, by being often repeated, neither does truth lose any of its beauty by being seldom promulgated.

-*Hunter v. Martin* (1814) Supreme Court of Appeals of Virginia

He who sees the truth, let him proclaim it, without asking who is for it or who is against it.

-Henry George, *The Land Question*

PART VI

THE MATERIAL WORLD

ONE

Ability

No man's abilities are so remarkably shining as not to stand in need of a proper opportunity, a patron, and even the praises of a friend to recommend them to the notice of the world.

-Pliny the Younger, *Epistles*

In the country of the blind, the one-eyed man is king.

-Spanish Proverb

A horse never runs so fast as when he has other horses to catch up and outpace.

-Ovid, *The Art of Love*

No one knows what he can do until he tries.

-Publilius Syrus, *Sententiae*

The same man cannot be skilled in everything; each has his special excellence.

-Euripides, *Rhesus*

The world cares very little about what a man or woman knows; it is what a man or woman is able to do that counts. An educated man standing on the corners of the street with his hands in his pockets is of no more value to the world than an ignorant man doing the same thing

-Booker T. Washington, address in Selma, Alabama, 5 June 1895

The weakest among us has a gift, however seemingly trivial, which is peculiar to him and which worthily used will be a gift also to his race.

-John Ruskin, "Of Truth", *Modern Painters*

No one is expected to achieve the impossible.

-French Proverb

Natural abilities are like natural plants; they need pruning by study.

-Francis Bacon, *Essays*

There is hardly anybody good for everything, and there is scarcely anybody who is absolutely good for nothing.

-Lord Chesterfield, letter to his son, 2 January 1748

The question for each man to settle is not what he would do if he had the means, time, influence and educational advantages; the question is what he will do with the things he has. The moment a young man ceases to dream or to bemoan his lack of opportunities and resolutely looks his conditions in the face, and resolves to change them, he lays the corner-stone of a solid and honorable success.

-Hamilton Wright Mabie, "Making the Most of Leisure", *Success*, November 1903

Each man is capable of doing one thing well. If he attempts several, he will fail to achieve distinction in any.

-Plato, *The Republic*

Anyone can hold the helm when the sea is calm.

-Publilius Syrus, *Sententiae*

The winds and waves are always on the side of the ablest navigators.

-Edward Gibbon, *The History of the Decline and Fall of the Roman Empire*

To be possessed of a vigorous mind is not enough; the prime requisite is rightly to apply it.

-Rene Descartes, *Discourse on the Method*

The house praises the carpenter.

-Ralph Waldo Emerson, *Journals*

The possession of great powers no doubt carries with it a contempt for mere external show.

-James A. Garfield, *The Works of James Abram Garfield*

Natural abilities are like natural plants, that need pruning by study; and studies themselves do give forth directions too much at large, except they be bounded in by experience.

-Francis Bacon, "Of Studies", *Essays*

Most do violence to their natural aptitude, and thus attain superiority in nothing.

-Baltasar Gracian, *The Art of Worldly Wisdom*

TWO

Action

One principal reason why men are so often useless is, that they neglect their own profession, and divide and shift their attention among a multitude of objects and pursuits.

-Nathanael Emmons, sermon in Oxford, 13 April 1791

Of all sad words of tongue or pen, the saddest are these: "It might have been!"

-John Greenleaf Whittier, "Maud Muller", *Poetical Works*

Every action of our lives touches on some chord that will vibrate in eternity.

-Edwin Hubbel Chapin, quoted in *Memory Gems for the Young* (1877) by Charles Northend

Do every act of your life as if it were your last.

-Marcus Aurelius, *Meditations*

Action springs not from thought, but from a readiness for responsibility.

-Dietrich Bonhoeffer, letter to Renate and Eberhard Bethge (1944)

They sicken of the calm, who knew the storm.

-Dorothy Parker, "Fair Weather", *Sunset Gun*

We are always getting ready to live, but never living.

-Ralph Waldo Emerson, *Journals,* 12April 1834

There are but three classes of men: the retrograde, the stationary, the progressive.

-Johann Kaspar Lavater, *Aphorisms of Man*

Nothing will ever be attempted, if all possible objections must first be overcome.

-Samuel Johnson, *Rasselas, Prince of Abyssinia*

I cannot do everything,
But still I can do something;
And because I cannot do everything,
I will not refuse to do the something that I can do.

-Edward Everett Hale, *Ten Times One is Ten*

Action springs not from thought, but from a readiness for responsibility.

-Dietrich Bonhoeffer, *Letters and Papers from Prison*

Our grand business is, not to see what lies dimly at a distance, but to do what lies clearly at hand.

-Thomas Carlyle, "Signs of the Times", *Essays*

It is a bad plan that admits of no modification.

-Publilius Syrus, *Moral Sayings*

Never undertake anything for which you wouldn't have the courage to ask the blessings of heaven.

-Georg Christoph Lichtenberg

You cannot run away from a weakness; you must sometimes fight it out or perish; and if that be so, why not now, and where you stand?

-Robert Louis Stevenson, *The Amateur Emigrant*

Determine never to be idle. No person will have occasion to complain of the want of time, who never loses any. It is wonderful how much may be done, if we are always doing.

-Thomas Jefferson, letter to Martha Jefferson, 5 May 1787

The man who insists upon seeing with perfect clearness before he decides, never decides.

-Henri Frederic Amiel, *Journal Intime*, 17 December 1856

Action will remove the doubt that theory cannot solve.

-Chinese Proverb

The great thing in this world is not so much where we stand, as in what direction we are moving.

-Oliver Wendell Holmes Sr., *The Autocrat of the Breakfast-table*

A journey of a thousand miles must begin with a single step.

-Chinese Proverb

Action may not always bring happiness, but there is no happiness without action.

-Benjamin Disraeli, *Lothair*

Well done is better than well said.

-Benjamin Franklin, *Poor Richard's Almanack*

Our chief defect is that we are more given to talking about things than to doing them.

-Jawaharlal Nehru, "Freedom from Fear", speech in Wardha, India, 1 November 1952

Do what you can, with what you've got, where you are.

-Theodore Roosevelt, *Theodore Roosevelt: An Autobiography*

If he would move the world, he must first move himself.

-Socrates, quoted in *The California Teacher*, March 1869

Many people can't see opportunity when it is dressed in overalls

-Saying

Thou, O God, dost sell us all good things at the price of labor.

-Leonardo Da Vinci, *The Notebooks*

A mighty flame followeth a tiny spark.

-Dante Alighieri, "Paradiso", *The Divine Comedy*

It is the greatest of all mistakes, to do nothing because you can only do little.

-Sydney Smith, "On the Conduct of the Understanding" lecture at Royal Institution

Effort is only effort when it begins to hurt.

-Jose Ortega Y Gasset, *In Search of Goethe from Within*

I never did anything worth doing by accident, nor did any of my inventions come indirectly through accident.

-Thomas A. Edison, interview in *The Review of Reviews* – Vol. VIII (1893)

Conviction is worthless till converted into conduct.

-Thomas Carlyle, *Sartor Resartus*

What use is a good head if the legs won't carry it?

-Yiddish Proverb

I have always thought the actions of men the best interpreters of their thoughts.

-John Locke, *An Essay Concerning Human Understanding*

The world cares very little what you or I know, but it does care a great deal about what you or I do.

-Booker T. Washington, address to African Methodist Episcopal Zion Church, 30 July 1903

It isn't the plays that win. It's the execution.

-Knute Rockne

One has to try to strike the jugular and let the rest go.

-Oliver Wendell Holmes Jr., address to Massachusetts Supreme Court, 25 November 1899

All hard work brings a profit, but mere talk leads only to poverty.

-The Bible (NIV), Proverbs 14:23

Either lead, follow, or get out of the way.

-Saying

The great end of life is not knowledge but action.

-Thomas Henry Huxley, "Technical Education", address to the Working Men's Club and Institute, 1 Dec. 1877

Men are much more apt to agree in what they do than in what they think.

-Johann Wolfgang von Goethe

The beginnings of all things are small.

-Marcus Tullius Cicero, *De Finibus*

The first blow is half the battle.

-Oliver Goldsmith, *She Stoops to Conquer*

The beginning is the most important part of the work.

-Plato, *The Republic*

There is a tide in the affairs of men
Which, taken at the flood, leads on to fortune;
Omitted, all the voyage of their life
Is bound in shallows and in miseries.
On such a full sea are we now afloat;
And we must take the current when it serves,
Or lose our ventures.

-William Shakespeare, *Julius Caesar*

It is the greatest of all mistakes, to do nothing because you can only do little.

-Sydney Smith, lecture "On the Conduct of the Understanding" at Royal Institution

What a man knows should find its expression in what he does.

-Christian Nestell Bovee, *Intuitions and Summaries of Thought*

The reflections on a day well spent furnish us with joys more pleasing than ten thousand triumphs.

-Thomas a' Kempis, *The Imitation of Christ*

For the things we have to learn before we can do them, we learn by doing them.

-Aristotle, *Nicomachean Ethics*

Action is the proper fruit of knowledge.

-Thomas Fuller, *Gnomologia*

Be content to act, and leave the talking to others.

-Baltasar Gracian, *The Art of Worldly Wisdom*

Were I to await perfection, my book would never be finished.

-Chinese Proverb

Well begun is half done.

-Horace, *Satires, Epistles, and Art of Poetry*

Know ye not, each thing we prize
Does from small beginnings rise?

-Mary Anne Lamb, "The Brother's Reply", *Poetry for Children*

Irresolution is a worse vice than rashness. He that shoots best, may sometimes miss the mark; but he that shoots not at all, can never hit it.

-Owen Felltham, Resolves, Divine, Moral and Political

I agree with the man who said he had read the "Acts" of the Apostles, but never their "Resolutions."

-Horace Mann, "Demands of the Age on Colleges", speech in Ohio, 5 October 1854

THREE

ADVERSITY

Victories that are cheap, are cheap. Those only are worth having which come as the result of hard fighting.

-Henry Ward Beecher, *Royal Truths*

If you would not have affliction visit you twice, listen at once to what it teaches.

-James Burgh, *The Dignity of Human Nature*

He that has never known adversity is but half acquainted with others, or with himself.

- Charles Caleb Colton, *Lacon*

Obstacles are those frightful things you see when you take your eyes off the goal.

-Hannah More

Men think God is destroying them because he is tuning them. The violinist screws up the key till the tense cord sounds the concert pitch; but it is not to break it, but to use it tunefully, that he stretches the string upon the musical rack.

-Henry Ward Beecher, *Life Thoughts*

He that has never known adversity is but half acquainted with others, or with himself. Constant success shows us but one side of the world, for, as it surrounds us with friends who will tell us only our merits, so it silences those enemies from whom alone we can learn our defects.

-Charles Caleb Colton, *Lacon*

A smooth sea never made a skillful mariner.

-English Proverb

The harder the conflict, the more glorious the triumph. What we obtain too cheap, we esteem too lightly; 'tis dearness only that gives everything its value.

-Thomas Paine, *The American Crisis,* 23 December 1776

Adversity is sometimes hard upon a man; but for one man who can stand prosperity, there are a hundred that will stand adversity.

-Thomas Carlyle, *On Heroes, Hero-worship, and the Heroic in History*

Every path has its puddle.

-English Proverb

The furnace of affliction refines us from earthly drossiness, and softens us for the impression of God's own stamp.

–Robert Boyle, quoted in *A Dictionary of the English Language* (1818) by Samuel Johnson

Little minds are tamed and subdued by misfortune; but great minds rise above it.

-Washington Irving, "Philip of Pokanoket", *The Sketch Book of Geoffrey Crayon*

The block of granite which was an obstacle on the pathway of the weak, becomes a steppingstone on the pathway of the strong.

-George Henry Lewes, *The Life of Goethe*

He that wrestles with us strengthens our nerves and sharpens our skill. Our antagonist is our helper.

-Edmund Burke, *Reflections on the Revolution in France*

Prosperity is not without many fears and distastes, and adversity is not without comforts and hopes.

-Francis Bacon, "Of Adversity", *Essays*

There has never yet been a man in our history who led a life of ease whose name is worth remembering.

-Theodore Roosevelt, speech at state fairgrounds in Concord, N.H., 28 August 1902

The tree that never had to fight
For sun and sky and air and light,
But stood out in the open plain
and always got its share or rain,
Never became a forest king
but lived and died a scrubby thing.
The man who never had to toil to gain
and farm his patch of soil,
Who never had to win his share
Of sun and sky and light and air,
never became a manly man
But lived and died as he began.
Good timber does not grow with ease,
The stronger wind, the stronger trees.
The further sky, the greater length.
The more the storm, the more the strength
by sun and cold, by rain and snow,
In trees and men good timbers grow.
Where thickest lies the forest growth
We find the patriarchs of both.
And they hold counsel with the stars
Whose broken braches show the scars
Of many winds and much of strife.
This is the common law of life.

-Douglas Malloch, "Good Timber"

In the day of prosperity be joyful, but in the day of adversity consider.

-The Bible (KJV), Ecclesiastes 7:14

If adversity hath killed his thousand, prosperity hath killed his ten thousand: therefore adversity is to be preferred; the one deceives, the other instructs; the one is miserably happy, the other happily miserable; and therefore many philosophers have voluntarily sought adversity and commend it in their precepts.

-Robert Burton, *The Anatomy of Melancholy*

Stars may be seen from the bottom of a deep well, when they cannot be discerned from the top of a mountain. So are many things learned in adversity which the prosperous man dreams not of.

-Charles Haddon Spurgeon, *The Saint and His Saviour*

They took away what should have been my eyes,
(But I remembered Milton's Paradise)
They took away what should have been my ears,
(Beethoven came and wiped away my tears)
They took away what should have been my tongue,
(But I talked with God when I was young)
He would not let them take away my soul,
Possessing that, I still possess the whole.

-Helen Keller, *The Story of My Life*

Adversity has the same effect on a man that severe training has on the pugilist - it reduces him to his fighting weight.

-Josh Billings, *Josh Billings' Wit and Humor*

Adversity has the effect of eliciting talents, which in prosperous circumstances would have lain dormant.

-Horace, quoted in *The Treasury of Knowledge* (1833) by Edwin Williams

A stumble may prevent a fall.

-Thomas Fuller, *Gnomologia*

It is said that in some countries trees will grow, but will bear no fruit, because there is no winter there.

-John Bunyan, *Seasonal Counsel*

He knows not his own strength that hath not met adversity.

-Ben Jonson, *Discoveries*

Adversity has ever been considered as the state in which a man most easily becomes acquainted with himself, being free from flatterers.

-Samuel Johnson, *The Rambler*, 23 June 1750

Outward attacks and troubles rather fix than unsettle the Christian, as tempests from without only serve to root the oak faster.

-Hannah More, "Mistakes in Religion", *Practical Piety*

At the timberline where the storms strike with the most fury, the sturdiest of trees are found.

-Unknown

That which we acquire with most difficulty we retain the longest, as those who have earned a fortune are commonly more careful of it than those who have inherited one.

-Charles Caleb Colton, *Lacon*

Prosperity doth best discover vice; but adversity doth best discover virtue.

-Francis Bacon, "Of Adversity", *Essays*

The opposition is indispensable. A good statesman, like any other sensible human being, always learns more from his opponents than from his fervent supporters.

-Walter Lippmann, "The Indispensable Opposition", in *Atlantic Monthly*, August 1939

Many men owe the grandeur of their lives to their tremendous difficulties.

-Charles Haddon Spurgeon, *The Sword and the Trowel*

Difficulties strengthen the mind, as well as labor does the body.

-Lucius Annaeus Seneca (the younger), *Moral Letters to Lucilius*

FOUR

Age

I regard them [aged] as travelers who have gone on a journey which I too may have to go, and of whom I ought to inquire whether the way is smooth and easy or rugged and difficult.

-Socrates, quoted in *The Republic* by Plato

Winter, which strips the leaves from around us, makes us see the distant regions they formerly concealed; so does old age rob us of our enjoyments, only to enlarge the prospect of eternity before us.

-Jean Paul Richter, quoted in *New York Mirror,* 8 April 1837

The years teach much which the days never know.

-Ralph Waldo Emerson, "Experience", *Essays*

Before you contradict an old man, my fair friend, you should endeavor to understand him.

-George Santayana, *Dialogues in Limbo*

A man's age represents a fine cargo of experiences and memories.

-Antoine de Saint-Exupéry, *Wartime Writings*

While one finds company in himself and his pursuits, he cannot feel old, no matter what his years may be.

-Amos Bronson Alcott, quoted in *A Dictionary of Thoughts* (1891) by Tryon Edwards

Age considers; youth ventures.

-Hermann Raupach

With the ancient is wisdom; and in length of days understanding.

-The Bible (*KJV*), Job 12:12

FIVE

CHANGE

Condradiction is not a sign of falsity, nor the lack of contradiction a sign of truth.

-Blaise Pascal, *Pensées*

God, give us grace to accept with serenity
the things that cannot be changed, courage
to change the things which should be changed,
and the wisdom to distinguish the one from the other.

-Reinhold Niebuhr, "The Serenity Prayer"

Can the Ethiopian change his skin, or the leopard his spots?

-The Bible (*NIV*), Jeremiah 13:23

Weep not that the world changes - did it keep a stable, changeless state, 'twere cause indeed to weep.

-William Cullen Bryant, “Mutation”

You cannot step twice into the same river; for other waters are ever flowing on to you.

-Heraclitus, *On the Universe*

Men cannot bear to be deprived long together of anything they are used to; not even of their fears.

-Walter Savage Landor, "Lucullus and Caesar", *Imaginary Conversations*

Things will change, whether we like it or no.

-George Eliot, *Silas Marner*

No matter how far you have gone on a wrong road, turn back.

-Turkish Proverb

The hearts of the great can be changed.

-Homer, *Iliad*

If you board the wrong train, it is no use running along the corridor in the other direction.

-Dietrich Bonhoeffer, *The Way to Freedom*

To change and to improve are two different things.

-German Proverb

Loyalty to petrified opinions never yet broke a chain or freed a human soul in this world – and never will.

-Mark Twain, "Consistency", speech (1887)

It's an ill plan that cannot be changed.

-Latin Proverb

All changes, even the most longed for, have their melancholy; for what we leave behind us is a part of ourselves; we must die to one life before we can enter another.

-Anatole France, *The Crime of Sylvestre Bonnard*

If anyone accuses me of contradicting myself, I reply: Because I have been wrong once, or oftener, I do not aspire to be always wrong.

-Luc de Clapiers, Marquis de Vauvenargues *Reflections and Maxims*

There are those who would misteach us that to stick in a rut is consistency, and a virtue; and that to climb out of the rut is inconsistency, and a vice.

-Mark Twain, "Consistency", speech (1887)

Everybody thinks of changing humanity, and nobody thinks of changing himself.

-Leo Tolstoy, "Three Methods of Reform" in *Pamphlets*

If you want to make enemies, try to change something.

-Woodrow Wilson, address in Detroit, Michigan, 10 July 1916

A man must be able to cut a knot, for everything cannot be untied.

-Henri Frederic Amiel, *Journal Intime*, 15 August 1851

But touch a solemn truth in collision with a dogma of a sect, though capable of the clearest proof, and you will soon find you have disturbed a nest, and the hornets will swarm about your eyes and hand, and fly into your face and eyes.

-John Adams, letter to John Taylor (1814)

It is not easy to straighten in the oak the crook that grew in the sapling.

-Gaelic Proverb

Change is not made without inconvenience, even from worse to better.

-Richard Hooker, quoted in *A Dictionary of the English Language* (1755) by Samuel Johnson

Two roads diverged in a wood, and I -
I took the one less travelled by,
And that has made all the difference.

-Robert Frost, "The Road Not Taken", *Mountain Interval*

There are some remedies worse than the disease.

-Publilius Syrus, *Sententiae*

Time is a sort of river of passing events, and strong is its current; no sooner is a thing brought to sight than it is swept by and another takes its place, and this too will be swept away.

-Marcus Aurelius, *Meditations*

What is the use of running when we are not on the right road?

-German Proverb

You never need think you can turn over any old falsehood without a terrible squirming and scattering of the horrid little population that dwells under it.

-Oliver Wendell Holmes Sr., *The Autocrat of the Breakfast-table*

If you want the present to be different from the past, study the past.

-Baruch Spinoza

When people once begin to deviate, they do not know where to stop.

-King George III, quoted in *The Friend,* 1842

Reform, like charity, must begin at home.

-Thomas Carlyle, "Hero-worship", *Past and Present*

Just remember, when you should grab something, grab it; when you should let go, let go.

-Unknown

SIX

CIRCUMSTANCES

There are no conditions to which a man cannot become accustomed, especially if he sees that all around him are living in the same way.

-Leo Tolstoy, *Anna Karenina*

Success is to be had by those who make things happen despite their circumstances. Failures are those who quit because they believed chance played a more important role than choice.

– J.S. Felts

He that observeth the wind shall not sow; and he that regardeth the clouds shall not reap.

-The Bible (*KJV*), Ecclesiastes 11:4

The wounded gladiator forswears all fighting, but soon forgetting his former wound resumes his arms.

–Ovid, *Letters from the Black Sea*

The greater part of our happiness or misery depends upon our dispositions, and not upon our circumstances.

-Martha Washington, letter to Mercy Otis Warren, 26 December 1789

No change of circumstances can repair a defect of character.

-Ralph Waldo Emerson, “Character”, *Essays*

When the best things are not possible, the best may be made of those that are.

-Richard Hooker, *Of the Lawes of Ecclesiastical Politie*

Man is not the creature of circumstances, circumstances are the creatures of men. We are free agents, and man is more powerful than matter.

-Benjamin Disraeli, *Vivian Grey*

Shallow men believe in luck, believe in circumstances — it was somebody’s name, or he happened to be there at the time, or it was so then, and another day would have been otherwise. Strong men believe in cause and effect.

-Ralph Waldo Emerson, "Worship", *The Conduct of Life*

Circumstances are the rulers of the weak; they are but the instruments of the wise.

-Samuel Lover, *Rory O'More*

We learn geology the morning after the earthquake.

-Ralph Waldo Emerson, "Considerations by the Way", *The Conduct of Life*

People are always blaming their circumstances for what they are. I don't believe in circumstances. The people who get on in this world are the people who get up and look for the circumstances they want, and if they can't find them, make them.

-George Bernard Shaw, *Mrs. Warren's Profession*

There is no such thing as an accident. What we call by that name is the effect of some cause which we do not see.

-Voltaire, *"Letter of Memmius to Cicero"*

SEVEN

CITIZENSHIP

No people ever recognize their dictator in advance. He never stands for election on the platform of dictatorship.

-Dorothy Thompson, quoted in "Judiciary," *Time*, March 1, 1937

The public has more interest in the punishment of an injury than he who receives it.

-Cato the Elder

Governments arise either out of the people or over the people.

-Thomas Paine, *The Rights of Man*

All free governments are managed by the combined wisdom and folly of the people.

-James A. Garfield, letter to unknown person, 21 April 1880

Why build these cities glorious
If man unbuilded goes?
In vain we build the world, unless
The builder also grows.

-Edwin Markham, “Man-Making”

Laws too gentle are seldom obeyed; too severe, seldom executed.

-Benjamin Franklin, *Poor Richard's Almanack*

In the homes of America are born the children of America, and from them go out into American life, American men and women. They go out with the stamp of these homes upon them; and only as these homes are what they should be, will they be what they should be.

-Josiah Gilbert Holland, "The Institution of Home", *Titcomb's Letters to Young People, Single and Married*

Each citizen should play his part in the community according to his individual gifts.

-Plato, *The Republic*

No government is better than the men who compose it.

-John F. Kennedy, address in Springfield, Ohio, 17 October 1960

The whole history of civilization is strewn with creeds and institutions which were invaluable at first, and deadly afterwards.

-Walter Bagehot, *Physics and Politics*

The men who have changed the universe have never accomplished it by changing officials but always by inspiring the people.

-Napoleon Bonaparte, *Maxims*

Our country, right or wrong! When right, to be kept right; when wrong, to be put right.

-Carl Schurz, remarks in U.S. Senate, 29 February 1872

To put the world right in order, we must first put the nation in order; to put the nation in order, we must first put the family in order; to put the family in order, we must first cultivate our personal life; we must first set our hearts right.

-Confucius

In the long-run every Government is the exact symbol of its People, with their wisdom and unwisdom.

-Thomas Carlyle, "Captains of Industry", *Past and Present*

The ruin of a nation begins in the homes of its people.

-African Proverb

Every reform, however necessary, will by weak minds be carried to an excess, that itself will need reforming.

-Samuel Taylor Coleridge, *Biographia Literaria*

I have no expectation that any man will read history aright, who thinks that what was done in a remote age, by men whose names have resounded far, has any deeper sense than what he is doing today.

-Ralph Waldo Emerson, "History", *Essays*

It does not require a majority to prevail but rather an irate, tireless minority keen to set brush fires in people's minds.

-Unknown

The Roman Republic fell, not because of the ambition of Caesar or Augustus, but because it had already long ceased to be in any real sense a republic at all. When the sturdy Roman plebeian, who lived by his own labor, who voted without reward according to his own convictions, and who with his fellows formed in war the terrible Roman legion, had been changed into an idle creature who craved nothing in life save the gratification of a thirst for vapid excitement, who was fed by the state, and who directly or indirectly sold his vote to the highest bidder, then the end of the republic was at hand, and nothing could save it. The laws were the same as they had been, but the people behind the laws had changed, and so the laws counted for nothing.

-Theodore Roosevelt, “Nationalism and Democracy” *The Outlook,* 25 March, 1911

The worth of a State, in the long run, is the worth of the individuals composing it.

-John Stuart Mill, *On Liberty*

The punishments which the wise suffer, who refuse to take part in government is to live under the government of worse men.

-Plato, quoted in *Society and Solitude* by Ralph Waldo Emerson

Where the roots of private virtue are diseased, the fruit of public probity cannot but be corrupt.

-Felix Adler, founding address of New York Society for Ethical Culture, 15 May 1876

The first requisite of a good citizen in this republic of ours is that he shall be able and willing to pull his weight.

-Theodore Roosevelt, speech in New York, 11 November 1902

The strength of a nation, especially of a republican nation, is in the intelligent and well-ordered homes of the people.

-Lydia Sigourney, "Industry", *Letters to Young Ladies*

If ever the time should come, when vain and aspiring men shall possess the highest seats in government, our country will stand in need of its experienced patriots to prevent its ruin.

-Samuel Adams, letter to James Warren, 24 October 1780

It is not always the same thing to be a good man and a good citizen.

-Aristotle, *Nicomachean Ethics*

EIGHT

COMMITMENT

Chance favors the prepared mind.

-Louis Pasteur, lecture at University of Lille in France, 7 December 1854

If a man has not discovered something that he will die for, he isn't fit to live.

-Martin Luther King Jr., speech in Detroit, Michigan, 23 June 1963

Whatsoever thy hand findeth to do, do it with thy might.

-The Bible (*KJV*), Ecclesiastes 9:10

My great concern is not whether God is on our side; my great concern is to be on God's side.

-Abraham Lincoln

It is not best to swap horses while crossing the river.

-Abraham Lincoln, reply to National Union League, 9 June 1864

Commitment means staying loyal to what you said you were going to do, long after the mood you said it in has left you.

-Saying

Who draws his sword against the prince must throw away the scabbard.

-English Proverb

I had sooner that you believed half-a-dozen truths intensely than a hundred only feebly.

-Charles Haddon Spurgeon, *The Soul Winner*

Steady and undissipated attention to one object, is a sure mark of a superior genius.

-Lord Chesterfield, letter to his son, 14 April 1747

To do two things at once is to do neither.

-Publilius Syrus, *Sententiae*

And one may say boldly that no man has a right perception of any truth who has not been reacted on by it so as to be ready to be its martyr.

-Ralph Waldo Emerson, "Fate", *The Conduct of Life*

Better is it that thou shouldest not vow, than that thou shouldest vow and not pay.

-The Bible (*KJV*), Ecclesiastes 5:5

NINE

COMPLACENCY

I went past the field of the sluggard,
past the vineyard of the man who lacks judgment;
thorns had come up everywhere,
the ground was covered with weeds,
and the stone wall was in ruins.
I applied my heart to what I observed
and learned a lesson from what I saw:
A little sleep, a little slumber,
a little folding of the hands to rest-
and poverty will come on you like a bandit
and scarcity like an armed man.

-The Bible (*NIV*), Proverbs 24:30-34

Between the great things we cannot do and the small things we will not do, the danger is that we shall do nothing.

-Adolphe Monod, quoted in *Record of Christian Work*, January,1904

He that is too secure is not safe.

-Thomas Fuller, *Gnomologia*

Consider how many millions of people come into, and go out of, the world, ignorant of themselves and of the world they have lived in.

-William Penn, *Some Fruits of Solitude*

TEN

Consequences

There are in nature neither rewards nor punishments; there are consequences.

-Robert G. Ingersoll, *The Christian Religion*

Take away the cause, and the effect ceases; what the eye never sees, the heart never rues.

-Miguel de Cervantes, *Don Quixote*

These deeds that are taking place around you, touch upon chords that extend by a thousand connections, visible and invisible, and vibrate in eternity.

-Edwin Hubbel Chapin, *Duties of Young Men*

You can't unscramble scrambled eggs.

-American Proverb

Whatsoever a man soweth, that shall he also reap.

-The Bible (*KJV*), Galatians 6:7

Quite often good things have hurtful consequences. There are instances of men who have been ruined by their money or killed by their courage.

-Aristotle, *Nicomachean Ethics*

It will generally be found that men who are constantly lamenting their ill luck are only reaping the consequences of their own neglect, mismanagement, and improvidence, or want of application.

-Samuel Smiles, *Self-Help*

If you board the wrong train, it is no use running along the corridor in the other direction.

-Dietrich Bonhoeffer

ELEVEN

Contentment

A wise man will desire no more than what he may get justly, use soberly, distribute cheerfully, and leave contently.

-Benjamin Franklin, *Poor Richard's Almanack*

We are all of us richer than we think we are.

-Michel de Montaigne, "Of Physiognomy", *Essays*

Before we set our hearts too much upon anything, let us examine how happy those are, who already possess it.

-Francois de La Rochefoucauld, *Moral Maxims and Reflections*

The lust for comfort, that stealthy thing that enters the house a guest, and then becomes a host, and then a master.

-Khalil Gibran, "Houses", *The Prophet*

It is not how much we have, but how much we enjoy, that makes happiness.

-Charles Haddon Spurgeon, *John Ploughman's Talk*

To be secure, be humble; to be happy, be content.

-James Hurdis, *The Village Curate*

Everything has its wonders, even darkness and silence, and I learn whatever state I may be in, therein to be content.

-Helen Keller, *The Story of My Life*

Do not spoil what you have by desiring what you have not; but remember that what you now have was once among the things only hoped for.

-Epicurus, "Vatican Sayings"

The use we make of our fortune determines its sufficiency. A little is enough if used wisely, and too much if expended foolishly.

-Christian Nestell Bovee, *Intuitions and Summaries of Thought*

The heart is great which shows moderation in the midst of prosperity.

-Lucius Annaeus Seneca (the elder), *Suasoriae*

If your desires be endless, your cares and fears will be so too.

-Thomas Fuller, *Gnomologia*

Do not wade far out into the dangerous sea of this world's comfort. Take the good that God provides you, but say of it, "It passeth away;" for, indeed, it is but a temporary supply for a temporary need. Never suffer your goods to become your God.

-Charles Haddon Spurgeon, sermon, "The Peace of God", 6 January 1878

If all our misfortunes were laid in one common heap, where everyone might choose his portion, most people would be contented to take their own.

-Socrates, quoted in *Plutarch's Morals*

To be satisfied with what one has; that is wealth. As long as one sorely needs a certain additional amount, that man isn't rich.

-Mark Twain, open letter to Cornelius Vanderbilt, published in *Packard's Monthly* (1869)

He that is discontented in one place will seldom be happy in another.

-Aesop, "The Ass and His Masters", *Fables*

Thousands upon thousands are yearly brought into a state of real poverty by their great anxiety not to be thought poor.

-William Cobbett, *Advice to Young Men*

I have learned, in whatsoever state I am, therewith to be content.

-The Bible (*KJV*), Philippians 4:11

For many men, the acquisition of wealth does not end their troubles, it only changes them.

-Lucius Annaeus Seneca (the younger)

We should scarcely desire things ardently if we were perfectly acquainted with what we desire.

-Francois de La Rochefoucauld, *Reflections or Sentences and Moral Maxims*

Our desires always increase with our possessions; the knowledge that something remains yet unenjoyed, impairs our enjoyment of the good before us.

-Samuel Johnson, *The Adventurer*, 26 June 1753

Beggars should be no choosers.

-John Heywood, *Proverbs*

It is preoccupation with possessions, more than anything else that prevents men from living freely and nobly.

-Bertrand Russell, *Principles of Social Reconstruction*

Fortify yourself with contentment, for this is an impregnable fortress.

-Epictetus, *Enchiridion*

If money be not thy servant, it will be thy master. The covetous man cannot so properly be said to possess wealth, as that may be said to possess him.

-Pierre Charron, quoted in *The Rule of Life* (1766)

To secure a contented spirit, measure your desires by your fortune, and not your fortune by your desires.

-Jeremy Taylor, quoted in *A Dictionary of the English Language* (1818) by Samuel Johnson

A bird in the hand is worth two in the bush.

-Miguel de Cervantes, *Don Quixote*

I am always content with that which happens; for I know that what God chooses is better than what I choose.

-Epictetus, *Discourses*

Let your conversation be without covetousness; and be content with such things as ye have: for he hath said, I will never leave thee, nor forsake thee.

-The Bible (*KJV*), Hebrews 13:5

Contentment is a pearl of great price.

–John Balguy, "The Vanity and Vexation of Irregular Desires", *Sermons*

TWELVE

Death

Live as you will wish to have lived when you are dying.

-Christian Furchtegott Gellert, quoted in Synopsis of German Grammar (1899) by Edward Althaus

Only death reveals what a nothing the body of man is.

-Juvenal, *Satires*

Death, so called, is a thing which makes men weep,
And yet a third of Life is passed in sleep.

-Lord Byron, *Don Juan*

Is death the last sleep? No, it is the last final awakening.

-Walter Scott, quoted in *Gleason's Pictorial* (1853)

As men, we are all equal in the presence of death.

-Publilius Syrus, *Moral Sayings*

When a man knows he is to be hanged in a fortnight, it concentrates his mind wonderfully.

-Samuel Johnson, quoted in *Life of Samuel Johnson* (1791) by James Boswell

I have fought the good fight, I have finished the race, I have kept the faith.

-The Bible (*NIV*), 2 Timothy 4:7

Men sometimes upon the hour of departure do speak and reason above themselves; for then the soul, beginning to be freed from the ligaments of the body, reasons like herself, and discourses in a strain above mortality.

–Joseph Addison, *Spectator*

It is no happiness to live long, nor unhappiness to die soon; happy is he that hath lived long enough to die well.

-Francis Quarles, *Enchiridion*

If you would not be forgotten as soon as you are dead, either write things worth reading or do things worth writing.

-Benjamin Franklin, *Poor Richard's Almanack*

A man's dying is more the survivors' affair than his own.

-Thomas Mann, *The Magic Mountain*

The graveyards are full of indispensable men.

-Saying

The worst evil of all is to leave the ranks of the living before one dies.

-Lucius Annaeus Seneca (the younger), "On Peace of Mind", *Moral Essays*

We brought nothing into this world, and it is certain we can carry nothing out.

-The Bible (*KJV*), 1 Timothy 6:7

A ship spreads her white sails to the morning breeze and starts for the ocean. I stand watching her until she fades on the horizon, and someone at my side says, 'She is gone.' Gone where? The loss of sight is in me, not in her. Just at the moment when someone says, 'She is gone,' there are others who are watching her coming. Other voices take up the glad shout, 'Here she comes,' and that is dying.

-Henry Scott Holland

One may live as a conqueror, a king or a magistrate; but he must die as a man. The bed of death brings every human being to his pure individuality; to the intense contemplation of that deepest and most solemn of all relations, the relation between the creature and his Creator. Here it is that fame and renown cannot assist us; that all external things must fail to aid us; that even friends, affection and human love and devotedness cannot succor us.

-Daniel Webster, address to Suffolk Bar Association in Boston, 12 September 1845

For tis not in mere death that men die most.

-Elizabeth Barrett Browning, *Aurora Leigh*

Will this matter to me as I'm dying? Answer that question and you'll know where to spend your time and energy.

- J.S. Felts

THIRTEEN

Debt

Thousands upon thousands are yearly brought into a state of real poverty by their great anxiety not to be thought poor.

-William Cobbett, *Advice to Young Men*

Debt is a trap which man sets and baits himself, and then deliberately gets into.

-Josh Billings, *Josh Billings' Old Farmer's Allminax* (1870)

Beware of little expenses; a small leak will sink a great ship.

-Benjamin Franklin, *Poor Richard's Almanack*

Spend less than you earn and you'll never be in debt.

-Amish Proverb

The borrower is servant to the lender.

-The Bible (*KJV*), Proverbs 22:7

Debt is the worst poverty.

-Thomas Fuller, *Gnomologia*

Proportion your expenses to what you have, not what you expect.

-English Proverb

A great fortune is a great slavery.

-Lucius Annaeus Seneca (the younger), "To Polybius on Consolation", *Moral Essays*

None is so wretched as the poor man who maintains the semblance of wealth.

-Charles Haddon Spurgeon, *The Salt-Cellars*

It is hard to pay for bread that has been eaten.

-Danish Proverb

FOURTEEN

Desire

First deserve, then desire.

-English Proverb

The Creator has not given you a longing to do that which you have no ability to do.

-Orison Swett Marden, How to Get what You Want

Delight yourself in the LORD and he will give you the desires of your heart.

-The Bible (NIV), Psalms 37:4

What the eye sees not, the heart craves not.

-Dutch Proverb

The desire for imaginary benefits often involves the loss of present blessings.

-Aesop, "The Kites and the Swans", *Fables*

Do not spoil what you have by desiring what you have not; remember that what you now have was once among the things you only hoped for.

-Epicurus, "Vatican Sayings"

How few are our real wants! And how easy is it to satisfy them! Our imaginary ones are boundless and insatiable.

-Julius Charles Hare, *Guesses at Truth*

Before we passionately desire a thing, we should examine the happiness of its possessor.

-Francois de la Rochefoucauld, *Moral Maxims*

Boredom: the desire for desires.

-Leo Tolstoy, *Anna Karenina*

He who desires but acts not, breeds pestilence.

-William Blake, "Proverbs of Hell", *The Marriage of Heaven and Hell*

The desires of man increase with his acquisitions.

-Samuel Johnson, *The Idler*, 11 November, 1758

The desire of the righteous ends only in good, but the hope of the wicked in wrath.

-The Bible (*NIV*), Proverbs 11:23

Rule your desires lest your desires rule you.

-Publilius Syrus, *Sententiae*

'Tis much easier to suppress a first desire, than to satisfy all those that follow it.

-Francois de la Rochefoucauld, *Moral Maxims*

It is much easier to extinguish a first desire than to satisfy those which follow it.

-La Rochefoucauld, *Maxims*

FIFTEEN

DISCONTENT

Discontent is the first step in the progress of a man or a nation.

-Oscar Wilde, A Woman of No Importance

Content makes poor men rich; discontent makes rich men poor.

-Benjamin Franklin, *Poor Richard's Almanack*

The discontented man finds no easy chair.

-Benjamin Franklin, *Poor Richard's Almanack*

The great error of our nature is, not to know where to stop, not to be satisfied with any reasonable acquirement; not to compound with our condition; but to lose all we have gained by an insatiable pursuit after more.

-Edmund Burke, *A Vindication of Natural Society*

He that is discontented in one place will seldom be happy in another.

-Aesop, "The Ass and His Masters", *Fables*

SIXTEEN

FAILURE

The greatest test of courage on earth is to bear defeat without losing heart.

-Robert G. Ingersoll, speech on 100th anniversary of Declaration of Independence in Peoria, IL., 4 July 1876

Doing what's right is no guarantee against misfortune.

-William McFee, *Casuals of the Sea*

Little minds are tamed and subdued by misfortune; but great minds rise above them.

-Washington Irving, *Philip of Pokanoket*

Many of life's failures are men who did not realize how close they were to success when they gave up.

-Thomas A. Edison

When any calamity has been suffered, the first thing to be remembered, is, how much has been escaped.

–Samuel Johnson, quoted in *The Saturday Magazine*, 30 July 1836

The credit belongs to the man who is actually in the arena; whose face is marred by the dust and sweat and blood; who strives valiantly; who errs and comes short again and again, because there is no effort without error or shortcoming; who knows the great enthusiasms, the great devotions and spends himself in a worthy cause; who at the best, knows in the end the triumph of high achievement, and who, at worst, if he fails, at least fails while daring greatly; so that his place shall never be with those cold and timid souls who know neither victory or defeat.

-Theodore Roosevelt, "Citizen in a Republic" speech delivered at the Sorbonne, Paris, France, 23 April 1910

Never confuse a single defeat with a final defeat.

-F. Scott Fitzgerald

There are defeats more triumphant than victories.

-Michel de Montaigne, "Of Cannibals", *Essays*

Half the failures in life arise from pulling in one's horse as he is leaping.

-Julius Charles Hare, *Guesses at Truth*

It ain't no disgrace for a man to fall, but to lie there and grunt is.

-Josh Billings, *Josh Billings' Old Farmer's Allminax* (1876)

There are occasions when it is undoubtedly better to incur loss than to make gain.

-Titus Maccius Plautus, *The Captives*

Ignorance is a blank sheet, on which we may write; but error is a scribbled one, on which we must first erase.

-Charles Caleb Colton, *Lacon*

There is no failure except in no longer trying.

-Elbert Hubbard, *The Fra*, July 1913

Show me a thoroughly satisfied man, and I will show you a failure.

-Thomas A. Edison, quoted in *The Turning Wheel* (1934) by Arthur Pound

Failure is, in a sense, the highway to success, inasmuch as every discovery of what is false leads us to seek earnestly after what is true, and every fresh experience points out some form of error which we shall afterwards carefully avoid.

-John Keats, quoted in *Other Men's Minds* (1800) by Edwin Davies

Because they had no root, they withered away.

-The Bible (*KJV*), Matthew 13:6

If you think you're beaten, you are;
If you think you dare not, you don't;
If you'd like to win, but think, you can't
It's almost a cinch you won't.
If you think you will lose, you're lost;
For out in the world we find,
Success begins with a fellow's will,
It's all in the state of mind.
If you think you're outclassed, you are;
You've got to think high to rise.
You've got to hustle before
You can ever win a prize.
Life's battles don't always go
To the stronger or faster man,
But sooner or later the man who wins
Is the one who thinks he can.

-Walter D. Wintle, "The Man Who Thinks He Can"

But he [Jesus] said to me [Paul], "My grace is sufficient for you, for my power is made perfect in weakness." Therefore I will boast all the more gladly about my weaknesses, so that Christ's power may rest on m.e.

-The Bible (*KJV*), 2 Corinthians 12:9

I would rather fail in a cause that I know someday will triumph, than to win in a cause that I know someday will fail.

-Woodrow Wilson

Defeat may be victory in disguise.

-Henry Wadsworth Longfellow, "Loss and Gain", *In the Harbor*

What is defeat? Nothing but education, nothing but the first step to something better.

-Wendell Phillips, "Harper's Ferry", speech in Brooklyn, New York, 1 Nov. 1859

We climb to heaven most often on the ruins of our cherished schemes, finding our failures were successes.

-Amos Bronson Alcott, quoted in *The Guardian*, April 1874

We learn wisdom from failure much more than from success: We often discover what will do, by finding out what will not do; and he who never made a mistake, never made a discovery.

-Samuel Smiles, *Self-Help*

We failed, but in the good providence of God apparent failure often proves a blessing.

-Robert E. Lee, letter to George W. Jones, 22 March 1869

Ninety-nine percent of the failures come from people who have the habit of making excuses.

-George Washington Carver

Show me a man who has never failed, and I will show you a man who has never succeeded.

- J.S. Felts

By speaking of our misfortunes we often relieve them.

-Pierre Corneille, *Ployeucte*

If you would not have affliction visit you twice, listen at once to what it teaches.

-James Burgh, *The Dignity of Human Nature*

No man is entirely free from weakness and imperfection in this life.

-John Adams, diary entry, 19 February 1756

It is better to fail in originality, than to succeed in imitation. He who has never failed somewhere, that man can not be great. Failure is the true test of greatness.

-Herman Melville, *Hawthorne and His Mosses*

SEVENTEEN

JUSTICE

I will be as harsh as truth and as uncompromising as justice. On this subject I do not wish to think, or speak, or write, with moderation. No! No! Tell a man whose house is on fire to give a moderate alarm; tell him to moderately rescue his wife from the hands of the ravisher; tell the mother to gradually extricate her babe from the fire into which it has fallen; but urge me not to use moderation.

-William Lloyd Garrison, *The Liberator*, 1 January 1831

We must reject the idea that every time a law's broken, society is guilty rather than the lawbreaker. It is time to restore the American precept that each individual is accountable for his actions.

-Ronald Reagan, speech at the Republican National Convention in Miami, FL, 31 July 1968

I would remind you that extremism in the defense of liberty is no vice! And let me remind you also that moderation in the pursuit of justice is no virtue.

-Barry Goldwater, acceptance speech at Republican National Convention, 16 July 1964

I submit that an individual who breaks a law that conscience tells him is unjust, and willingly accepts the penalty by staying in jail in order to arouse the conscience of the community over its injustice, is in reality expressing the very highest respect for law.

-Martin Luther King Jr., letter from a Birmingham jail, 16 April 1963

He threatens many that hath injured one.

-Ben Jonson, *The Fall of Sejanus*

If you study the history and records of the world you must admit that the source of justice was the fear of injustice.

-Horace, *Satires*

Neutrality consists in having the same weights and measures for each.

-Napoleon Bonaparte, *Maxims*

It is better to risk saving a guilty man than to condemn an innocent one.

-Voltaire, *Zadig*

In matters of government, justice means force as well as virtue.

-Napoleon Bonaparte, *Maxims*

Mankind censure injustice, fearing that they may be victims of it and not because they shrink from committing it.

-Plato, *The Republic*

Abuse a man unjustly, and you will make friends for him.

-Edgar Watson Howe, *Country Town Sayings*

Injustice is relatively easy to bear; what stings is justice.

-H.L. Mencken, *Prejudices: Third Series*

Justice will not condemn even the Devil himself wrongfully.

-Thomas Fuller, Gnomologia

Speak softly and carry a big stick.

-Theodore Roosevelt, "National Duties", speech at Minnesota State Fair, 2 September 1901

Do not withhold good from those who deserve it, when it is in your power to act.

-The Bible (*NIV*), Proverbs 3:27

He hears but half who hears one party only.

-Aeschylus, *The Eumenides*

If an injury has to be done to a man it should be so severe that his vengeance need not be feared.

-Niccolo Machiavelli, *The Prince*

Power is no blessing in itself. . . [except] when it is used to protect the innocent.

-Jonathan Swift, "On Mutual Subjection", *Three Sermons*

The certainty of punishment, even more than its severity, is the preventive of crime.

-Tryon Edwards, *A Dictionary of Thoughts*

The object of punishment is three-fold: for just retribution; for the protection of society, for the reformation of the offender.

-Tryon Edwards, *A Dictionary of Thoughts*

In the history of man it has been very generally the case, that when evils have grown insufferable, they have touched the point of cure.

-Edwin Hubbel Chapin, *Christianity: The Perfection of True Manliness*

Justice discards party, friendship, kindred, and is therefore always represented as blind.

-Joseph Addison, *The Guardian*, 4 July 1713

Justice is always violent to the party offending, for every man is innocent in his own eyes.

-Daniel Defoe, *The Shortest Way With the Dissenters*

If [the law] is of such a nature that it requires you to be an agent of injustice to another, then, I say, break the law.

-Henry David Thoreau, *Civil Disobedience*

Justice is truth in action.

-Joseph Joubert, *Pensées of Joubert*

Pardon one offense, and you encourage the commission of many more.

-Publilius Syrus, *Sententiae*

Compassion is a virtue that cannot always be exercised, as in some cases mercy to the guilty is cruelty to the innocent.

-Unknown

EIGHTEEN

LIBERTY

When bad men combine, the good must associate; else they will fall, one by one, an unpitied sacrifice in a contemptible struggle.

-Edmund Burke, *Thoughts on the Cause of the Present Discontents*

I would remind you that extremism in the defense of liberty is no vice! And let me remind you also that moderation in the pursuit of justice is no virtue.

-Barry Goldwater, acceptance speech at Republican National Convention, 16 July 1964

In a free system, literacy is as imperative as ignorance is necessary in a slave system.

-Horace Mann Bond, *The Education of the Negro in the American Social Order*

A day, an hour of virtuous liberty, is worth a whole eternity in bondage.

-Joseph Addison, *Cato*

Judges ought to remember that their office is *jus dicere*, and not *jus dare*; to interpret law, and not to make law, or give law.

-Francis Bacon, "Of Judicature", *Essays*

Freedom to differ is not limited to things that do not matter much. That would be a mere shadow of freedom. The test of its substance is the right to differ as to things that touch the heart of the existing order.

-Justice Robert Jackson, *West Virginia State Board v. Barnette* (1943)

Better that we should die fighting than be outraged and dishonored. Better to die than live in slavery.

-Emmeline Pankhurst

In the eyes of empire builders men are not men, but instruments.

-Napoleon Bonaparte, *Maxims*

Give me the liberty to know, to utter, and to argue freely according to conscience, above all liberties.

-John Milton, *Areopagitica*

What country can preserve its liberties, if its rulers are not warned from time to time, that this people preserve the spirit of resistance?

-Thomas Jefferson, letter to Col. William S. Smith, 13 Nov. 1787

When a prisoner sees the door of his dungeon open, he dashes for it without stopping to think where he shall get his dinner outside.

-George Bernard Shaw, preface to *Back to Methuselah*

The spirit of improvement is not always a spirit of liberty, for it may aim at forcing improvements on an unwilling people.

-John Stuart Mill, *On Liberty*

Power must never be trusted without a check.

-John Adams, letter to Thomas Jefferson, 2 February 1816

I disapprove of what you say, but I will defend to the death your right to say it.

-Evelyn Beatrice Hall (S. G. Tallentyre), *The Friends of Voltaire*

Any excuse will serve a tyrant.

-Aesop, "The Wolf and The Lamb", *Fables*

Nor should we listen to those who say "The voice of the people is the voice of God," for the turbulence of the mob is always close to insanity.

-Alcuin, letter to Charlemagne (800 A.D.)

He that is good is free, though he be a slave; he that is evil is a slave, though he be a king.

-Saint Augustine, *The City of God*

Depend upon it, that the lovers of freedom will be free.

-Edmund Burke, speech to the electors of Bristol, 6 September 1780

The people never give up their liberties but under some delusion.

-Edmund Burke, speech at county meeting of Buckinghamshire (1784)

Among a people generally corrupt, liberty cannot long exist.

-Edmund Burke, letter to the sheriffs of Bristol, 3 April 1777

The condition upon which God hath given liberty to man is eternal vigilance; which condition if he break, servitude is at once the consequence of his crime, and the punishment of his guilt.

-John Philpot Curran, speech, "Right of Election of Lord Mayor of Dublin", 10 July 1790

Power concedes nothing without a demand. It never did, and it never will. Find out just what people will submit to, and you have found out the exact amount of injustice and wrong which will be imposed upon them; and these will continue until they are resisted with either words or blows, or with both. The limits of tyrants are prescribed by the endurance of those whom they suppress.

-Frederick Douglass, letter to Gerrit Smith, 30 March, 1849

Those who would give up essential liberty to purchase a little temporary safety deserve neither liberty nor safety.

-Benjamin Franklin, *An Historical Review of the Constitution and Government of Pennsylvania*

The voice of the people has been said to be the voice of God; and, however generally the maxim has been quoted and believed, it is not true in fact. The people are turbulent and changing; they seldom judge or determine right.

-Alexander Hamilton, address at Federal Convention, 18 June 1787

If ye love wealth better than liberty, the tranquility of servitude, than the animating contest for freedom, go from us in peace. We ask not your counsels or arms. Crouch down and lick the hands which feed you ... and may posterity forget that ye were our countrymen.

-Samuel Adams, *On American Independence*

Where books are burned, men also, in the end, are burned.

-Heinrich Heine, *Almansor*

Is life so dear, or peace so sweet, as to be purchased at the price of chains and slavery? Forbid it, Almighty God! I know not what course others may take; but as for me, give me liberty or give me death!

-Patrick Henry, speech in Virginia Convention, 23 March 1775

If all mankind minus one, were of one opinion, and only one person were of the contrary opinion, mankind would be no more justified in silencing that one person, than he, if he had the power, would be justified in silencing mankind.

-John Stuart Mill, *On Liberty*

Necessity is the plea for every infringement of human freedom. It is the argument of tyrants; it is the creed of slaves.

-William Pitt, speech to Parliament, 18 Nov. 1783

Liberty means responsibility. That is why most men dread it.

-George Bernard Shaw, *Man and Superman*

I think that we should be men first, and subjects afterwards. It is not desirable to cultivate a respect for the law, so much as for the right. The only obligation which I have a right to assume, is to do at any time what I think right.

-Henry David Thoreau, *Civil Disobedience*

To be prepared for war is one of the most effectual means of preserving peace.

-George Washington, address to Congress, 8 January 1790

There are a thousand hacking at the branches of evil to one who is striking at the root.

-Henry David Thoreau, *Walden*

One form of inequality is to try to make unequal things equal.

-Aristotle, *Politics*

A government which robs Peter to pay Paul can always depend on the support of Paul.

-George Bernard Shaw, *Everybody's Political What's What*

By gnawing through a dyke, even a rat may drown a nation.

-Edmund Burke, quoted in *A Dictionary of Thoughts* (1891) by Tryon Edwards

It is seldom that liberty of any kind is lost all at once.

-David Hume, "Of the Liberty of the Press", *Essays, Moral and Political*

The greatest dangers to liberty lurk in the insidious encroachment by men of zeal, well-meaning but without understanding.

-Louis D. Brandeis, dissenting opinion in *Olmstead v. United States* (1928)

A people that values its privileges above its principles soon loses both.

- Dwight D. Eisenhower, first inaugural address, 20 January 1953

Yield to all and you will soon have nothing to yield.

-Aesop, "The Man and His Two Wives", *Fables*

A government that is big enough to give you all you want is big enough to take it all away.

-Barry Goldwater, speech in West Chester, PA, 21 Oct. 1964

Freedom suppressed and again regained bites with keener fangs than freedom never endangered.

-Marcus Tullius Cicero, *De Officiis (On Duties)*

He that would make his own liberty secure must guard even his enemy from oppression.

-Thomas Paine, *Dissertation on First Principles of Government*

The root of the kingdom is in the state. The root of the state is in the family. The root of the family is in the person of its head.

-Mencius, *The Life and Works of Mencius*

Guard with jealous attention the public liberty. Suspect everyone who approaches that jewel. Unfortunately, nothing will preserve it, but downright force. Whenever you give up that force, you are inevitably ruined.

-Patrick Henry, speech in Virginia on Federal Constitution, 4 June 1788

Freedom is a fragile thing and is never more than one generation away from extinction. It is not ours by inheritance; it must be fought for and defended constantly by each generation, for it comes only once to a people. Those who have known freedom, and then lost it, have never known it again.

-Ronald Reagan, first address as Governor of California, 5 January 1967

None are so hopelessly enslaved, as those who falsely believe they are free.

-Johann Wolfgang von Goethe, *Goethe's Opinions* (1853)

Under a government which imprisons any unjustly, the true place for a just man is also a prison.

-Henry David Thoreau, *Civil Disobedience*

The people go...
from slavery to spiritual faith
from spiritual faith to courage
from courage to liberty
from liberty to abundance
from abundance to selfishness
from selfishness to apathy
from apathy to dependence
from dependence back to slavery

-Unknown

The time to guard against corruption and tyranny, is before they shall have gotten hold of us. It is better to keep the wolf out of the fold, than to trust to drawing his teeth and claws after he shall have entered.

-Thomas Jefferson, *Notes on the State of Virginia*

The greatest menace to freedom is an inert people.

-Louis D. Brandeis, concurring opinion in *Whitney v. California* (1927)

If a law commands me to sin I will break it; if it calls me to suffer, I will let it take its course unresistingly. The doctrine of blind obedience and unqualified submission to any human power, whether civil or ecclesiastical, is the doctrine of despotism, and ought to have no place among Republicans and Christians.

-Angelina Emily Grimke, *An Appeal to the Christian Women of the South*

A state which dwarfs its men, in order that they may be more docile instruments in its hands, even for beneficial purposes, will find that with small men no great thing can really be accomplished.

-John Stuart Mill, *On Liberty*

Put not your trust in princes.

-The Bible (*KJV*), Psalms 146:3

How strangely will the tools of a Tyrant pervert the plain meaning of words!

-Samuel Adams, letter to John Pitts, 21 January 21 1776

Don't expect to build up the weak by pulling down the strong.

-Calvin Coolidge, speech to Massachusetts State Senate, 7 Jan. 1914

It is error alone which needs the support of government. Truth can stand by itself.

-Thomas Jefferson, *Notes on the State of Virginia*

Experience hath shewn, that even under the best forms [of government] those entrusted with power have, in time, and by slow operations, perverted it into tyranny.

-Thomas Jefferson, A Bill For the More General Diffusion of Knowledge (1778)

No people ever recognize their dictator in advance. He never stands for election on the platform of dictatorship.

-Dorothy Thompson, quoted in "Judiciary," *Time*, March 1, 1937

All free governments are managed by the combined wisdom and folly of the people.

-James A. Garfield, letter to Burke Aaron Hinsdale, 21 April 1880

The spirit of liberty is not merely, as multitudes imagine, a jealousy of our own particular rights, an unwillingness to be oppressed ourselves, but a respect for the rights of others, and unwillingness that any man, whether high or low, should be wronged, and trampled underfoot.

-William Ellery Channing, "Importance of Religion to Society", *Discourses, Reviews and Miscellanies*

A politician... is a man who thinks of the next election; while the statesman thinks of the next generation.

-James Freeman Clarke, "Wanted, a Statesman!" *Old and New* magazine, December 1870

There are two freedoms: the false, where a man is free to do what he likes; the true, where a man is free to do what he ought.

-Charles Kingsley, preface to *Alton Locke*

It is better to die on your feet than to live on your knees!

-Proverb

The things that will destroy America are prosperity at any price, peace at any price, safety first instead of duty first, the love of soft living and the get-rich-quick theory of life.

-Theodore Roosevelt, letter to S. Stanwood Menken, 10 January 1917

It is a general popular error to suppose the loudest complainers for the public to be the most anxious for its welfare.

-Edmund Burke, *Observations on a Late Publication on the Present State of the Nation*

The true danger is when liberty is nibbled away, for expedients, and by parts.

-Edmund Burke, letter to the sheriffs of Bristol, 3 April 1777

Since the general civilization of mankind, I believe there are more instances of the abridgment of freedoms of the people by gradual and silent encroachment of those in power than by violent and sudden usurpations.

-James Madison, speech in the Virginia Convention, 16 June 1788

If there is no struggle, there is no progress. Those who profess to favor freedom, and yet depreciate agitation, are men who want crops without plowing up the ground. They want rain without thunder and lightning. They want the ocean without the awful roar of its many waters. This struggle may be a moral one; or it may be a physical one; or it may be both moral and physical; but it must be a struggle.

-Frederick Douglass, "West India Emancipation", speech in New York, 4 August 1857

Were we directed from Washington when to sow and when to reap, we should soon want bread.

-Thomas Jefferson, *Autobiography of Thomas Jefferson*

Let us with caution indulge the supposition that morality can be maintained without religion . . . reason and experience both forbid us to expect that national morality can prevail in exclusion of religious principle.

-George Washington, farewell address to people of United States, 17 September 1796

Those who expect to reap the blessings of freedom, must, like men, undergo the fatigue of supporting it.

-Thomas Paine, *The American Crisis*, 12 September 1777

All men having power ought to be distrusted to a certain degree.

-James Madison, speech in Constitutional Convention, 11 July, 1787

Liberty has never come from the government. Liberty has always come from the subjects of it. The history of liberty is a history of resistance. The history of liberty is a history of limitations of governmental power, not the increase of it.

-Woodrow Wilson, speech to New York Press Club, 9 September 1912

Men fight for liberty, and win it with hard knocks.
Their children, brought up easy, let it slip away again, poor fools.
And their grandchildren are once more slaves.

-D.H. Lawrence, "Liberty's Old Old Story", *Pansies*

To disarm the people . . . the best and most effectual way to enslave them.

-George Mason, speech at Virginia Ratifying Convention, 14 June 1788

The supreme power in America cannot enforce unjust laws by the sword; because the whole body of the people are armed, and constitute a force superior to any band of regular troops.

-Noah Webster, An Examination of the Leading Principles of the Federal Constitution

To preserve liberty, it is essential that the whole body of the people always possess arms, and be taught alike, especially when young, how to use them.

-Richard Henry Lee, *Additional Letters from the Federal Farmer*

A free people ought to be armed.

-George Washington, address to Congress, 8 January, 1790

When a strong man, fully armed, guards his house, his possessions are safe.

-The Bible (*NIV*), Luke 11:21

To take from one, because it is thought his own industry and that of his fathers has acquired too much, in order to spare to others, who, or whose fathers, have not exercised equal industry and skill, is to violate arbitrarily the first principle of association, the guarantee to everyone the free exercise of his industry and the fruits acquired by it.

-Thomas Jefferson, letter to Joseph Milligan, 6 April 1816

Here in America we are descended in blood and in spirit from revolutionaries and rebels - men and women who dared to dissent from accepted doctrine. As their heirs, may we never confuse honest dissent with disloyal subversion.

-Dwight D. Eisenhower, speech at Columbia University, 31 May 1954

The truth is, all might be free if they valued freedom, and defended it as they ought.

-Samuel Adams, essay in the *Boston Gazette*, 14 October 1771

NINETEEN

LIFE

The present is the living sum-total of the whole past.

-Thomas Carlyle, "Characteristics", *Critical and Miscellaneous Essays*

If you suffer, thank God! It is a sure sign that you are alive.

-Elbert Hubbard, A Thousand and One Epigrams

Each day should be passed as though it were our last.

-Publilius Syrus, *Sententiae*

Living consists not in the length of days, but in the use of time; a man may have lived long, and yet lived but a little.

-Michel de Montaigne, “That to Study Philosophy is to Learn to Die”, *Essays*

Life can only be understood backwards, but it must be lived forwards.

-Soren Kierkegaard, *Journal*

If you can't live longer, live deeper.

-Italian Proverb

We have to do with the past only as we can make it useful to the present and the future.

-Frederick Douglass, "What to the Slave Is the Fourth of July?" speech in New York, 5 July 1852

These are three ingredients in the good life: learning, earning, and yearning.

-Christopher Morley, *Parnassus on Wheels*

Use your health, even to the point of wearing it out. That is what it is for. Spend all you have before you die; and do not outlive yourself.

-George Bernard Shaw, *The Doctor's Dilemma*

The greatest use of life is to spend it for something that will outlast it.

-William James, quoted in *The Thought and Character of William James* (1935)

Measurement of life should be proportioned rather to the intensity of the experience than to its actual length.

-Thomas Hardy, *A Pair of Blue Eyes*

I recommend to you to take care of the minutes; for the hours will take care of themselves.

-Lord Chesterfield, letter to his son, 6 November 1747

Chaos often breeds life, when order breeds habit.

-Henry Adams, *The Education of Henry Adams*

Man's life is like iron.
If you use it, it wears out.
If not, the rust consumes it.

-Cato the Elder, quoted in *The Attic Nights* by Aulus Gellius

A man who dares to waste one hour of time has not discovered the value of life.

-Charles Darwin, letter to his sister Susan, 4 August 1836

If you can keep your head when all about you
are losing theirs and blaming it on you;
If you can trust yourself when all men doubt you,
but make allowance for their doubting too;
If you can wait and not be tired by waiting,
or being lied about, don't deal in lies,
Or being hated, don't give away to hating,
And yet don't look too good, nor talk too wise;
If you can dream - and not make dreams your master;
If you can think - and not make thoughts your aim,
If you can meet with Triumph and Disaster,
and treat those two imposters just the same:
If you can bear to hear the truth you've spoken
twisted by knaves to make a trap for fools,
Or watch the things you gave your life to, broken,
and stoop and build 'em up with worn-out tools;
If you can make one heap of all your winnings
and risk it on one turn of pitch-and-toss,

And lose, and start again at your beginnings
and never breathe a word about your loss:
If you can force your heart and nerve and sinew
to serve your turn long after they are gone,
And so hold on when there is nothing in you
except the will which says to them: "Hold on!"
If you can talk with crowds and keep your virtue,
or walk with Kings nor lose the common touch,
If neither foes nor loving friends can hurt you,
If all men count with you, but none too much:
If you can fill the unforgiving minute with
sixty seconds' worth of distance run,
Yours is the earth and everything that's in it, and –
which is more - you'll be a Man my son!

-Rudyard Kipling, "If -", *Rewards and Fairies*

You will give yourself relief, if you perform every act in life as though it were your last.

-Marcus Aurelius, *Meditations*

We are always getting ready to live, but never living.

-Ralph Waldo Emerson, *Journals*

Make it your ambition to lead a quiet life [and] to mind your own business.

-The Bible *(NIV)*, 1 Thessalonians 4:11

The life of every man is a diary in which he means to write one story, and writes another; and his humblest hour is when he compares the volume as it is with what he vowed to make it.

-James M. Barrie, *The Little Minister*

Half of our mistakes in life arise from feeling where we ought to think, and thinking where we ought to feel.

-John Churton Collins

To every thing there is a season, and a time to every purpose under the heaven.
A time to be born, and a time to die; a time to plant, and a time to pluck up that which is planted;
A time to kill, and a time to heal; a time to break down, and a time to build up;
A time to weep, and a time to laugh; a time to mourn, and a time to dance;
A time to cast away stones, and a time to gather stones together; a time to embrace, and a time to refrain from embracing;
A time to get, and a time to lose; a time to keep, and a time to cast away;
A time to rend, and a time to sew; a time to keep silence, and a time to speak;
A time to love, and a time to hate; a time of war, and a time of peace.

-The Bible (*KJV*), Ecclesiastes 3:1-8

Four things to learn:
To think clearly without hurry or confusion;
To love everybody sincerely;
To act in everything with the highest motives;
To trust God unhesitatingly.

-Helen Keller, diary entry, 18 October, 1894

I bargained with Life for a penny,
And Life would pay no more,
However I begged at evening
When I counted my scanty store;
For Life is a just employer,
He gives you what you ask,
But once you have set the wages,
Why, you must bear the task.
I worked for a menial's hire,
Only to learn, dismayed,
That any wage I had asked of Life,
Life would have paid.

-Jessie B. Rittenhouse, "My Wage", *The Door of Dreams*

Biography is the best form of history.

-Josh Billings, quoted in Edge-tools of Speech (1899) by Maturin Murray Ballou

I went to the woods because I wished to live deliberately. . . and not, when I came to die, discover that I had not lived . . . I wanted to live deep and suck out all the marrow of life. . . to put to rout all that was not life.

-Henry David Thoreau, *Walden*

Most people are so absorbed in making a living that they forget to make a life.

-Orison Swett Marden, *The Young Man Entering Business*

The less of routine, the more of life.

-Amos Bronson Alcott, *Table-Talk*

I would rather be ashes than dust!
I would rather that my spark should burn out in a brilliant blaze
than it should be stifled by dry rot.
I would rather be a superb meteor, every atom of me in magnificent glow,
than a sleepy and permanent planet.
The proper function of man is to live, not to exist.
I shall not waste my days in trying to prolong them.
I shall use my time!

-Jack London, *Jack London and His Times* (1939) by Joan London

A man in old age is like a sword in a shop window. Men that look upon the perfect blade do not imagine the process by which it was completed. Man is a sword. Daily life is the workshop, and God is the artificer; and those cares which beat him upon the anvil, and file his edge, and eat in, acid-like, the inscription upon his hilt,--these are the very things that fashion the man.

-Henry Ward Beecher, *Life Thoughts*

Four things do not come back: the Spoken Word, the Sped Arrow, the Past Life, and the Neglected Opportunity.

-Arab Proverb

Seven Social Sins:
Politics without principle,
pleasure without conscience,
wealth without work,
knowledge without character,
business without morality,
science without humanity,
worship without sacrifice.

-Mahatma Gandhi, *Young India*, 22 October 1925

To laugh is to risk appearing a fool,
To weep is to risk appearing sentimental.
To reach out to another is to risk involvement,
To expose feelings is to risk exposing your true self.
To place your ideas and dreams before a crowd is to risk their loss.
To love is to risk not being loved in return,
To live is to risk dying,
To hope is to risk despair,
To try is to risk failure.
But risks must be taken because the greatest hazard in life is to risk nothing.
Only a person who risks is free.

-Unknown author

- The secret of life is in knowing who you are, not what you are.
- What you make of your life is dependent upon you.
- It is always better to assume no one can/will keep a secret.
- You should remember every promise made and keep it to the letter.
- Do not be ashamed to stand up for the truth, even when it's unpopular.
- When no one else is watching, know that God is.
- You become like those you surround yourself with; choose wisely.
- Keep your priorities in order, and above all succeed at home first.
- If you spend less than you earn, you will never see debt.
- It's not what you gain in life, but what you save that makes you rich.
- Always be yourself. Never pretend to be something you're not.
- Know that character is more important than wealth.
- Treat others as you would like to be treated.
- Remember, everybody makes mistakes, including you, so learn to forgive.
- Honesty is the best policy, so never compromise your integrity.
- Be quick to take responsibility for your actions.
- Hope for the best, but always have a plan for the worst.

- Learn from your failures and do not be afraid to fail often.
- Growth never occurs in comfort. Learn to thrive in adversity.
- Know that life is not fair, but it is not unfair either.
- Never forget, you are always communicating in all that you do or don't do.
- Relationships are and will always be more important than things.
- Remember, that most people are not against you, they are simply for themselves.
- Know what you can change, and let go of the rest.
- Life is short; don't put off till tomorrow what can be done today.
- Don't dwell on the past, for it can't be changed.
- You will reap what you sow, and the hidden will eventually become known.
- You need to know when to let go - when to walk away.
- Remember, not getting what you want is sometimes a blessing.
- If you're waiting for someone else to act, you are part of the problem.
- While words are sometimes necessary, your actions will always speak louder.
- You can endure a lot more pain than you will ever know - Don't quit!
- Always finish stronger than you started and you will be successful.
- Remember, life is a marathon, not a sprint.

- ❖ Always make sure you are on God's side, and do what matters for eternity.
- ❖ The lessons of life will be continually repeated until they are learned.

-J.S. Felts, "Maxims for Life & Living"

But the fruit of the Spirit is love, joy, peace, patience, kindness, goodness, faithfulness, gentleness, self-control.

-The Bible (*NIV*), Galatians 5:22-23

TWENTY

Money

What is wealth? Money - or what's worth money? Would you take a million dollars for your health, or your eyesight, or your wife and child? Certainly not! Well, then, what do you mean by complaining of having too little? Good heavens, man, you're a millionaire!

-Channing Pollock, *The Adventures of a Happy Man*

If money be not thy servant, it will be thy master. The covetous man cannot so properly be said to possess wealth, as that may be said to possess him.

-Pierre Charron, quoted in *The Rule of Life* (1766)

The love of money is the root of all evil.

-The Bible (*KJV*), 1 Timothy 6:10

He that trusteth in his riches shall fall.

-The Bible (*KJV*), Proverbs 11:28

He that is of the opinion that money will do everything may well be accused of doing everything for money.

-Benjamin Franklin, *Poor Richard's Almanack*

Dishonest money dwindles away, but he who gathers money little by little makes it grow.

-The Bible (NIV), Proverbs 13:11

Money is a good servant, but a bad master.

-French Proverb

Riches are not an end of life, but an instrument of life.

-Henry Ward Beecher, *Proverbs from Plymouth Pulpit*

It's good to have money and the things that money can buy, but it's good, too, to check up once in a while and make sure you haven't lost the things money can't buy.

-George Horace Lorimer, *Old Gorgon Graham*

TWENTY-ONE

Past & Future

Every saint has a past, and every sinner has a future.

-Oscar Wilde, A Woman of No Importance

Those who cannot remember the past are condemned to repeat it.

-George Santayana, *The Life of Reason*

But with every deed you are sowing a seed,
Though the harvest you may not see.

-Ella Wheeler Wilcox, "You Never Can Tell", *Custer*

Never let the future disturb you. You will meet it, if you have to, with the same weapons of reason which today arm you against the present.

-Marcus Aurelius, *Meditations*

Of this I am quite sure, that if we open a quarrel between the past and the present, we shall find that we have lost the future.

-Winston Churchill, speech in the House of Commons, June 18, 1940

The man who thinks only of his own generation is born for few.

-Lucius Annaeus Seneca (the Younger), *Moral Letters to Lucilius*

Of this I am quite sure, that if we open a quarrel between the past and the present, we shall find we have lost the future.

-Winston Churchill, speech in the House of Commons, 18 June 1940

The past speaks to us in a thousand voices, warning and comforting, animating and stirring to action. What its great thinkers have thought and written on the deepest problems of life, shall we not hear and enjoy?

-Felix Adler, address of New York Society for Ethical Culture, 15 May 1876

TWENTY-TWO

PATIENCE

Time eases all things.

-Sophocles, *Oedipus Rex*

My brethren, count it all joy when ye fall into divers temptations; Knowing this, that the trying of your faith worketh patience. But let patience have her perfect work, that ye may be perfect and entire, wanting nothing. If any of you lack wisdom, let him ask of God, that giveth to all men liberally, and upbraideth not; and it shall be given him.

-The Bible (*KJV*), James 1:2-5

If you are patient in one moment of anger, you will escape a hundred days of sorrow.

-Chinese Proverb

He that can have patience, can have what he will.

-Benjamin Franklin, *Poor Richard's Almanack*

Be patient in bearing with the defeats and infirmities of others, of what sort so ever they may be, for that thou thyself also hast many, which must be suffered by others. If thou canst not make thyself such a one as thou wouldest, how canst thou expect to have another in all things to thy liking? We would have others perfect, and yet we amend not our own faults.

-Thomas a' Kempis, *The Imitation of Christ*

Never cut what you can untie.

-Joseph Joubert, *Some of the Thoughts of Joseph Joubert*

The strongest of all warriors are these two - Time and Patience.

-Leo Tolstoy, *War and Peace*

Blessings may appear under the shape of pains, losses, and disappointments; but let him have patience, and he will see them in their proper figures.

-Joseph Addison, *The Guardian*, 25 July 1713

How poor are they that have not patience! What wound did ever heal but by degrees?

-William Shakespeare, *Othello*

Patience is bitter, but its fruit is sweet.

-Jean-Jacques Rousseau, *Julie, or the New Heloise*

Let us not become weary in doing good, for at the proper time we will reap a harvest if we do not give up.

-The Bible (*NIV*), Galatians 6:9

We must bear with others, but first we must learn to bear with ourselves, and to have patience with our own imperfections.

-Saint Francis de Sales, *Selections From the Letters of S. Francis de Sales* (1856)

The principle part of faith is patience.

-George MacDonald, *Weighed and Wanting*

A man's wisdom gives him patience.

-The Bible (*NIV*), Proverbs 19:11

TWENTY-THREE

PERSEVERANCE

Not only so, but we also rejoice in our sufferings, because we know that suffering produces perseverance; perseverance, character; and character, hope.

-The Bible (*NIV*), Romans 5: 3-4

He that can't endure the bad will not live to see the good.

-Yiddish Proverb

No great thing is created suddenly, any more than a bunch of grapes or a fig. If you tell me that you desire a fig, I answer you, that there must be time. Let it first blossom, then bear fruit, then ripen.

-Epictetus, *Discourses*

Clear your mind of cant'.

-Samuel Johnson, quoted in *Life of Samuel Johnson* (1791) by James Boswell

Go as far as you can see, and when you get there, you will see further.

-Saying

Every artist was first an amateur.

-Ralph Waldo Emerson, "Progress of Culture", *Letters and Social Aims*

Success is to be measured not so much by the position that one has reached in life as by the obstacles which he has overcome.

-Booker T. Washington, Up From Slavery

When nothing seemed to help, I would go and look at a stone-cutter hammering away at his rock, perhaps a hundred times without as much as a crack showing in it. Yet at the hundred-and-first blow it will split in two, and I knew it was not the last blow that did it, but all that had gone before.

-Jacob A. Riis, *The Making of an American*

I think and think for months and years. Ninety-nine times, the conclusion is false. The hundredth time I am right.

-Albert Einstein

Much rain wears the marble.

-William Shakespeare, *King Henry VI*

Little strokes fell great oaks.

-Benjamin Franklin, *Poor Richard's Almanack*

Take your needle, my child, and work at your pattern, it will come out a rose by and by. Life is like that, one stitch at a time taken patiently, and the pattern will come out all right like the embroidery.

-Oliver Wendell Holmes Sr., *The Guardian Angel*

The man who removes a mountain begins by carrying away small stones.

-Chinese Proverb

Though thy beginning was small, yet thy latter end should greatly increase.

-The Bible (*KJV*), Job 8:7

Any man can work when every stroke of his hands brings down the fruit rattling from the tree to the ground; but to labor in season and out of season, under every discouragement . . . that requires a heroism which is transcendent.

-Henry Ward Beecher, "Labor and Harvest", *The Original Plymouth Pulpit*

Without perseverance talent is a barren bed.

-Welsh Proverb

Nothing in the world can take the place of persistence. Talent will not; nothing is more common than unsuccessful individuals with talent. Genius will not; unrewarded genius is almost a proverb. Education will not; the world is full of educated derelicts. Persistence and determination alone are omnipotent.

-Unknown

By perseverance the snail reached the Ark.

-Charles Haddon Spurgeon, *The Salt-Cellars*

I'm a little wounded, but I am not slain;
I will lay me down to bleed a while, then I'll rise and fight again.

-"Johnie Armstrong" (Scottish Ballad)

Never give in! Never give in! Never, never, never, never . . . In nothing great or small, large or petty, never give in except to convictions or honor and good sense!

-Winston Churchill, address at Harrow School, 29 October, 1941

And let us not be weary in well doing; for in due season we shall reap, if we faint not.

-The Bible (*KJV*), Galatians 6:9

The creation of a thousand forests is in one acorn.

-Ralph Waldo Emerson, "History", *Essays*

Slow and steady wins the race.

-Aesop, "The Hare and The Tortoise", *Fables*

This one thing I do, forgetting those things which are behind, and reaching forth unto those things which are before, I press toward the mark for the prize of the high calling of God in Christ Jesus.

-The Bible (*KJV*), Philippians 3:13-14

Perseverance is more prevailing than violence; and many things which cannot be overcome when they are together, yield themselves up when taken little by little.

-Quintus Sertorius, quoted in *Plutarch's Lives*

For a just man falleth seven times, and riseth up again.

-The Bible (*KJV*), Proverbs 24:16

They that wait upon the Lord shall renew their strength; they shall mount up with wings as eagles; they shall run, and not be weary, and they shall walk, and not faint.

-The Bible (*KJV*), Isaiah 40:31

Blessed are the poor in spirit: for theirs is the kingdom of heaven.
Blessed are they that mourn: for they shall be comforted.
Blessed are the meek: for they shall inherit the earth.
Blessed are they which do hunger and thirst after righteousness: for they shall be filled.
Blessed are the merciful: for they shall obtain mercy.
Blessed are the pure in heart: for they shall see God.
Blessed are the peacemakers: for they shall be called the children of God.
Blessed are they which are persecuted for righteousness' sake: for theirs is the kingdom of heaven.
Blessed are ye, when men shall revile you, and persecute you, and shall say all manner of evil against you falsely, for my name sake.

-The Bible (*KJV*), Matthew 5:3-11

All things are difficult before they are easy.

-Thomas Fuller, *Gnomologia*

Many strokes overthrow the tallest oak.

-John Lyly, *Euphues: The Anatomy of Wit*

The best way out is always through.

-Robert Frost, "A Servant to Servants", *North of Boston*

My brethren, count it all joy when ye fall into divers temptations; Knowing this, that the trying of your faith worketh patience. But let patience have her perfect work, that ye may be perfect and entire, wanting nothing. If any of you lack wisdom, let him ask of God, that giveth to all men liberally, and upbraideth not; and it shall be given him.

-The Bible (*KJV*), James 1:2-5

If you should put even a little on a little, and should you do this often, soon this too would become big.

-Hesiod, *Works and Days*

What you are to be, you are now becoming.

-Saying

It is always darkest just before the day dawneth.

-Thomas Fuller (2), *Pisgah Sight*

The promised land always lies on the other side of a wilderness.

-Havelock Ellis, *The Dance of Life*

Time eases all things.

-Sophocles, *Oedipus Rex*

When the apple is ripe it will fall.
-Irish Proverb
Did you tackle that trouble that came your way
With a resolute heart and cheerful?
Or hide your face from the light of day
With a craven soul and fearful?
Oh, a trouble's a ton, or a trouble's an ounce,
Or a trouble is what you make it.
And it isn't the fact that you're hurt that counts,
But only how did you take it?
You are beaten to earth? Well, well, what's that?
Come up with a smiling face.
It's nothing against you to fall down flat,
But to lie there--that's disgrace.
The harder you're thrown, why the higher you bounce;
Be proud of your blackened eye!
It isn't the fact that you're licked that counts;
It's how did you fight - and why?

-Edmund Vance Cooke, "How Did You Die?" *Impertinent Poems*

Many littles make a much.

-Miguel de Cervantes, *Don Quixote*

Rome was not built in one day.

-John Heywood, *Proverbs*

What is now proved was once, only imagin'd.

-William Blake, "Proverbs of Hell", *The Marriage of Heaven and Hell*

Time is generally the best doctor.

-Ovid, quoted in *Treasury of Thought* (1894) by Maturin Murray Ballou

When you get into a tight place, and everything goes against you till it seems as if you couldn't hold on a minute longer, never give up then, for that's just the place and time that the tide'll turn.

-Harriet Beecher Stowe, *Old Town Folks*

Greater is he that is in you, than he that is in the world.

-The Bible (*KJV*), 1 John 4:4

If you can't win, make the fellow ahead of you break the record.

-Saying

Errors, like straws, upon the surface flow;
He who would search for pearls, must dive below.

-John Dryden, *All For Love* (Prologue)

I can do all things through Christ which strengthened me.

-The Bible (*KJV*), Philippians 4:13

Better late than never.

-English Proverb

Most of the things worth doing in the world were said to be impossible before they were done.

-Louis D. Brandeis

TWENTY-FOUR

Power

Power will intoxicate the best hearts, as wine the strongest heads. No man is wise enough, nor good enough to be trusted with unlimited power.

-Charles Caleb Colton, *Lacon*

All power tends to corrupt and absolute power corrupts absolutely.

-Lord Acton, letter to Bishop Mandell Creighton, 5 April 1887

An honest man can feel no pleasure in the exercise of power over his fellow citizens.

-Thomas Jefferson, letter to John Melish, 13 January 1813

It is a strange desire which men have, to seek power and lose liberty.

-Francis Bacon, "Ornamenta Rationalia", *The Works of Francis Bacon*

We have, I fear, confused power with greatness.

-Stewart L. Udall, commencement address at Dartmouth College, 13 June 1965

The worst pain a man can have is to know much and be impotent to act.

-Herodotus, *Histories*

Power must never be trusted without a check.

-John Adams, letter to Thomas Jefferson, 2 February 1816

TWENTY-FIVE

PROCRASTINATION

Yesterday is ashes; tomorrow wood. Only today does the fire burn brightly.

-Eskimo Proverb

Delay always breeds danger; and to protract a great design is often to ruin it.

-Miguel de Cervantes, *Don Quixote*

One of these days is none of these days.

-English Proverb

Procrastination is the thief of time.

-Edward Young, *Night Thoughts*

Through indecision opportunity is often lost.

-Latin Proverb

If we try to avoid making choices, that is in itself a choice.

-Saying

Make up your mind to act decidedly and take the consequences. No good is ever done in this world by hesitation.

-Thomas Henry Huxley, letter to Dohrn, 17 October 1873

I do not believe in a fate that falls on men however they act; but I do believe in a fate that falls on them unless they act.

-G.K. Chesterton, "On Holland", *Generally Speaking*

It has been my observation that most people get ahead during the time that others waste.

-Henry Ford

Know the true value of time; snatch, seize, and enjoy every moment of it. No idleness, no laziness, no procrastination; never put off till to-morrow what you can do to-day.

-Lord Chesterfield, letter to his son, 26 December 1749

Our chief defect is that we are more given to talking about things than to doing them.

-Jawaharlal Nehru, "Freedom from Fear", speech in Wardha, India, 1 November 1952

Never put off till tomorrow what you can do today.

-Thomas Jefferson, letter to Thomas Jefferson Smith, 21 February 1825

Irresolution is a worse vice than rashness. He that shoots best, may sometimes miss the mark; but he that shoots not at all, can never hit it.

-Owen Feltham, *Resolves, Divine, Moral and Political*

TWENTY-SIX

PURPOSE

God is preparing his heroes... and when the opportunity comes, he can fit them into their places in a moment, and the world will wonder where they came from.

-Albert Benjamin Simpson, *The Holy Spirit*

If you bear the cross unwillingly, you make it a burden, and load yourself more heavily; but you must bear it.

-Thomas a' Kempis, *The Imitation of Christ*

The fishermen know that the sea is dangerous and the storm is terrible, but they have never found these dangers sufficient reason for remaining ashore.

-Vincent Van Gogh, letter to Theo van Gogh, 16 May 1882

What makes life dreary is want of motive.

-George Eliot, *Daniel Deronda*

If we have our own 'why' of life we shall get along with almost any 'how'.

-Friedrich Nietzsche, *Twilight of the Idols*

Without a purpose, nothing should be done.

-Marcus Aurelius, *Meditations*

Our plans miscarry because they have no aim. When a man does not know what harbor he is making for, no wind is the right wind.

-Lucius Annaeus Seneca (the younger), *Moral Letters to Lucilius*

Be not simply good; be good for something.

-Henry David Thoreau, letter to Harrison Blake, 27 March 1848

Firmness of purpose is one of the most necessary sinews of character, and one of the best instruments of success. Without it, genius wastes its efforts in a maze of inconsistencies.

-Ezra Sampson, "Of the Importance of Learning to Say, No", *The Brief Remarker*

If one advances confidently in the direction of his dreams, and endeavors to live the life which he has imagined, he will meet with a success unexpected in common hours.

-Henry David Thoreau, *Walden*

So will I go in unto the king, even though it is against the law. And if I perish, I perish.

-The Bible (*NIV*), Esther 4:16

Many a man curses the rain that falls upon his head, and knows not that it brings abundance to drive away hunger.

-Giovanni Battista Basile, "The Merchant", *The Pentameron*

God considered not action, but the spirit of the action. It is the intention, not the deed wherein the merit or praise of the doer consists.

-Peter Abelard, *Ethics*

No great man lives in vain. The history of the world is but the biography of great men.

-Thomas Carlyle, *On Heroes, Hero-worship, and the Heroic in History*

Every calling is great when greatly pursued.

-Oliver Wendell Holmes Jr., "The Law", speech to Suffolk Bar Association, 5 Feb. 1885

Vexed sailors curse the rain
For which poor shepherds prayed in vain.

-Edmund Waller, "To Phyllis", *Poetical Works*

If the highest aim of a captain were to preserve his ship, he would keep it in port forever.

-Thomas Aquinas, *Summa Theologica*

He too serves a certain purpose who only stands and cheers.

-Henry Adams, *The Education of Henry Adams*

It is the cause and not the death that makes the martyr.

-Napoleon Bonaparte, *Aphorismes politiques* (1848)

Do not free a camel of the burden of his hump. You may be freeing him from being a camel.

-G.K. Chesterton, "The Suicide of Thought", *Orthodoxy*

It is better to lose the saddle than the horse.

-Italian Proverb

In arguing of the shadow we forgo the substance.

-John Lyly, *Euphues: The Anatomy of Wit*

Set your affection on things above, not on things on the earth.

-The Bible (*KJV*), Colossians 3:2

The innkeeper loves the drunkard, but not for a son-in-law.

-Jewish Proverb

First, say to yourself what you would be; and then do what you have to do.

-Epictetus, *Discourses*

Surely there are in every man's life certain rubs, doublings, and wrenches, which pass a while under the effects of chance, but at the last, well examined, prove the very hand of God.

-Thomas Browne, *Religio Medici*

Hell is paved with good intentions.

-Samuel Johnson, quoted in *Life of Samuel Johnson* (1791) by James Boswell

More men fail through lack of purpose than through lack of talent.

-Unknown

A ship in harbor is safe, but that is not what ships are built for.

-John A. Shedd, *Salt from My Attic*

He is no fool who gives what he cannot keep to gain what he cannot lose.

-Jim Elliot, journal entry, 28 October 1949

The man without a purpose is like a ship without a rudder.

-Thomas Carlyle, quoted in *A Dictionary of Thoughts* (1891) by Tryon Edwards

They never fail who die in a great cause.

-Lord Byron, *Marino Faliero*

Every individual has a place to fill in the world, and is important in some respect, whether he chooses to be so or not.

-Nathaniel Hawthorne, Passages from the American Note-books

To repel one's cross is to make it heavier.

-Henri Frederic Amiel, *Journal Intime*, 30 December 1850

Whatever our place allotted to us by Providence, that for us is the post of honor and duty. God estimates us, not by the position we are in, but by the way in which we fill it.

-Thomas Edwards, quoted in *The Growing World* (1880)

You'll never be able to fulfill your purpose, until your life quits being about you.

- J.S. Felts

TWENTY-SEVEN

Risk

One doesn't discover new lands without consenting to lose sight of shore for a very long time.

-Andre Gide, *The Counterfeiters*

It is when we all play safe that we create a world of utmost insecurity.

-Dag Hammarskjold, speech, 15 May 1956

Take calculated risks. That is quite different from being rash.

-George S. Patton, letter to his son, Cadet Patton, 6 June 1944

You don't learn to hold your own in the world by standing on guard, but by attacking, and getting well-hammered yourself.

-George Bernard Shaw, *Getting Married*

Cautious, careful people, always casting about to preserve their reputation and social standing, can never bring about a reform. Those who are really in earnest must be willing to be anything or nothing in the world's estimation.

-Susan B. Anthony, "On the Campaign for Divorce Law Reform" (1860)

To conquer without risk is to triumph without glory.

-Pierre Corneille, *Le Cid*

Risk what may be spared, not what is necessary.

-Johann Georg von Zimmermann, quoted in *Mental Recreation* (1831)

TWENTY-EIGHT

SUCCESS

Two roads diverged in a wood, and I -
I took the one less travelled by,
And that has made all the difference.

-Robert Frost, "The Road Not Taken", *Mountain Interval*

Do not abstain from sowing for fear of the pigeons.

-French Proverb

If it falls your lot to be a street sweeper, sweep streets as Raphael painted pictures, sweep streets as Michelangelo carved marble, sweep streets as Beethoven composed music, sweep streets as Shakespeare wrote poetry. Sweep streets so well that all the hosts of Heaven and earth will have to pause and say, "Here lived a great street sweeper who swept his job well."

-Martin Luther King Jr., *The Measure of a Man*

Only those who dare to fail greatly can ever achieve greatly.

-Robert F. "Bobby" Kennedy, speech in Capetown, South Africa, 6 June 1966

Success doesn't come from what you occasionally do, but what you consistently do.

-Saying

No man is truly great who is great only in his lifetime. The test of greatness is the page of history.

-William Hazlitt, "The Indian Jugglers", *Table Talk*

I cannot give you the formula for success, but I can give you the formula for failure, which is: Try to please everybody.

-Herbert Bayard Swope, speech, 20 December 1950

The very first step towards success in any occupation is to become interested in it.

-William Osler, "The Master-Word in Medicine", *Aequanimitas*

Self-trust is the first secret of success.

-Ralph Waldo Emerson, "Success", *Society and Solitude*

No man was ever great by imitation.

-Samuel Johnson, *Rasselas*

He has achieved success who has lived well, laughed often, and loved much;
Who has gained the respect of intelligent men, the trust of pure women and the love of little children;
Who has filled his niche and accomplished his task;
Who has left the world better than he found it,
Whether an improved poppy, a perfect poem, or a rescued soul;
Who has never lacked appreciation of earth's beauty or failed to express it;
Who has always looked for the best in others and given them the best he had;
Whose life was an inspiration;
His memory a benediction.

-Bessie A. Stanley, "Success"

Pray that success will not come any faster than you are able to endure it.

-Elbert Hubbard, *The Philistine*, December 1901

Success is not greedy, as people think, but insignificant. That's why it satisfies nobody.

-Lucius Annaeus Seneca (the younger), *Moral Letters to Lucilius*

It is no use saying "We are doing our best." You have got to succeed in doing what is necessary.

-Winston Churchill, spoken in the British House of Commons, 7 March 1916

There is only one decisive victory: the last.

-Carl Von Clausewitz

It is not the going out of port, but the coming in, that determines the success of a voyage.

-Henry Ward Beecher, *Proverbs from Plymouth Pulpit*

A dwarf standing on the shoulders of a giant may see farther than a giant himself.

-Robert Burton, *The Anatomy of Melancholy*

The secret of success is constancy of purpose.

-Benjamin Disraeli, speech in London, 24 June 1872

It is better to fail in originality than to succeed in imitation. He who has never failed somewhere, that man cannot be great. Failure is the true test of greatness.

-Herman Melville, "Hawthorne and His Mosses", in *The Literary World,* 17 August 1850

I am glad that the eight-hour day had not been invented when I was a young man. If my life had been made up of eight-hour days, I do not believe I could have accomplished a great deal. This country would not amount to as much as it does if the young men of fifty years ago had been afraid that they might earn more than they were paid for.

-Thomas A. Edison

The world knows nothing of its greatest men.

-Henry Taylor, *Philip Van Artevelde*

He who undertakes too much seldom succeeds.

-Dutch Proverb

One must lose a minnow to catch a salmon.

-French Proverb

TWENTY-NINE

TRIALS

What was hard to bear is sweet to remember.

-Portuguese Proverb

Nine times out of ten the best thing that can happen to a young man is to be tossed overboard and compelled to sink or swim.

-James A. Garfield, quoted in *The Life and Work of James A. Garfield* (1881) by John Ridpath

No pain, no palm; no thorns, no throne; no gall, no glory; no cross, no crown.

-William Penn, *No Cross, No Crown*

The gem cannot be polished without friction, nor man perfected without trials.

-Chinese Proverb

Times of general calamity and confusion have ever been productive of the greatest minds. The purest ore is produced from the hottest furnace, and the brightest thunderbolt is elicited from the darkest storms.

-Charles Caleb Colton, *Lacon*

In order to try whether a vessel be leaky, we first prove it with water, before we trust it with wine.

-Charles Caleb Colton, Lacon

Therefore whosoever heareth these sayings of mine, and doeth them, I will liken him unto a wise man, which built his house upon a rock: And the rain descended, and the floods came, and the winds blew, and beat upon that house; and it fell not: for it was founded upon a rock. And every one that heareth these sayings of mine, and doeth them not, shall be likened unto a foolish man, which built his house upon the sand: And the rain descended, and the floods came, and the winds blew, and beat upon that house; and it fell: and great was the fall of it.

-The Bible (*KJV*), Matthew 7:25

A house built on sand is, in fair weather, just as good, as if builded on a rock. A cobweb is as good as the mightiest chain cable when there is no strain on it. It is trial that proves one thing weak and another strong.

-Henry Ward Beecher, *Royal Truths*

Behold, I have refined thee, but not with silver; I have chosen thee in the furnace of affliction.

-The Bible (KJV), Isaiah 48:10

True gold does not fear the test of fire.

-Chinese Proverb

Every man deems that he has precisely the trials and temptations which are the hardest of all for him to bear; but they are so, because they are the very ones he needs.

-Lydia Maria Child, *Letters from New York*

The mother eagle teaches her little ones to fly by making their nest so uncomfortable that they are forced to leave it and commit themselves to the unknown world of air outside. And just so does our God to us. God stirs up our comfortable nests, and pushes us over the edge of them, and we are forced to use our wings to save ourselves from fatal falling. Read your trials in this light, and see if your wings are being developed.

-Hannah Whitall Smith, *The Christian's Secret of a Happy Life*

THIRTY

Warfare

Believe that you can whip the enemy, and you have won half the battle.

-J.E.B. Stuart

Tis safest, when in fear, to force the attack.

-Lucius Annaeus Seneca (the younger), "Hippolytus", *Tragedies*

We are never more in danger than when we think ourselves most secure, nor in reality more secure than when we seem to be most in danger.

-William Cowper, letter to Rev. William Unwin, 3 August 1782

Take calculated risks. That is quite different from being rash.

-George S. Patton, letter to his son, Cadet Patton, 6 June 1944

Fear is stronger than arms.

-Aeschylus, *Agamemnon*

In case of defence 'tis best to weigh the enemy more mighty than he seems.

-William Shakespeare, *Henry V*

It is an unfortunate fact that we can secure peace only by preparing for war.

-John F. Kennedy, campaign address in Seattle, Wash., 6 September 1960

Victory at all costs, victory in spite of all terror, victory however long and hard the road may be; for without victory there is no survival.

-Winston Churchill, speech in the House of Commons, 13 May 1940

The best fighter is never angry.

- Lao Tzu, *Tao Te Ching*

If you want to go fast, go alone; If you want to go far, go together.

-African Proverb

Our security is not a matter of weapons alone. The arm that wields them must be strong, the eye that guides them clear, the will that directs them indomitable.

-Franklin D. Roosevelt, message to Congress, 16 May 1940

To lead an uninstructed people to war, is to throw them away.

-Confucius, *Analects*

Never contend with a man who has nothing to lose.

-Baltasar Gracian, *The Art of Worldly Wisdom*

He that is taken and put into prison or chains is not conquered, though overcome; for he is still an enemy.

-Thomas Hobbes, *Leviathan*

The first blow is half the battle.

-Oliver Goldsmith, *She Stoops to Conquer*

He who fights with monsters might take care lest he thereby become a monster. And when you gaze long into an abyss the abyss also gazes into you.

-Friedrich Nietzsche, *Beyond Good and Evil*

Discipline is the soul of an army. It makes small numbers formidable; procures success to the weak, and esteem to all.

-George Washington, general orders, 29 July 1757

When you see a rattlesnake poised to strike, you do not wait until it has struck before you crush him.

-Franklin Delano Roosevelt, radio address, 11 September 1941

If a madman were to come into this room with a stick in his hand, no doubt we should pity the state of his mind; but our primary consideration would be to take care of ourselves. We should knock him down first, and pity him afterwards.

-Samuel Johnson, quoted in *Life of Samuel Johnson* (1791) by James Boswell

We are outnumbered; there is only one thing to do. We must attack!

-Andrew Cunningham, before attacking the Italian fleet at Taranto, 11 Nov. 1940

It is fatal to enter any war without the will to win it.

-Douglas MacArthur, speech to Republican National Convention, 7 July 1952

There is many a boy here today who looks on war as all glory, but boys, it is all hell.

-William T. Sherman, speech in Columbus, Ohio, 11 August 1880

Moderation in war is imbecility.

-Thomas Babington Macaulay, "John Hampden", *Essays*

In war, more than anywhere else in the world, things happen differently from what we had expected, and look differently when near, to what they did at a distance.

-Carl Von Clausewitz, *On War*

There is a violence that liberates, and a violence that enslaves; there is a violence that is moral, and a violence that is immoral.

-Benito Mussolini, speech in Udine, Italy, 20 Sept. 1922

A man surprised is half beaten.

-Thomas Fuller, *Gnomologia*

Never interrupt your enemy when he is making a mistake.

-Napoleon Bonaparte

Let him who desires peace prepare for war.

-Flavius Vegetius Renatus, *De Re Militari*

There is no little enemy.

-Italian Proverb

A sword never kills anybody; it's a tool in the killer's hand.

-Lucius Annaeus Seneca (the younger), *Moral Letters to Lucilius*

The mere absence of war is not peace.

-John F. Kennedy, State of the Union address, 14 Jan. 1963

We sleep safe in our beds because rough men stand ready in the night to visit violence on those who would do you harm.

-George Orwell

Thus we may know that there are five essentials for victory:
(1) He will win who knows when to fightand when not to fight.
(2) He will win who knows how to handle both superior and inferior forces.
(3) He will win whose army is animated by the same spirit throughout all its ranks.
(4) He will win who, prepared himself, waits to take the enemy unprepared.
(5) He will win who has military capacity and is not interfered with by the sovereign.

-Sun Tzu, *The Art of War*

In cases of defense 'tis best to weigh
The enemy more mighty than he seems.

-William Shakespeare, *King Henry V*

A pint of sweat will save a gallon of blood.

-George S. Patton, letter to his troops, November 1942

The best armor is to keep out of range.

-Italian Proverb

Whoever fights monsters should see to it that in the process he does not become a monster.

-Friedrich Nietzsche, *Beyond Good and Evil*

You must not fight too often with one enemy, or you will teach him all your art of war.

-Napoleon Bonaparte, quoted in *Representative Men* by Ralph Waldo Emerson

Know your enemy and know yourself and you can fight a hundred battles without disaster.

-Sun Tzu, *The Art of War*

Sweat saves blood.

-Alexander von Kluck

The two most powerful warriors are patience and time.

-Leo Tolstoy, *Bethink Yourselves*

To be prepared for war is one of the most effective means of preserving peace.

-George Washington, first annual message to Congress, 8 January 1790

The supreme art of war is to subdue the enemy without fighting.

-Sun Tzu, *The Art of War*

The art of war is simple enough. Find out where your enemy is. Get at him as soon as you can. Strike him as hard as you can, and keep moving on.

-Ulysses S. Grant, letter to a friend (1863)

It is fatal to enter any war without the will to win it.

-Douglas MacArthur, speech at Republican National Convention, Chicago, Ill., 7 July 1952

Do not hit at all if you can help it, but never hit soft!

-Theodore Roosevelt, speech in New York City, 17 March 1905

Whoever is first in the field and awaits the coming of the enemy, will be fresh for the fight; whoever is second in the field and has to hasten to battle will arrive exhausted.

-Sun Tzu, *The Art of War*

You don't hurt 'em if you don't hit 'em.

-Lewis B. "Chesty" Puller, *The Marine Corps Gazette*, January 1963

If you know the enemy and know yourself, you need not fear the result of a hundred battles. If you know yourself but not the enemy, for every victory gained you will also suffer a defeat. If you know neither the enemy nor yourself, you will succumb in every battle.

-Sun Tzu, *The Art of War*

All warfare is based on deception. Hence, when able to attack, we must seem unable; when using our forces, we must seem inactive; when we are near, we must make the enemy believe we are far away; when far away, we must make him believe we are near.

-Sun Tzu, *The Art of War*

So in war, the way is to avoid what is strong and to strike at what is weak.

-Sun Tzu, *The Art of War*

THIRTY-ONE

WORK

If you work at that which is before you . . . expecting nothing, fearing nothing, but satisfied with your present activity according to nature, and with heroic truth in every word and sound which you speak, you will live happy. And there is no man who is able to prevent this.

-Marcus Aurelius, *Meditations*

Many people can't see opportunity when it is dressed in overalls

-Saying

Thou, O God, dost sell us all good things at the price of labor.

-Leonardo Da Vinci, *The Notebooks*

The work praises the man.

-Irish Proverb

Measure not the work
Until the day's out and the labour done,
Then bring your gauges.

-Elizabeth Barrett Browning, *Aurora Leigh*

All hard work brings a profit, but mere talk leads only to poverty.

-The Bible (*NIV*), Proverbs 14:23

By nature, men are nearly alike; by practice, they get to be wide apart.

-Confucius, *Analects*

Labor is discovered to be the grand conqueror, enriching and building up nations more surely than the proudest battles.

-William Ellery Channing, *On War*

Whatever you do, work at it with all your heart, as working for the Lord, not for men.

-The Bible (NIV), Colossians 3:23

Whenever it is possible, a boy should choose some occupation which he should do even if he did not need the money.

-William Lyon Phelps

Labor disgraces no man; unfortunately, you occasionally find men who disgrace labor.

-Ulysses S. Grant, speech in Birmingham, England (1877)

It is quality rather than quantity that matters.

-Lucius Annaeus Seneca (the younger)

Their work will be shown for what it is, because the Day will bring it to light.

-The Bible (*NIV*), 1 Corinthians 3:13

Work spares us from three evils: boredom, vice and need.

-Voltaire, *Candide*

Genius begins great works; labour alone finishes them.

-Joseph Joubert, *Pensées of Joubert*

Whatever is worth doing at all, is worth doing well.

-Lord Chesterfield, letter to his son, 10 March 1746

The artist finds a greater pleasure in painting than in having completed the picture.

-Lucius Annaeus Seneca (the younger), *Moral Letters to Lucilius*

Always do more than is required of you.

-George S. Patton

When love and skill work together, expect a masterpiece.

-Charles Reade, *Put Yourself in His Place*

THIRTY-TWO

YOUTH

When I was a child, I talked like a child, I thought like a child, I reasoned like a child. When I became a man, I put childish ways behind me.

-The Bible (*NIV*), 1 Corinthians 13:11

Young men are fitter to invent than to judge; fitter for execution than for counsel; and fitter for new projects than for settled business.

-Francis Bacon, "Of Youth and Age", *Essays*

But the LORD said to me, "Do not say, 'I am only a child.' You must go to everyone I send you to and say whatever I command you. Do not be afraid of them, for I am with you and will rescue you," declares the LORD.

-The Bible (*NIV*), Jeremiah 1:7-8

Tell me what are the prevailing sentiments that occupy the minds of your young men, and I will tell you what is to be the character of the next generation.

-Edmund Burke, quoted in *Selections for Sabbath Reading* (1857) by W.J. Tuck

It is very natural for young men to be vehement, acrimonious and severe. For as they seldom comprehend at once all the consequences of a position, or perceive the difficulties by which cooler and more experienced reasoners are restrained from confidence, they form their conclusions with great precipitance. Seeing nothing that can darken or embarrass the question, they expect to find their own opinion universally prevalent, and are inclined to impute uncertainty and hesitation to want of honesty, rather than of knowledge.

-Samuel Johnson, *The Rambler*, 14 May 1751

AUTHOR INDEX

A

B

C

D

E

F

G

Gibbon, Edward (1737-1794) English Historian, Statesman · 158, 180, 261, 425
Gibran, Khalil (1883-1931) Lebanese Artist, Poet, Writer · 25, 50, 146, 204, 402, 464
Gide, Andre (1869-1951) French Novelist, Essayist · 180, 384, 544
Gladstone, William (1809-1898) British Prime Minister · 189, 271
Goethe, Johann Wolfgang von (1749-1832) German Poet, Dramatist, Philosopher · 285, 331, 337, 377
Goldsmith, Oliver (1730-1774) Irish Writer, Physician · 53, 150, 322, 433, 556
Goldwater, Barry (1909-1998) U.S. Senator · 487, 491, 498
Goncharov, Ivan (1812-1891) Russian novelist · 362
Goodier, Alban (1869-1939) Archbishop of Bombay, Writer · 36
Gorky, Maxim (1868-1936) Russian Author · 31, 228
Gough, John B. (1817-1886) English Social Reformer, Lecturer · 225, 346
Gracian, Baltasar (1601-1658) Spanish prose writer · 152, 155, 172, 213, 226, 353, 363, 364, 381, 426, 434, 556
Grant, Ulysses S. (1822-1885) 18th President of U.S., Union General · 560, 564
Gregory I, Saint (Gregory the Great) (c. 540 - 604) Catholic Pope · 345
Gregory, William Henry (1817-1892) Irish Writer · 235
Greville, Fulke (1717-1806) English Statesman and Author · 26
Grimke, Angelina Emily (1805-1879) American Abolitionist and Suffragist · 500
Guest, Edgar A. (1881-1959) American Poet · 169, 187

H

Hale, Edward Everett (1822-1909) American Author, Unitarian Clergyman · 77, 428
Hale, Matthew (1609-1676) Lord Chief Justice of England · 389
Hall, Evelyn Beatrice (1868-1956) English Writer · 493
Hamilton, Alexander (1755-1804) American Statesman, Founding Father · 258, 326, 495
Hamilton, Robert Browning (1880-1950) American Poet · 62
Hammarskjold, Dag (1905-1961) Secretary General of United Nations · 544
Hammond, Henry (1605-1660) English Churchman · 123
Hand, Learned (1872-1961) American Jurist · 88
Hardy, Thomas (1840-1928) English Novelist and Poet · 507
Hare, Julius Charles (1795-1855) English Theological Writer · 94, 352, 391, 476, 481
Harvey, John (c. 19th Century) Methodist Minister · 49
Hawthorne, Nathaniel (1804-1864) American Novelist & Writer · 382, 543
Hazlitt, William (1778-1830) English Writer · 25, 37, 67, 280, 326, 547
Hegel, George (1770-1831) German Philosopher · 50
Heine, Heinrich (1797-1856) German Poet, Journalist · 495
Helps, Sir Arthur (1813-1875) English Writer · 56, 68, 147, 373
Henley, William Ernest (1849-1903) English Poet · 64

Henry, Matthew (1662-1714) English Clergyman · 8, 36, 91, 363, 416
Henry, Patrick (1736-1799) American Revolutionary War Statesman · 279, 495, 498
Henshaw, Joseph (1608-1679) English Bishop of Peterborough · 308
Heraclitus (c.535-c.475 B.C.) Greek Philosopher · 95, 262, 446
Herbert, Edward (1583-1648) English Diplomat, Historian, Poet, and Philosopher · 101
Herbert, George (1593-1633) Welsh Poet, Orator and Priest · 105, 142, 157, 173, 195, 231, 302, 381
Herodotus (484-c. 425 B.C.) Greek Historian, "Father of History" · 18, 534
Hesburgh, Theodore Martin (1917-2015) Catholic Priest, President of Univ. of Notre Dame · 167
Heschel, Abraham (1907-1972) Jewish Rabbi and Theologian · 229, 360
Hesiod (c. 700 BC) Greek Poet · 529
Hesse, Hermann (1877-1962) German-Swiss poet, Novelist · 331
Heywood, John (1497-1580) English Playwright · 467, 531
Hickson, William Edward (1803-1870) British Writer · 259
Hill, Aaron (1685-1750) English Dramatist, Writer · 356
Hitler, Adolf (1889-suicide in 1945) German Chancellor, Leader of Nazi Party · 348
Hobbes, Thomas (1588–1679) English Philosopher · 556
Hoffer, Eric (1902- 1983) American Philosopher, Writer · 215
Holcroft, Thomas (1745-1809) English Dramatist and Poet · 254
Holland, Henry Scott (1847-1918) Professor of Divinity at the University of Oxford · 471
Holland, Josiah Gilbert (1819-1881) American Novelist & Poet · 33, 168, 203, 338, 343, 454
Holmes Jr., Oliver Wendell (1841-1935) U.S. Supreme Court Justice · 159, 432, 540
Holmes Sr., Oliver Wendell (1809-1894) American Physician & Writer · 17, 172, 183, 201, 238, 256, 264, 418, 430, 449, 526
Holmes, John Andrew (1841-1935) American Writer, Minister · 405
Home, Henry (1696-1782) Scottish Philosopher · 32
Homer (c.700 B.C.) Greek Poet · 111, 239, 241, 383, 446
Hooker, Richard (1554-1600) Anglican Theologian · 448, 451
Horace (65 - 8 B.C.) Roman Poet · 135, 177, 238, 434, 441, 487
Howe, Edgar Watson (1853-1937) American Novelist, Newspaper & Magazine Editor · 19, 199, 297, 354, 385, 488
Hubbard, Elbert (1856-1915) American Writer, Publisher · 109, 141, 152, 153, 165, 181, 186, 482, 506, 548
Hugo, Victor (1802-1885) French Poet, Novelist, Dramatist · 31, 71, 106, 121, 239, 325
Hume, David (1711-1776) Scottish Philosopher, Historian 402, 497
Hurdis, James (1763-1801) English Poet, Clergyman, Oxford Professor · 115, 465
Hutcheson Jr., Joseph C. (1879-1973) Judge for Court of Appeals for the Fifth Circuit · 175

I

J

K

L

Livy, [Titus Livius] (59 BC-AD 17) Roman historian · 73, 137, 306, 415
Locke, John (1632-1704) English Philosopher · 157, 166, 167, 172, 174, 262, 290, 292, 305, 307, 312, 325, 404, 409, 412, 431
London, Jack (1876-1916) American Author · 81, 512
Longfellow, Henry Wadsworth (1807-1882) American Poet · 45, 186, 188, 223, 266, 269, 276, 295, 318, 389, 484
Lorimer, George C. (1838-1904) American Baptist Preacher · 92
Lorimer, George Horace (1869-1937) Editor of The Saturday Evening Post · 518
Lover, Samuel (1797-1868) Irish Songwriter, Novelist · 452
Lowell, James Russell (1819-1891) American Poet, writer, diplomat, and abolitionist · 35, 81, 280, 323
Lubbock, John (1834-1913) British Statesman · 32, 247, 297, 387
Luther, Martin (1483-1546) German Monk & Theologian · 96, 105, 218, 399, 416
Lyly, John (c. 1553 - 1606) English Writer · 529, 541

M

Mabie, Hamilton Wright (1846-1916) American Essayist, Author · 425
MacArthur, General Douglas (1880-1964) American General · 44, 557, 561
Macaulay, Thomas Babington (1800-1859) English Poet & Historian · 241, 557
MacDonald, George (1824-1905) Scottish Author, Poet, & Christian Minister · 105, 108, 235, 236, 243, 301, 356, 414, 523
Machiavelli, Niccolo (1469-1527) Italian Philosopher · 53, 212, 252, 381, 489
MacLaren, Alexander (1826-1910) English Non-conformist Minister · 342
Madison, James (1751-1836) Fourth President of the United States, Founding Father · 502, 503
Maimonides, Moses (1135-1204) Jewish Rabbi, Physician, and Philosopher · 372, 410
Malloch, Douglas (1877 - 1938) American Poet · 439
Mann, Horace (1796-1859) American Education Reformer, Abolitionist · 28, 166, 261, 362, 402, 416, 418, 435
Mann, Thomas (1875-1955) German Novelist · 275, 325, 371, 470
Marden, Orison Swett (1850-1924) American Writer · 475, 512
Markham, Edwin (1852-1940) American Poet · 454
Marshall, Peter (1902-1949) Chaplain of the United States Senate · 112, 222, 349
Martial (1st century) Roman Poet · 112, 247
Mason, George (1725-1792) Delegate Constitutional Convention, Founding Father · 504
McFee, William (1881-1966) Writer · 480
Melville, Herman (1819-1891) American Novelist & Poet · 21, 207, 353, 355, 485, 549
Mencius (372 - 289 BC) Chinese Philosopher · 174, 498
Mencken, H.L. (1880-1956) Journalist, Satirist, Social Critic · 219, 291, 419, 488

N

O

Orwell, George (1903-1950) English Author & Journalist · 558
Osler, Sir William (1849-1919) Canadian Physician · 11, 547
Ovid (43 BC - 17 AD) Roman Poet · 17, 82, 179, 285, 287, 423, 451, 531

P

Paine, Thomas (1737-1809) American Patriot, Quaker · 27, 250, 320, 336, 339, 348, 357, 369, 437, 453, 498, 503
Palmer, Roundell (1812-1895) Lord Chancellor of Great Britain · 341
Panin, Ivan (1855-1942) Discovered numeric patterns in the text of the Hebrew and Greek Bible · 35, 150
Pankhurst, Emmeline (1858-1928) British Suffragette Movement Leader · 492
Parker, Dorothy (1893-1967) American Writer & Poet · 428
Parker, Theodore (1810-1860) American Unitarian Minister · 315, 378, 414
Pascal, Blaise (1623-1662) French Mathematician, Philosopher · 51, 102, 104, 112, 126, 147, 204, 269, 289, 290, 367, 410, 445
Pasteur, Louis (1822-1895) French Chemist, Bacteriologist · 458
Patmore, Coventry (1823 – 1896) English Poet · 408
Patton, General George S. (1885-1945) American General in WW I & II · 23, 207, 253, 259, 374, 544, 554, 559, 565
Peguy, Charles (1873-1914) French Poet · 376, 412
Peirce, Charles Sanders (1839-1914) American Physicist & Philosopher · 414
Penn, William (1644-1718) English Quaker, Founder of Pennsylvania · 37, 41, 100, 158, 171, 210, 219, 289, 414, 461, 551
Pershing, General John J. (1860-1948) United States Army Officer · 206
Petrarch (1304-1374) Italian Poet 29
Petronius (c. AD 27 – 66) Roman Courtier · 203
Phaedrus (c.15 BC - c.AD 50) Roman Fabulist · 247, 250, 367
Phelps, William Lyon (1865 - 1943) Author · 86, 226, 564
Phillips, Wendell (1811-1884) American Abolitionist & Orator · 484
Pierce, Robert · 87
Pink, A.W. (1886-1952) Evangelist, Biblical Scholar · 127
Pitt, William (1759-1806) English Statesman · 496
Plato (c. 428-348 B.C.) Athenian Philosopher, Disciple of Socrates · 111, 171, 193, 228, 263, 270, 291, 299, 318, 425, 433, 454, 457, 488
Plautus, Titus Maccius (c. 254-184 B.C.) Roman Comic Playwright · 137, 482
Pliny the Elder (23-79 A.D.) Author, Natural Philosopher, Military Commander · 265
Pliny the Younger (61-113 A.D.) Lawyer, Author, and Magistrate of Ancient Rome · 192, 423
Plutarch (c.46-127 A.D.) Greek Historian · 8, 24, 25, 67, 267, 336, 342
Pollock, Channing (1880-1946) American Playwright & Writer · 393, 517

Pollock, Frederick (1845-1937) English Jurist and Writer · 155
Polybius (c. 200 BC-c. 118 BC) Greek Historian · 133
Pope, Alexander (1688-1744) English Poet · 1, 58, 101, 163, 172, 232, 266, 300, 304, 350, 361, 381
Pound, Ezra (1885-1972) American Poet · 271
Prentice, George D. (1802-1870) Newspaper Editor · 181
Proust, Marcel (1871-1922) French Novelist · 26, 32, 258
Puller, Lewis B. · 561

Q

Quarles, Francis (1592-1644) English Poet · 470

R

Racine, Jean (1639-1699) French Dramatist · 95, 406
Raupach, Hermann Friedrich (1728-1778) German Composer · 444
Ravenhill, Leonard (1907-1994) British Evangelist · 85
Reade, Charles (1814-1884) English Novelist and Dramatist 229
Reagan, Ronald (1911-2004) 40th President of the United States · 143, 486, 498
Renatus, Flavius Vegetius (c. 390) Roman Historian & Military Strategist · 558
Richter, Jean Paul (1763-1825) German Author · 21, 35, 146, 443
Riis, Jacob A. (1849-1914) American Muckraker Journalist · 525
Rittenhouse, Jessie B. (1869-1948) American Poet and Author · 511
Robertson, Frederick William (1816-1853) English Divine · 10, 92, 126, 133, 406, 420
Robinson, James Harvey (1863-1936) American Historian · 269
Rockne, Knute (1888-1931) Football Coach · 432
Rodin, Auguste (1840-1917) French artist & Sculptor · 280
Rogers, Will (1879-1935) American Comedian and Actor · 156, 204, 271
Roland, Madame (1754-1793) French Revolutionist · 385
Rommel, Erwin (1891-1944) German Field Marshall · 286
Roosevelt, Franklin Delano (1882-1945) 32nd President of the U.S. · 18, 112, 363, 410, 556
Roosevelt, Theodore (1858-1919) 26th President of U.S. · 183, 211, 345, 361, 430, 438, 456, 457, 481, 488, 502, 561
Rousseau, Jean-Jacques (1712-1778) Genevan Philosopher · 82, 290, 377, 522
Roux, Joseph (1834-1886), French Priest & Writer · 31, 37, 279
Ruskin, John (1819-1900) Author, Poet · 112, 127, 262, 291, 424
Russell, Bertrand (1872-1970) British Mathematician, Philosopher · 18, 31, 304, 467
Rutherford, Samuel (1600-1661) Scottish Presbyterian Theologian & Author · 121
Ryle, J. C. (1816-1900) Anglican Bishop · 126, 417

S

Sa'di (1210-c.1291) Persian Poet · 20, 264, 365

T

U

V

W

Webster, Daniel (1782-1852) American Statesman · 367, 471
Webster, Noah (1758-1843) American Lexicographer, Author · 504
Weil, Simone (1909-1943) French Philosopher · 134
Wesley, John (1703-1791) Theologian, Founder of Methodism · 90, 120, 308, 407
Wesley, Susanna (1669-1742) Mother of John and Charles Wesley · 134
Whately, Richard (1787-1863) English Theological Writer, Archbishop of Dublin · 151, 179, 257, 417, 418
Whewell, William (1794–1866) Anglican Priest, Philosopher, Scientist, and Theologian · 394
Whistler, James McNeill (1834-1903) British Painter & Etcher · 412
Whitehead, Alfred North (1861-1947) British Mathematician, Philosopher · 257, 326
Whittier, John Greenleaf (1807-1892) American Poet, Abolitionist · 335, 427
Wilcox, Ella Wheeler (1850-1919) American Author & Poet · 519
Wilde, Oscar (1854-1900) Irish Writer · 15, 253, 274, 324, 406, 478, 519
Wilder, Laura Ingalls (1867 - 1957) American Author · 91
Williams, Charles Walter Stansby (1886-1945) British Author & Theologian · 100
Williams, Roger, (1603-1684) English Theologian, Anglo-American Clergyman · 90, 243
Wilson, Woodrow (1856-1924) 28th President of U.S. · 214, 447, 483, 504
Wintle, Walter D. (c.19th and 20th century) Poet · 483
Witherspoon, John (1723-1794) Signer of Declaration, Clergyman · 19, 22
Wright, Orville (1871-1948) American Inventor · 299
Wright, Sir Robert (c. 1634-1689) Lord Chief Justice · 157
Wrigley Jr., William (1861-1932) Chewing Gum Industrialist · 238

Y

Yeats, William Butler (1865-1939) Irish Poet, Dramatist · 175, 265
Young, Edward (1683-1765) English Literary Critic, Poet and Dramatist · 101, 343, 535

Z

Zimmermann, Johann Georg von (1728-1795) Swiss Philosopher 415, 545

Made in United States
Orlando, FL
15 December 2021

11803722R00361